Copyright © 2019 Kathy Diekroeger

All rights reserved. This book or any portion thereof may not be reproduced or used in any manner whatsoever without the express written permission of the author.

First edition.

Front cover images and sketches by Anthony Lanza.
Book design by Bernadette Marciniak.

Contents

Introduction		5
Chapter 1 — Pick Me! Pick Me!		7
Chapter 2 — Sign Here (or Not)		37
Chapter 3 — Put Me In, Coach		53
Chapter 4 — The "Off" Season		83
Chapter 5 — Play Ball!		99
Chapter 6 — Safe at Home?		127
Chapter 7 — Take Me Out to the Ballgame		161
Chapter 8 — On the Road (Again)		195
Chapter 9 — Just a Bit Outside		223
Chapter 10 — Curveballs and Changeups		245
Chapter 11 — Yer Outta Here!		275
Chapter 12 — Grand Slam!		301
Roster of Players		307
Acknowledgments		317

Introduction

"Another book about baseball? Are you kidding? Hasn't enough been written about this?"

I've watched a lot of baseball: Little League, Pony League, Babe Ruth League, Fall Ball, Travel Ball, Middle School Baseball, High School Baseball, College Baseball, Collegiate Summer Leagues, and Professional Baseball. My three boys have participated in all of those leagues and they have a lot of stories. The craziest stories, and I believe the best, are about what goes on in minor league baseball. Some of the stories are funny, some are sad, some are simply unbelievable, as in, you can't make this stuff up. When they would sit around with their former teammates and tell stories, I would say, "You guys have got to write this stuff down, you're not going to remember everything." But as far as I knew, they hadn't written them down. So I started to think that maybe I should.

Then one day in 2016, I got a text from my son. He was playing minor league baseball in Florida. It was 11:06 AM in late June and the temperature was 90 degrees with about 90% humidity.

> What are you up to this weekend?

> Bus trip headed to port Charlotte. Air conditioning broken. Should have quit this morning 😂

That's when it hit me. That was a typical day in the life of a minor league baseball player, a life that few people really understand. Those crazy untold stories I had been listening to about life in the minor leagues needed to be told, and I was in a position to do it. I wanted a breadth of experiences, so I set out to collect stories from a lot of minor league players. Not just any minor league players. Players I knew personally. Players who went to college with my own sons, players whose classmates have graduated and are doing some really cool things. Players who are living the dream, who many of their classmates would trade places with in a heartbeat. How many times have these guys wanted to quit, go somewhere else, get a real job and not have to put up with this crazy lifestyle?

The fact is, most players don't just quit midseason. In a typical year, almost 1,000 players enter the system. Many get released before, during and after the season. Many get injured and therefore have to reluctantly walk away. Many voluntarily retire, but very few actually quit midseason.

Everyone knows that baseball is a game of failure. We've all heard "even the great hitters fail 70% of the time". But despite the long bus rides and rundown hotels and crappy food, despite the rainouts and weather delays, minor league players keep going. There's always the hope that they'll make it to the bigs. And then life gets better. Or does it?

Some people may wonder why I've confined my stories to 28 guys from one college program. After all, the minor leagues are incredibly diverse. Players come from not just all around the country but from all around the world. They can be as young as 18 or as old as their late 30's. Nevertheless, as I interviewed those young men who I knew, it was clear to me that they'd had quite a breadth of experience across the minor leagues. Some were drafted in the first round and some were drafted in the 47th. Some ended their careers without even getting out of Rookie ball and some have made it to the big leagues. They represent every single minor league and 68 of the 192 teams in those leagues. Collectively, they have 88 seasons of minor league experience. Maybe another book will focus on a different group of guys. For me, these are the guys whose stories I am choosing to tell.

All of the players mentioned in the book will be introduced by their first and last names as part of their personal draft stories in the first two chapters. After that, they will be referred to only by their first names. Some players have asked that some of their stories remain anonymous and I have honored their wishes.

This book is not an attempt to highlight or profile any particular player. I believe each player's story is unique and each player's journey is just as interesting and important as the next. Gathered together, this is a collection of stories that I believe represent the lifestyle of minor league baseball. I hope you learn a lot, laugh a lot, and maybe even shed a few tears. Enjoy!

Chapter 1
Pick Me! Pick Me!

Most professional baseball players begin their careers with the MLB first-year player draft. When you think about the draft, you might imagine that all the players are sitting in a large studio on TV, cameras focused on them waiting for their names to be called. And when they hear their name, they stand up, hug their family, high five their friends, take a selfie, and walk to the podium for a picture in their new team's jersey and cap. Or maybe you picture them in their living rooms surrounded by loved ones, gathered in front of the TV, all cheering and clapping when the player's name is called.

But that's not always how it goes. During the 2018 draft, a total of only six players were sitting in the TV studio. And yes, every year many players are surrounded by family and friends and they do cheer in jubilation. However, there are many more who are not. A college player might be playing a postseason game when his name is called. A high schooler might be at his graduation or his graduation party. Some players are alone. Some don't even know their name is selected until their phone rings and it's a scout. Really? Yes.

Furthermore, even though for many players the draft is a dream come true, it can also be a disappointment. Some players are thrilled just to be drafted, but others might view being selected in the second round as a disappointment. And frankly, most eligible players don't get drafted at all.

So what really happens on draft day? What goes through the minds of the players? You're about to get a day-by-day inside look at the draft, and it's not what you expect.

****

The Major League Baseball first-year player draft is held every year in June among the 30 Major League clubs. The clubs select players in reverse order of their won-lost records at the close of the previous regular season – so the worst team picks first and the best team picks last, regardless of league. There are now 40 rounds. Up until the year 2012, there were 50 rounds.

The draft takes place over three days. The first day consists of rounds one and two, plus competitive balance rounds A and B, which are additional selections granted to certain teams following each of those rounds. (See Note 1.) In 2018, there were a total of 78 players selected on day one of the draft.

Rounds three through ten occur on day two, and rounds 11 through 40 occur on day three. There were a total of 1214 players drafted in the 2018 draft. That's a lot, but not when you consider the number of players that are eligible each year.

Who is eligible for the draft? Baseball players do not have to "declare" for the draft. Simply put, a player is eligible for selection in the MLB Amateur Draft if the player is a high school graduate who has not yet attended college or has completed his junior year of college. Players must be a resident of the United States, Canada, or other US territories (e.g. Puerto Rico) and have never before signed a Major League or Minor League contract. (See Note 2.) Each year there are over 140,000 draft eligible players.

Senior High School Players	114,159
Junior and Senior NCAA Players	12,581
Junior College Players (NJCAA and COA)	13,695
Total Draft Eligible Players	140,435

Source: The High School Baseball Web[1]

How hard is it to get drafted? In the 2018 draft, 1214 players were selected from the approximately 140,000 draft eligible players. That's less than 0.9%, or about one of every 116 baseball players. Not just 116 average baseball players but good baseball players, many of whom are playing college and junior college ball. Every single year. If the odds are that low, why isn't everyone who's drafted jumping up and down in jubilation? As you'll see, it's all about the expectations.

****

"Nothing's a done deal until the end, it doesn't matter what this scout or that scout or this GM tells you until it's officially happened."

It was the first day of the draft, June 6, 2013. The draft started at 4:00 PM on the West Coast and Mark Appel, who had a legitimate chance to be the #1 overall pick, was at a friend's house with his family. His senior season with the Stanford baseball team had ended and graduation was still a week away, so he was able to get off campus and drive across the Bay. The TV was tuned in to the MLB

---
[1] hsbaseballweb.com/inside_the_numbers.htm

Network and his computer was streaming the draft on MLB.com.

> "The first two picks were the Astros and the Cubs. I had confidence that I would be one of those first two picks and so my agent asked me if I had a choice where I'd like to go. Obviously I said Houston because it was my hometown and the opportunity to play for that team would be incredible. Then I got a call from the GM of the Astros and he said, 'Congratulations, we're going to take you with the first pick.' It was an incredible phone call. I came back out into the living room about 30 seconds before the pick was called. People were asking me what was going to happen and I was like, 'You're just going to have to watch.' I got picked and everyone started screaming and hootin' and hollering and stuff like that. My whole family was there, a lot of family and friends. I was just so thankful and so excited to be part of the Astros organization, it was a great day." Mark Appel, drafted #1 overall by the Houston Astros, 2013. Signed for $6.35 million.

That worked out really well for Mark in 2013 but this wasn't the first time he was drafted in the first round. We'll get to that later. And by the way, did he mention an agent? Isn't it against NCAA rules to hire an agent? Yes and no. High school baseball players are permitted to hire an agent for professional league contract negotiations, but the relationship must be severed if the student decides to enroll in college and play baseball. Those who decide to enter the MLB draft after spending three years in college are permitted to hire an advisor. The advisor may assist the student with the decision-making process, but cannot act as the student's agent. (See Note 3.)

Not everyone uses an agent/advisor. Generally players projected to go in the top ten rounds have one, but because they generally take a 5% cut of the signing bonus, players need to weigh that cost against their likely signing bonus.

In the first round of the draft, teams are given four minutes to announce their selections. In 2016, the Miami Marlins had just made their selection at #7, and commissioner Bob Manfred announced, "The San Diego Padres are now on the clock." Cal Quantrill hadn't pitched at all his junior season at Stanford. Moreover, his sophomore year was cut short by Tommy John surgery, an increasingly common procedure among pitchers to reconstruct the ulnar collateral ligament in their elbows. But his freshman year he had been Stanford's ace pitcher and among other accolades, he had been Pac-12 Freshman of the Year in 2014. He was projected to go high in the draft his junior year.

"There was a lot happening that weekend and I was graduating the next day. My grandparents and my parents came to Palo Alto and we had two hotel rooms. We got the TV up and running – I think we hooked up one of the computers and we stole my teammate Griffin Weir's login for the MLB network. It was a real hodgepodge set up, definitely not one of the those ones you see when you're watching the draft. Ours wasn't like 40 family members with a live broadcast and all. But we were pretty excited. We had a good idea of the range of where we were going, but we weren't 100% sure it was going to happen. Nothing's a done deal until the end, it doesn't matter what this scout or that scout or this GM tells you until it's officially happened. It was kind of wild, at the last second we were pretty sure we'd go 8th to the Padres and then the Marlins called and they said, 'We're going to take you at 7.' Then we had to go back to the drawing board and ask ourselves, is this a good fit, is this a good option? The Marlins ended up taking a high school lefty. Then the Padres followed and took me at 8. It was definitely exciting. And it was funny because after it happened, I did a couple interviews and then I was thinking, OK, gotta go to bed because I gotta be up early to go walk the Wacky Walk and all that crazy stuff at graduation." Cal Quantrill, drafted #8 overall by the San Diego Padres, 2016. Signed for $3.963 million.

> "We hooked up one of the computers and we stole my teammate's login for the MLB network. It was a real hodgepodge set up, definitely not one you see when you're watching the draft."

While some guys like Cal are in the middle of graduation festivities, some are still playing baseball in the college postseason. In 2014, Alex Blandino, junior infielder for Stanford, was one of those guys.

"We were on the road in Nashville playing in the Super Regionals and there was a lot going on. Draft day was the night before our first game and I was in the hotel with my parents. I was watching and honestly, I didn't know what to expect. Then I got a call from my advisor saying, 'Hey, the Reds want to take you at 29 at slot, what do you think about that?' I had about three minutes to decide if I wanted to accept or not. They were one of the teams we liked and they liked me, so I was like, 'Yeah, let's do it.' Then a couple minutes later the selection came on the TV and there was excitement for sure. Part of me was relieved just to know how it was going to happen because all year — your whole life — that's what you're working towards. There are certain moments in your career where things that you do matter and you're rewarded for them or you are not rewarded for them. Getting into college is one point where you're rewarded. Then you have to play three years, and all the years matter but definitely the junior year matters the most. That's another point, the draft." Alex Blandino, drafted in the 1st round by the Cincinnati Reds, 2014. Signed for $1.788 million.

Alex was offered "slot," which is the dollar value assigned to that pick in the draft. The sum of the slot values for the first ten rounds of the draft for each major league club is known as their "signing bonus pool" for each draft. Teams don't have to pay slot, but if they spend more than their assigned bonus pool in total, they will incur a penalty. (See Note 4.) Therefore, if a team spends more than slot on a player in rounds one through ten, they'll have to spend less than slot on other player(s) in those rounds to avoid the penalty. You'll see an example of this later when we get to the "senior signs".

Alex and his family weren't the only ones celebrating in the hotel that evening.

"Honestly what made me the most happy was getting Snaps of my teammates who were also in the hotel watching the draft. I had no idea they were watching at all and they were going so crazy and they were happy for me when they saw I got drafted. When they sent me videos of them watching it and cheering for me, and being so excited, that actually almost made me happier because you're like a kid, you don't even know what the money is and you don't really realize how much your life changes until you get into

it. I definitely got a lot of texts from people and I had to respond but it took some time to go through them all for sure. It was very exciting and then we were also there to play Vanderbilt which was the more immediate thing I was concerned with at the time." Alex

****

"And then the first round ended and I felt a little bit disappointed."

After the first round, the pace of the draft picks up. Selections occur every 60 seconds starting with the competitive balance round A, followed by round two, then the competitive balance round B.

Stephen Piscotty had just helped his team win the Stanford Regional in 2012 and the draft was starting the next day.

"I remember after that game I couldn't sleep, it was such an exciting game and I knew that the draft was the next day. I felt like I had thrown everything I possible could at the scouts as far as performance, which put me in a great spot to get drafted in the first round. I had a mini draft party at the house. The whole family gathered around, along with a couple coaches that were near and dear to me throughout my entire life, going way back to Little League. I was pretty nervous and I was talking to Brodie my advisor, trying to understand what might happen. The consensus was that I would go mid-to-late first round. We were gathered around the TV and I remember around the 14th pick or 16th pick the Cleveland Indians were the first team to call. They wanted to draft me but they wanted to pay me well under slot value for that pick so that was the first draft room discussion. Do I tell them I'll sign for that? Do I want to take the first team that's willing to take me? I talked with my dad and my advisor and we were all thinking let's wait, they undervalue me. They want me in that spot but they don't want to pay me that, so we said pass. And sure enough they took someone else. And then there was another close call later in the first round. But it was getting towards the end of the first round and I was thinking, 'Oh no, I wonder if I'm going to go here.' And I remember the A's came on the

board and I thought that would be cool because they were my favorite team growing up. But they went with someone else. And then the first round ended and I felt a little bit disappointed. I remember my advisor called me and calmed me down, he said, 'It's going to be alright, it's going to happen.' And then the supplemental round started and it was one minute per pick and it became chaos. Things really started to accelerate and it got my heart rate going a little bit more. The Brewers called me and they wanted to pick me at spot 38 and at that point I was thinking, just sign, it doesn't matter who, let's just do it. Picks were flying off the board, we were watching the TV waiting for the Brewers to come on the clock." Stephen Piscotty

But Stephen wasn't drafted by the Brewers.

"The Cardinals were up and I had had no conversation with them at that point and I didn't know they were interested in me. But sure enough the Cardinals were at pick 36 and I heard, 'Stephen Piscotty, an outfielder from Stanford University' and that was that. So I ended up going two picks ahead of where I thought I was going to go. It was really exciting, I knew the Cardinals were a great organization. I knew it would be a little tough to get to the big leagues there because they'd just been in the World Series a couple years prior. But I had heard so many good things about their player development program, and to be drafted by them was really exciting at the end of the day." Stephen Piscotty, drafted in the supplemental 1st round by the St. Louis Cardinals, 2012. Signed for $1.43 million.

Mark, Cal, Alex and Stephen were all first rounders and they were all happy with their outcomes. But at some point, the first round ends and there are many guys who were hoping to be first rounders and weren't. In 2013 one of those players was Austin Wilson.

"Before the 2013 season, projections and mock drafts had me getting selected towards the end of the first round. The season had not gone the way I expected. I missed half the season due to injury and Stanford didn't make the playoffs. Fortunately I was able *to fly to Los Angeles to watch and enjoy the draft with my family and friends. The day of the draft I was anxious and nervous and did not know was what was going to happen. As every pick went by, it got more and more nerve-racking. Towards the end of the first round the Mariners informed me, my advisors and my parents that they were going to select me with their second round pick which was the 49th overall selection. Waiting for that to happen was definitely surreal. I let my family and friends know so when the Mariners were on the clock, we could get ready. Seeing my name get called on TV and being around my friends and family was incredible. Being able to go berserk with them and celebrate was one of the best experiences of my life." Austin Wilson, drafted in the 2nd round by the Seattle Mariners, 2013. Signed for $1.7 million.*

So what's the big deal about being a first rounder? Besides getting less money on average, the odds of making it to the Major Leagues drop the later a player is drafted.[2]

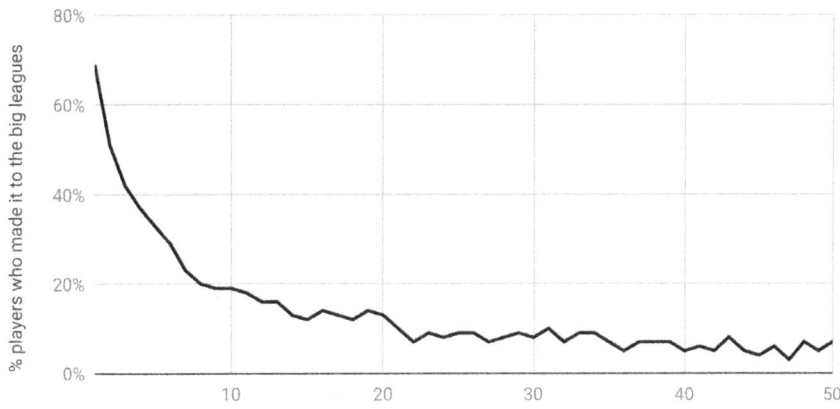

---

[2] Calculations made using data from draft years 2000-2012.

A first rounder has a 69% chance of making it to the Major Leagues while the odds for a second rounder are 51%. That number declines steadily to about 19% for a tenth rounder and then at or below 10% after the twentieth round. Players understandably feel the stress when their hopes of being a first rounder or a first-day pick don't materialize.

"I was a junior in college, a pitcher. At one point it was looking like I would be a first day draft pick so even though I still had a final to take, I flew home to Pennsylvania to be with my family. As it got closer to draft day, I was pretty sure I wasn't going to get picked on day one because only starters go on the first day and my coach had been using me as a closer. But my parents decided they wanted to have a draft party anyway so they invited 50 to 60 people over. I just knew I wasn't going to get drafted that day so I stayed in the office by myself and didn't even circulate. It was tough. And I didn't get drafted that day. At the end of the night I finally left the office and pretty much everyone had already gone home." Colton Hock, TBD...

At this point, after 75 names had been selected on the first day of the 2017 draft, it was almost midnight for Colton. Just like him, we'll have to wait until day two to find out what happened.

****

"Geez, I mean, the adrenaline was just running for the four or five hours where I had to sit through that process. It felt like forever."

On the second day of the draft, 240 players are selected over the course of rounds three through ten. Day two is not televised on the MLB Network but it is streamed live on MLB.com. It starts at 1:00 pm EST and names are called every 60 seconds.

"It was the second day of the draft. I hadn't been drafted on day one and I still had a final to take. I had to take it at some point that morning so I went to a friend's house who had good Wi-Fi and turned off my phone. About a half hour into the final my friend's mom came into the room crying, and told me I had been drafted in the 4th round. I didn't even realize I had been drafted. So I finished my final (and passed). When I turned my phone back on I had 262 messages and 33 missed calls." Colton Hock, drafted in the 4th round by the Miami Marlins, 2017. Signed for $500,000.

> "I finished my final (and passed). When I turned my phone back on I had 262 messages and 33 missed calls."

After missing out on his party the night before, things worked out pretty well for Colton. In case you're wondering if his parents threw another party...

"No, they did not. We had a beer together and then drove 45 minutes to a Lids store just to find a Marlins hat!" Colton

Five years earlier, Kenny Diekroeger was also drafted in the 4th round but his experience was colored by his earlier history with the draft.

"Draft day was more of a relief than anything else. I was thrilled to begin my pro ball experience — it was always a childhood dream of mine. But it was also the culmination of a somewhat disappointing three years. I chose to attend Stanford after being drafted in the 2nd round at the end of my senior year in high school. It definitely wasn't easy to say no to such an amazing opportunity. But ever since I stepped foot on campus there were expectations of me being drafted even higher than that. Other people bestowed those expectations on me and they became part of how I viewed myself as a player. I was lucky to play well enough during my freshman year to where those expectations got even higher. I did my best to tune it out, but looking back on it, I probably caved under the pressure. My sophomore and junior years were mediocre at best. So here I was on draft day at the end of my junior year of college, knowing I'd finally have that shot at a

major league career but also that I'd be drafted in a lower round than what I thought I was capable of." Kenny Diekroeger, drafted in the 4th round by the Kansas City Royals, 2012. Signed for $500,000.

For some guys it can still be stressful even though they end up going about where they expected from the beginning.

"It was the second day of the draft and I had a good idea I would go that day but I just didn't know when, so the whole day I was watching. At the time my brother Brett was playing for AAA Sacramento with the Giants and he came over to watch the draft with me. After the third round my advisor said, 'There's a chance you'll go to the Cardinals or the Mariners in the 4th round but if you don't you're for sure going to them in the 5th round if no one else takes you.' When the Mariners and the Cardinals didn't say my name in the 4th round I was like, 'Damn! alright next round, here we go.' It was painful. And then finally in the 5th round it happened. Immediately my brother and I embraced and hugged and we both started crying, it was pretty awesome. Then Brett had to leave an hour later for his game in Sacramento. After his game he said he showered in 10 seconds, put his clothes on and raced back down to celebrate. He got home at 11:30 PM and we were all still partying. My parents were there, my little brother was there, a bunch of my college friends made the drive from Palo Alto to Orinda, my high school buddies came over, my parents' friends came over and it turned into a big party. It was awesome, it was one of those nights I felt on top of the world." Drew Jackson, drafted in the 5th round by the Seattle Mariners, 2015. Signed for $335,400.

In some cases, the pick comes earlier than expected.

"The day of the draft I went over to my gym and worked out. I was checking the draft every once in a while and then came back home. I got a call from the Dodgers who said they were going to pick me, so we tuned in. But then we saw me go the pick before by the Mets, which was kinda random and cool. We had a decent amount of interest from the Mets in the beginning stages but they didn't call me during the draft which was

interesting. But they were definitely one of the higher ranking teams on my radar at that point." Chris Viall, drafted in the 6th round by the New York Mets, 2016. Signed for $250,500.

And in what is turning out to be a rare occurrence, the draft can go as expected.

"I feel like I'm one of the very few people that the draft worked out exactly the way I expected it to. So many people have different expectations and are either positively surprised or it turns out the way they don't want it to. I was told throughout I would go in the five-to-seven or six-to-eight round range and I ended up going in the sixth round. So on the first day of the draft I pretty much knew that I wasn't going to get drafted and didn't really hear from anyone. Then on the second day we went to a bar that my advisor's brother owns. It was myself, my advisor, my family and a couple of family friends. I think I started to get calls sometime around the 4th round and they started to ask if I would accept a certain number and what I would take. Going into the draft my advisor had advised me on a number that he thought was a good number for me to shoot for. The first couple of teams offered a number well below what my original number was so I was a little concerned, but my advisor said, 'No that's normal, you'll get a bunch of calls, they're just trying to gauge what is the least amount you would possibly sign for.' Sometime around the 5th round the Cardinals' scout texted me and asked me, 'Do you have any updated number or is it still at 250?' and I said, 'Yes, 250 is still my number.' Then about 20 minutes passed and it got to the 6th round, and about halfway through the 6th round — the Cardinals were picking at the end of the 6th round — he texted back and said, 'Hey, we're going to take you with our pick in the sixth round and it's going to be slot and we're going to include school.' Slot was a little bit below my number but with the school it was pretty much exactly my number. It was a pretty great feeling, and my parents and family went wild. We had the draft on the computer hooked up to the TV and saw my name go up on the screen for the Cardinals' pick in the 6th round and that was pretty much it. Then all the texts and phone calls started to flood in. I was super blessed, most people haven't been lucky enough to have it turn out exactly that way." Tommy Edman, drafted in the 6th round by the St. Louis Cardinals, 2016. Signed for $236,400.

Tommy mentioned his contract included "school." This refers to the fact that when a player is drafted, he can negotiate to have his remaining college education paid for by the MLB's Professional Baseball Scholarship Plan as part of his contract. (See Note 5.) Tommy went back to Stanford in the Fall of 2016 and finished his degree in Math and Computational Science, paid for by this plan.

Remember we're still on day two, in rounds three through ten. Most guys are excited and many are relieved to be among the top 300 or so players drafted through that point. But in some cases that excitement and relief turns into disappointment. There's the disappointment of not getting drafted where you expected and then there's the disappointment and frustration of not having the process itself go as planned. With names being called every 60 seconds and the slot values declining rapidly in rounds three through ten, it's important for guys to be near their phones.

"Rounds three through ten were on a day when we had a 1:00 PM game in Nashville and the draft started at noon there. I was hoping to go rounds three to five. I left my phone on the bus and I had given a bunch of scouts my advisor's phone number and the number I was comfortable signing with, so I was expecting after the game to be drafted. I got back on the bus and checked the draft board real quick and I still hadn't been selected. It was a pit in my stomach kind of feeling like, man, you're talking about $400K - $500K maybe even $600K in rounds three to five and when I got back on the bus it was the end of the 7th round and all of a sudden the slot's down to a buck sixty. I was thinking, man I don't know what happened. My phone had 40 or 50 missed calls and text messages from scouts and scouting directors, saying, 'Hey, will you take this? Will you take that?' And somehow the message got lost in translation that we were in the middle of a game. That was really frustrating. Even though I had an advisor, I think a lot of scouts would rather talk to the player than the advisor. On the ride back to the hotel I got drafted in the 8th round. From the back of the bus Bloom yelled, 'Congrats Slater' and I said, 'For what?' and he said, 'You just got drafted.' That was kinda funny." Austin Slater, drafted in the 8th round by the San Francisco Giants, 2014. Signed for $200,000.

Continuing into rounds nine and ten, there are still some guys who are pleasantly surprised.

"I was actually on the field at practice when I got drafted. We were doing bunting drills out on the field with Coach Nine and I came back into the locker room to a voicemail and then a text message from the Tigers' regional scout. That was the only call that day — one missed call and one text message. That was the first time I realized I was going to be a Tiger. I was talking to a few teams and I actually didn't talk to the Tigers very much, I talked to the local scout maybe one time before they drafted me. Going into that day I was really not expecting to hear from them, I was kind of expecting to hear from somebody else, but it was definitely a pleasant surprise. I guess they liked me enough to take me even though I missed the call. So that was my draft day story, I was doing bunting drills to come back into a voicemail in the locker room." Jake Stewart, drafted in the 9th round by the Detroit Tigers, 2012. Signed for $125,000.

It was approaching the end of the second day of the 2014 draft and it had been going on for over five hours. Players who wanted to be drafted in the top ten rounds were running out of time.

"We were playing in the Super Regionals at Vanderbilt and day two of the draft started during our game. After the game we found out Slater had been drafted and I remember I was really happy for him. It was still going on when I got back to my hotel room so I was following it and my name popped up. I was the last pick of the day. I got a bunch of texts and calls and I was super happy. I got a call from my scout and he said, 'We have $5,000 for you.' After we hung up I realized I had just agreed to a bad deal but I was happy to get drafted as a senior nonetheless. Then I had to take a Computer Science final so I had to turn off my phone for two hours. We had a game the next day so I didn't really celebrate." Danny Diekroeger, drafted in the 10th round by the St. Louis Cardinals, 2014. Signed for $5,000.

"After we hung up I realized I had just agreed to a bad deal but I was happy to get drafted as a senior nonetheless."

Only $5,000 in the tenth round? But slot was $137,500! That's a result of the bonus pool system mentioned earlier. Remember that a team has a set bonus pool for the draft, and if they exceed that number, there are penalties. So if they pay a little more than slot to the higher draft picks, they have to make it up somewhere. That usually leads to what is referred to as the "senior discount." While the best college players usually get drafted and sign after their junior year, seniors don't have the option to return to school and therefore have no negotiating leverage. It's a take-it-or-leave-it situation. In the 2018 draft, 20 of the 30 selections in the tenth round were college seniors and their average signing bonus was $9,375. In contrast, the average signing bonus for the remaining 10 selections in that round (college juniors and high school seniors) was $145,340.

Danny was the last pick of day two that year. A total of 315 players had been selected at that point but there were a lot of other guys still waiting. In 2013, Lonnie Kauppila was one of those players.

"Overall the draft process was pretty stressful I would say. As you know, you just have this certain perception in your head like, 'I think I'm going to go in these couple rounds, or in this particular range of rounds.' Everyone has that perception of watching the first round on TV, and everyone being there in person, but no, that's not how it goes. There are thousands of people waiting to get drafted and they're not all just sitting in the room waiting. I got a couple of phone calls on day two and I was thinking, 'Is my advisor gonna call, is it going to be today, is it going to be tomorrow?' As the day progressed nothing really happened, so we went on to day three." Lonnie Kauppila, TBD...

In 2017, it was a similar situation for Alex Dunlap.

"I made the trip back to Texas to be with my family during draft time. On the first day, I didn't expect any calls. But the second day was a little more tedious. I remember there were three or four teams that asked me directly if I was ready to accept an offer for the discounted senior price. I had already gotten my degree so I had no leverage, but if they could save a lot of money on me and were willing to take me early before the tenth

round, then absolutely, I was feeling lucky to get drafted. Being a senior with a broken hand, I was ready to go whenever. Geez, I mean, the adrenaline was just running for the four or five hours where I had to sit through that process. It felt like forever. The whole day I was sitting inside with my phone plugged into the wall beside me, just kinda tapping my foot. I couldn't really do anything but watch the board. It's a different situation when you don't have an advisor, it was just a sit and wait kinda game for me, I wasn't trying to make deals with teams or scouts or anything. I felt like I was going to have an aneurysm anytime the phone rang. Those two days were nerve-wracking. I had those four or five phone calls where they were checking in early saying, 'Hey I'm telling my guys if you're ready to go now then I'll let 'em know that and hopefully I'll give you a call back soon.' Those four teams, they didn't call me back. So I had to go to sleep that night, still empty-handed." Alex Dunlap, TBD...

It was about 5:30 PM Texas-time when Alex realized that day two of the draft wasn't going to be his day.

****

> "I definitely figured out that watching the draft is the worst thing to do."

Day three of the draft is not televised, but you can stream the audio live on MLB.com. On this final day, there are 30 rounds of players to select (rounds 11-40) for a total of 900 names. It's rapid fire and there is virtually no time between selections, just name after name after name. Particularly nerve-wracking is the fact that every name is called twice, first by the team itself, and then it is repeated by MLB's senior director of baseball operations, so it sounds like twice as many names are being called. In 2017, the draft started at 9:00 AM on the West Coast.

"It was the third day of the draft and it started early in the morning. I was all by myself in my suite at Stanford. I had spent the previous day watching all the rounds, and I got pretty worried overnight. I hadn't even talked to the Cardinals in several weeks and had *no idea they were interested. I saw my name pop up online in the 12th round on the draft tracker, like 10:00 AM. I felt relief more than excitement, I wasn't jumping up and down or anything. My phone started ringing, everyone started texting and calling me. The first call was from the scout who drafted me, then I called my parents." Andrew Summerville, drafted in the 12th round by the St. Louis Cardinals, 2017. Signed for $125,000.*

As a junior, Andrew was given a larger signing bonus than many of the seniors who were drafted ahead of him, partly because he had the option to turn it down and go back to school for his senior year.

For a bunch of guys, June 7, 2014 was a fun day. Much of this was enabled by Sahil Bloom who, after having his college career cut short by injuries, chose to spend the last year of his eligibility as a graduate assistant coach at Stanford.

"We were at the Super Regionals at Vanderbilt and it was the second game of that series, and the draft was going on during the game. I knew before the game that there were probably three to five guys on our team that had a chance at being selected that day, so I had my phone with me down in the bullpen. I was managing the bullpen as the graduate assistant coach at the time, so I knew everyone else was going to be playing and they were not going to be able to keep an eye out. Obviously it's an awesome moment, a big moment for everyone, so I thought that I would just have the draft tracker up on my phone in the event that any of them were selected so I could be a part of what would be a really cool moment for them." Sahil Bloom

Sneaking a phone into the bullpen! The first recipient of the good news was Wayne Taylor.

"That was a pretty exciting day. I remember it was before the game started. I was in the lineup that day and I was getting warmed up, I had just gotten done playing catch. For some reason I was over by the bullpen where Sahil was with the phone and he came up to me and was congratulating me and I had no idea why he was congratulating me. But that's how I found out. It was super exciting. Both of my parents were there too so it was

a special time to get to go over and talk to them. They told me all the details of the signing bonus and where I got picked and who picked me. Then I had to turn around and play a game so I had to get focused pretty quickly." Wayne Taylor, drafted in the 16th round by the Seattle Mariners, 2014. Signed for $100,000.

By the way, Wayne hit a walk off home run that day to force the third and final game of the series. When he was reminded about it, he said, "Yeah, that was probably one of the best baseball days of my life." It was also one of the best days of Dominic Jose's life.

"Dom was playing left field during the game and I was in the left field bullpen. I had just found out that he got drafted by the Yankees, which was his favorite team, and I figured he would be really excited about it. So when he ran out to left field for the inning to start, I kinda just called out to him and I pointed at him and he looked over at me like, what's going on? I just mouthed out, 'New York Yankees.' He got this amazing smile on his face and then he started flexing and he kinda started dancing in left field. It was such a cool moment because it's something a lot of these kids have worked towards their whole life and obviously they're in the midst of a really big moment with the Super Regional game and all the tension that's going on, but seeing someone with such real pure happiness in a moment like that — it was something that was really cool to be a part of. I still get the chills thinking about that." Sahil

Dom had a similar recollection.

"Yeah, I was playing left field and the bullpen was right there down the left field line and Sahil called out to me, 'Dominic! Dominic!' and I was like, 'What's going on?' and then he said, 'New York Yankees!' That was such a cool moment. I was so happy. I freaked out for a good two pitches. I've

"…He said, 'New York Yankees!' That was such a cool moment. I was so happy. I freaked out for a good two pitches. I've always been a big Yankee fan."

always been a big Yankee fan because when I was growing up they were right in the middle of their dynasty. They had Jeter, Mariano, Posada, Petit, all those great teams. I grew up watching those unbelievable playoff and World Series moments. My dad played a little bit for the Yankees too so when I got drafted by the Yankees it was a dream come true." Dominic Jose, drafted in the 24th round by the New York Yankees, 2014. Signed for $5,000.

There was still one more guy that Sahil was able to inform.

"The one with Brant was funny because I didn't know his first name was actually Mikel. It was getting into the late rounds that day and I was thinking to myself, 'Man this is really weird that Brant hasn't gotten drafted yet.' And then I remembered that earlier in the day there was someone drafted named Mikel Whiting and when I'd seen it pop up I was like, 'Oh shoot I wish that were Brant Whiting.' So then I decided just on a whim that maybe I should go back and check, so I checked and Mikel Whiting was listed as a catcher at Stanford, and I realized I had messed up. So a few rounds late I had to run down and tell Brant that he actually had been drafted. He had additional suspense unfortunately because of my lack of awareness of what his first name was." Sahil

"I heard Sahil was telling everybody before the game they were getting drafted so I was just sitting there going through all these thoughts in my head, like, I guess I didn't get drafted. So I was pretty pissed off going into that game, I went three for four against Vanderbilt which might have been because I was a little upset. Apparently I was drafted during the game, it was right after I hit a double. Later I found out the announcer said, 'Do you think he knows he just got drafted?' I didn't find out until the end of the game. I got back on the bus and got to my phone and there were like 20, 30, 40 messages, so that was pretty cool. The offer I got was $10,000, or $5,000 and a year of grad school so I obviously took the $5,000 and a year of grad school." Brant Whiting, drafted in the 30th round by the Los Angeles Dodgers, 2014. Signed for $5,000.

Fortunately, in some years the draft is midweek and therefore doesn't conflict with the weekend college playoff games.

Taking stock, we've heard from guys who were at home with family and friends, guys who were in hotel rooms and bars, holed up taking a final, guys who were in their dorms, on the practice field, on a bus, and in the middle of a game. But how about being in the air?

"My name was selected in the 18th round by the Dodgers when we were in the air flying to Tallahassee for Super Regionals. I found out when we landed in Lubbock, Texas to refuel. I turned on my phone and it was buzzing like crazy so I knew something had happened. I went to voicemail and the first one was from my dad saying, 'Congratulations,' and the next one was from the area scout. Then I looked at all the texts and stuff. It was kind of funny, I had a final the next morning so I was supposed to study that night but I couldn't really study. It would have been cool to be with my family but it was great to be with my teammates." Eric Smith, drafted in the 18th round by the Los Angeles Dodgers, 2012.

Eric's teammate Tyler Gaffney was on that same airplane headed to Florida State for the Super Regionals.

"I was on the plane when I got drafted. I was actually sleeping and our player personnel guy Kevin Bills woke me up. He said, 'You've been drafted,' and I pretty much went back to sleep. At this point it didn't matter where I was drafted, I just knew I was going to get an opportunity somewhere. I'd been told that I was going to be drafted in the first 10 rounds roughly but that didn't happen. It was the first year with the new draft rules and it kind of screwed me over that I played another sport. I was supposed to be drafted high because I played football and it actually had the reverse effect in that it hurt my status because people were afraid that I might not sign. So I got drafted in round 24. It was exciting but I guess it was a little bit of a letdown, based on how long I had to wait. I was ready for the Super Regionals — that was the most important thing. Getting drafted in the 20-40th round wasn't my priority." Tyler Gaffney, drafted in the 24th round by the Pittsburgh Pirates, 2012. Signed for $95,000.

In 2013, Lonnie had been disappointed that he wasn't selected on day two, but on day three he got the good news.

"You're seeing teams pick up players every 30 seconds it seems like, one by one, so it's going by pretty quickly and you're just kind of waiting for your phone to ring, honestly. I ended up getting a call from my advisor around the 16th round, he said, 'Hey they're going to take you.' That part was super exciting, that I eventually got taken." Lonnie Kauppila, drafted in the 16th round by the Seattle Mariners, 2013. Signed for $80,000.

Lonnie's teammate and fraternity brother Justin Ringo was also selected that day.

"It was senior year. I was pretty sure I was going to get drafted at some point but there was really no guarantee. Some of us were just huddled around the computer listening. I was sweating it for a while because I didn't know if the call was ever going to happen. I was hoping to get drafted in the ten-to-twenty round range and it was getting into the twentieth, twenty-fifth round and I was starting to get a little bit nervous. Then I got a phone call from the Cardinals' scout and he told me, 'We'd like to draft you if you're going to sign and your signing bonus is a thousand bucks' and I told him yeah." Justin Ringo, drafted in the 28th round by the St. Louis Cardinals, 2013. Signed for $1,000.

Four years later, Chris Castellanos went through a similar nerve-wracking experience.

"Everyone has a different crazy story about the draft, right? And it never pans out how anyone imagined it would. For me, I knew I was going to be a late draft pick and I didn't even know I was going to get picked to be honest with you, I was just hoping to get picked at some point on day three. I knew that one of the Mariners' scouts was interested in me and so I contacted him a few days before and he said, 'Yeah, you're on our draft board, you're going to be later in the draft.' I said, 'Fine, that works.' I didn't think about it until the morning of day three when I started thinking this could actually become a

reality today. I started following it on the draft tracker, refreshing, seeing names pop up, refreshing. Around the 17th round I got a text from the Mariners' scout saying that I would be coming up pretty soon, he told me to keep my phone ready. From that point on over the next couple of hours I kept monitoring my phone. Then the 24th round came along and he said, 'You stay ready right there, you're coming up.' It was just so nerve-wracking hearing that because I didn't know what that meant, it wasn't specific. I didn't know if it would be the next round or 15 rounds in the future. Finally the 30th round came and I was on the edge of my seat, I was stressing out and I was pacing. It was only me and my mom who were home because my sister was at school and my dad was at work. He didn't even know it was the draft, which was insane. And the funny thing was, he left his phone at home. When I gave him a call earlier it went straight to voicemail and then I realized his phone was sitting right next to me on the desk! Finally I got a call in the 31st round and it was the scout again and he said, 'You're on deck, we're going to pick you.' So I thought OK, on deck, the next round right? And sure enough the 32nd round comes by and it wasn't me. It was my future teammate Ryan Costello and I thought Costello was Castellanos at first, so that one was a false alarm. Finally I got the call in the 33rd round. It was a really cool moment for me and my mom." Chris Castellanos, drafted in the 33rd round by the Seattle Mariners, 2017. Signed for $5,000.

What about his dad?

"It turns out that my dad works with my aunt so I had to get a hold of her in order to get a hold of my dad. At first my aunt told him that I had news for him and he thought it was bad news, like someone had died or something. I said, 'Hey, Dad I've got good news for you, guess what just happened?' and he had no idea what happened, he didn't even know it was draft day. He was so happy. Then my girlfriend came over and we had to go find Mariners hats in Long Beach, California. Easier said than done, I guess you can say. I thought the assumption was that I would sign for $1,000. I thought that's what the going rate was, but it turns out that if you're a senior sign they might give you 5,000 bucks. Which was a lot of money for me because I was a broke college student." Chris

While Chris was stressing out at home in Long Beach, Jack Klein was stressing out in San Francisco.

"Two days before the draft the area scout for the Royals called me and said they were interested and he was asking me what I would sign for. I said I just wanted an opportunity to play, wherever you take me it would be an honor. They said that they were thinking of taking me on day two within the top ten rounds which I thought would be a really cool experience. So on day two I was watching the draft and I got a text from the Royals' area scout in the sixth round saying, 'Stay near your phone, I'm pulling for you, I hope we get you right here.' I was right there watching every single pick, waiting for who the Royals would pick. And it did not end up happening. Day two went by and I guess I was a little disappointed but at the same time it's expected as a senior. I definitely figured out that watching the draft is the worst thing to do. When you're watching it you're comparing yourself to every guy. I played against a lot of those guys since I was 14 years old, through circuits, summer showcases, summer ball, travel ball or even in my conference. I'd see someone get drafted ahead of me and whether it was true or not, I'd feel like, 'Dang, I thought I was better than that guy.' It's not healthy. Then on day three I went hitting while the draft was going on to clear my mind and relax. That day goes faster but there are a lot of names and I went a lot later than I had been selfishly hoping for. It's a weird thing, egotistically you want to get drafted high but at the end of the day it's still a huge honor just to be drafted. Getting drafted is a very special feeling, knowing that someone wants you to play with them, it's something that's hard to put into words. It ended up being an absolute blessing. I couldn't be happier here. The Royals have been a Class A organization." Jack Klein, drafted in the 34th round by the Kansas City Royals, 2017. Signed for $1,000.

And we haven't forgotten about Alex, who was sitting by his phone in 2017.

"On day three there were 18 rounds before I got drafted, it felt like forever. I was glued to the computer as much as I was glued to Twitter because every time I saw the name of one of my buddies go up it felt like a little further step for me. But apart from those little

moments of selfishness I was so pumped for everybody that got picked because it's an opportunity of a lifetime. Not many guys get that feeling. But I had to take a break, I had to turn the computer off and get out and get some fresh air. I drove down to my buddy's house. We were playing some Need for Speed on his PlayStation, and I got a text from Tyler Thorne and he congratulated me and I was like, 'What are you talking about Tyler?' and he was like, 'Dude, c'mon man, you just got drafted.' I was like, 'Are you kidding me?' I actually got a tweet, Stanford had tweeted out that I'd just gotten drafted and I finally got the call from the Nationals' scout that I'd been talking to. He said, 'Hey bud we just put your name up, are you ready to go play some pro ball?' It was a really backward string of events how I found out that I'd gotten drafted, as opposed to all the other stories where the scouts are deliberating with the player and they're trying to find out if it's enough money. For me it was a small check and an opportunity and I was just pumped to say yes. My buddy gave me a big hug, then I sped home and embraced my family. I was happy to be close to them, it was a great moment." Alex Dunlap, drafted in the 29th round by the Washington Nationals, 2017. Signed for $2,500.

****

"Three days came and went and I didn't get picked."

The draft is officially over after the 40th round. What happens to the other 99% of draft eligible guys who don't get drafted? It depends on who you are. The largest category of undrafted but eligible players are high school seniors, who can go on to college and hope to get drafted when they become eligible again, usually after their junior year. College players with remaining eligibility can continue to play in college and hope to get drafted the following year. Sam Lindquist was one of those guys in 2013.

"It was tricky, my junior year in college I knew I wanted to stay in school and the only way I would sign is if I went high. There were a lot of teams interested in me and some people told me I could go as high as the third round but more realistically it was seven to ten. I *had an advisor that looking back I realize wasn't the right fit. He was young and to be honest didn't know what he was doing and didn't have connections to the higher ups in the organizations. There may have been some misunderstanding between us, but I drew a clear line in the sand that I was going to stay in school unless I was drafted in the upper rounds. So the day came and went and I wasn't drafted by round ten. That night I got a lot of calls asking if I would sign the next day but I just told people no, I told them I was a pretty hard no, and they would be wasting that pick if they drafted me in those rounds. I was more than happy to stay for my senior year. I was a little surprised by the process, people tell you they know what's going on but really anything can happen on draft day. What was interesting is that when it was all over, the Mariners told me they were going to take me in the 7th round and I'm not sure if it was because of a misunderstanding on a number we had thrown out, but because they paid a guy in an earlier round over slot, that didn't leave enough for me. That's just the way things went. Later when I went back home to Seattle the Mariners invited me to a game and offered to sign me, but the most they could pay me was $100,000 so I said no." Sam Lindquist*

Sam went back for his senior year at Stanford and had another shot to be drafted in 2014.

"My senior year I got a different advisor, the guy I wish I had the year before, a really good guy, well regarded in the industry. It was a good move to go to him but I didn't have the same kind of year pitching and the outlook had changed for me. I went a lot later than I would have the year before. Who can honestly say what would have happened if I had him the year before? But if I had to do it over again I would do it 100 times that way." Sam Lindquist, drafted in the 37th round by the Seattle Mariners, 2014.

Sometimes there are other opportunities that deter players from wanting to get drafted their junior year.

"I think the opportunity was definitely present after my junior season but I was fortunate enough to get a really cool internship opportunity in New Zealand with the State

Department and I saw that as an opportunity that I'll either never have again or that I won't have for a very long time. I figured if I was good enough to get drafted this year, then I would just have to stay healthy and continue to prove myself and I'd be good enough to go for next year's draft. I put up a relatively high bar as far as signing bonus money, something that I felt justified turning away that internship, that opportunity, that life experience to go ahead and get started a year earlier. Ultimately I felt the offers that were made in my direction didn't meet that bar that I set, so I decided to go ahead and turn down the draft that year. I had a few phone calls and I had to say no to them. Those were tough decisions; I'm not going to lie. It wasn't easy, but I didn't want to back off the number that I set. I made it with conviction and I wanted to hold to it so that was very important to me. I ended up having the summer of my life, and came back for senior year." Alex Dunlap

Like Sam, Alex was only a junior so he could go back to school and he ultimately got drafted after senior year. But what happens to the seniors who have no more college eligibility? Is their dream over? Not necessarily. A player who is eligible to be selected and is passed over by every club becomes a free agent and may sign with any club until the player enters, or returns to, a four-year college full-time or enters, or returns to, a junior college.[3] And that's exactly what David Schmidt did.

"Leading up to the draft my senior year in college I hadn't really been playing much at Stanford but I had been doing well in practice and doing well in those mid-week games. So I was thinking yeah, I think I still have this, I think I still have what it takes to play and I'm definitely not ready to be done yet, so I was going to go play independent ball if it came down to it. I just started calling everybody who had ever shown interest, seeing if anyone was looking for a player and just letting people know that I was still interested in playing. Fortunately the Cardinals' scout that drafted me in high school was now with the Astros, and he was running a pre-draft showcase for the Astros down in Huntington Beach, California and he said, 'Yeah we'd be happy to have you out, no promises or

---

[3] mlb.mlb.com/mlb/draftday/faq.jsp

anything.' So why not, I went down and basically threw about 15-20 pitches and that was that. It was a pretty good day, I felt good about how I performed, but as you know there's a lot of variables and obviously not a lot of teams had shown interest prior to that. I was hoping that something would happen, I wasn't necessarily convinced that it would, but either way it was a good experience. Three days came and went and I didn't get picked. Then the day before graduation I got a call at 10:00 in the morning. It was a random number so I didn't recognize it but luckily I had my ringer on. I was sleeping in and it woke me up. I usually would have just ignored it but for some reason I hopped up and grabbed the phone and answered it. It was the California scout for the Astros, and he said, 'Hey, what do you think about signing as a free agent? We've got a spot open for ya, you can come out, we need you as soon as possible,' and I was like, 'Oh yeah, absolutely, I don't have to think twice about that.' A lot of the senior signs especially in the later rounds get like $1,000. A plane ticket and a thousand bucks. They didn't have to offer me anything but they offered me the same deal. I didn't really negotiate at the time, I was pretty happy to get a shot. I had no leverage whatsoever. I feel like I accepted a good deal. Next thing you know, I graduated a day later, they put me on a plane, flew me straight out to Kissimmee, Florida, did my physical, and that was the beginning of my minor league baseball career." David Schmidt, signed as a free agent by the Houston Astros, 2015. Signed for $1,000.

****

Whether they were drafted or picked up as free agents, players aren't officially professional baseball players until they've "signed." This process can be easy or hard. It can happen immediately or take up to a month. And just like the draft, it doesn't always go as expected. What is the signing process really like?

Chapter One Notes

1. Competitive Balance Draft picks were implemented in the 2012-16 Collective Bargaining Agreement to create an additional way for small-market and low-revenue clubs to add talent to their organizations. The 10 lowest-revenue clubs and the clubs from the 10 smallest markets are eligible to receive a Competitive Balance pick (fewer than 20 clubs are in the mix each year, as some clubs qualify under both criteria). All eligible teams are assigned a pick, either in Competitive Balance Round A or Round B. Round A falls between the first and second rounds of the Rule 4 draft, while Round B comes between the second and third. (http://m.mlb.com/glossary/transactions/competitive-balance-draft-picks)

2. The Major League Rules govern which players are eligible for selection in the Draft. The basic eligibility criteria can be described as follows: Generally, a player is eligible for selection if the player is a resident of the United States or Canada and the player has never before signed a Major League or Minor League contract. Residents of Puerto Rico and other territories of the United States are eligible for the Draft. Also considered residents are players who enroll in a high school or college in the United States, regardless of where they are from originally. The basic categories of players eligible to be drafted are:
- High school players, if they have graduated from high school and have not yet attended college or junior college;
- College players, from four-year colleges who have either completed their junior or senior years or are at least 21 years old; and
- Junior college players, regardless of how many years of school they have completed

(http://mlb.mlb.com/mlb/draftday/rules.jsp.) The NCAA also publishes some data on this. (http://www.ncaapublications.com/productdownloads/CBSA19.pdf)

3. According to the NCAA, high school baseball players who are drafted by a pro team are permitted to hire an agent for professional league contract negotiations, but the relationship must be severed if the student decides to enroll in college and play baseball. Those who decide to enter the MLB draft after spending three years in college – the minimum length of time required by the MLB for those who play baseball in college – are permitted to hire an advisor. The advisor may assist the student with the decision-making process, but cannot act as the student's agent. (http://www.ncaa.org/about/deciding-whether-go-pro.) For more information, see (https://www.ncaa.org/sites/default/files/2018DIENF_MLBEducational_Memo_20180419.pdf)

There's a lot of discussion about whether this rule makes any sense for the players who are trying to negotiate a professional contract. As one player put it, *"I think it's an absolutely ridiculous rule that you're asking teenagers, 20-year-olds with no work experience, to negotiate million dollar contracts...That's just craziness, that's like asking a brand new college grad to go be a CEO and negotiate a million dollar contract with some foreign nation, like it makes no sense, we're not capable of doing that kind of thing, and not to mention we have more important things to worry about like our own baseball and our own school."*

4. Since the new draft rules were put in place in 2012, each Major League club is assigned a signing bonus pool for each first year player draft. A club's signing bonus pool is the sum of the signing bonus values ("slots") that have been assigned to each of a club's selections in the first ten rounds of the draft (including any compensation rounds). For example, in the 2018 draft, the Detroit Tigers selected first, and the slot for that selection was $8,096,300. The San Francisco Giants selected second with a slot value of $7,494,600. The slot values go down until the last selection in the 10th round, which in 2018 was the Dodgers, with a slot value of $136,800. A Club will be assessed penalties if the total signing bonuses exceeds its signing bonus pool. Rounds 11 through 40 don't have slot values, but the portion of any signing bonus in excess of $125,000 provided to players selected after the tenth round will count toward a club's total signing bonuses. Penalties range from 75% to 100% tax on the pool overage and loss of draft picks in future years.

5. When a player is drafted, he can negotiate to have his college education paid for as part of his Minor League Uniform Player Contract. According to MLB.com, in the early 1960s, the Major League Baseball Clubs established the Professional Baseball Scholarship Plan to help baseball players further their college educations. Many players enter the Major or Minor Leagues before starting or completing their college educations. The Plan has been successful in assisting and motivating players to further their scholastic careers. To be eligible for benefits, a participant must be enrolled and attend classes at an accredited college/university or junior college in pursuit of an undergraduate degree. The maximum number of semesters allowed is eight; the maximum number of quarters/trimesters is twelve. The Plan does not cover trade, vocational or graduate schools. The maximum reimbursable amount is negotiated as part of their minor league contract. Unlike a college athletic scholarship, the MLB college scholarship is taxable. (http://mlb.mlb.com/mlb/official_info/scholarship.jsp?content=guide)

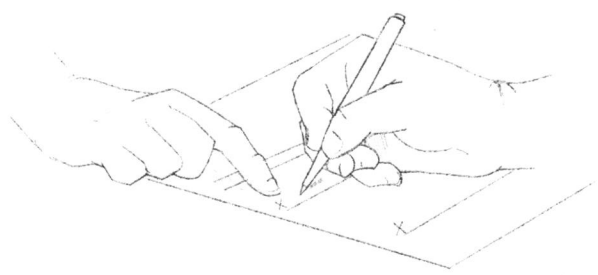

Chapter 2
Sign Here (or Not)

Draft day is over and many guys are excited to begin their professional baseball careers. Before they get started, however, they have to sign a Minor League Uniform Player Contract. It's not surprising that some guys don't sign right away, but what is surprising is that many don't sign at all. That seems odd given that this is a dream come true for so many baseball players, but as you'll see, there are several reasons to not sign and it's not all about the money.

****

"It was happening way too quick."

Once a player is drafted, he generally has up to a month to sign. For instance, in 2018 the draft was on June 4th, 5th and 6th, and the signing deadline was July 6th.[1] Most guys are anxious to get started so they sign within a few days and are expected to report to their teams quickly in order to get in a full summer of baseball with their new organizations.

"My advisor was mad at me that I agreed so quickly, he thought that I should hold out and wait and get more money, which a lot of people will do, but I was ready to go play. I didn't want to wait around or have them think differently of me. I was the 30th round pick, they expected me to go play." Brant

For those who are graduating or finishing up their college or high school seasons, the process can be a whirlwind.

"It was crazy, I ended up getting drafted and flying out three to four days later. I actually had to push it back a day. I said I probably won't be able to turn it around that quickly, I still had to unpack my stuff from college. They rushed me out to State College (Short Season A) as quickly as they could and I had my physical there." Tommy

"They wanted me to report to Arizona the next day. I said, 'Excuse me, excuse me, I have to go to graduation, I'm not missing graduation.' They said that would be fine. So we went to Disneyland the next day, then drove up to Stanford the following day. Right after graduation we drove the six hours back home to Southern California and then I got my stuff packed up and I was off first thing the next morning." Chris C.

"I got drafted on a Thursday and they actually wanted me to come the next morning and get my physicals and all that stuff done. I told them I had graduation on that Sunday, and we had just finished the season four days earlier. I asked them if it was OK if I were to come a little bit later and they said yes. It was nice for me to have a little bit of time at

---

[1] Until 2011, the signing deadline was August 15th. Since then, it has hovered around early to mid-July.

home after a full season and graduation and honestly just to move stuff out of my dor. and pack for the next journey. I graduated on Sunday and I left Monday morning. It was more time than before, so I was happy." Jack

"The draft happened, then I graduated college, and then that night everyone else went out partying and having fun and we drove to San Diego and signed the contract. Then the next morning I drove to Arizona and started. It was a very, very quick five days. It was a mess, it was happening way too quick." Cal

"Draft day was on June 14th and graduation was on the 18th. As soon as I walked across the stage I put on the Nationals cap and took a few photos. We came back home for a day, I packed up, and I flew out two to three days after graduation." Alex D.

One of the perks for the top draft picks is that they frequently get flown to the major league home city to sign their contracts and be given the star treatment before being assigned to their summer team. Stephen was a supplemental first round pick by the Cardinals so he was shown the red carpet in St. Louis.

"They brought me out to Busch Stadium and I got to take batting practice on the field. I remember Mark McGwire was the hitting coach at the time, so I got to meet him and take batting practice as he was watching. It was a really cool experience, my parents were out and my brother was with me. We went to the game that evening, they put us up in a suite. It was first class treatment, it was really cool." Stephen

Austin was selected in the second round by the Mariners and he had some fun in Seattle.

"My family and I flew out to Seattle. I got to take batting practice before the game. The Mariners had just flown in so they weren't going to hit on the field, so myself and another draft pick had the whole field to ourselves. We then watched the game. They put me on the Jumbotron and I got to wave to the crowd, and I got to talk with some of the players.

You feel like a rockstar but it's comical, they kind of give you a little tease, and a little taste like hey, if you do make it to the bigs this could be your life every day." Austin W.

If you're not a top round pick, you still might get flown to the major league home city, but the experience may not be the same. Tyler was the 24th round pick of the Pirates so he was flown to Pittsburgh to sign his contract.

"I wouldn't say it was the red carpet treatment. No one was directing me anywhere. I got to the hotel, I checked in by myself. They basically said there are two tickets in your room, go to the game. I went to the game, I sat in the seat by myself. I knew nobody around me. I had gone up to their office in the stadium to sign in the morning before the game and that was it. They said an intern would be giving me a ride the next day to State College, where I would be playing, and to be ready at this time." Tyler

****

"If you want to get the money you want, you have to hold out."

Some players don't sign right away. One player felt he had to hold out to get the money he felt he deserved.

"My advisor was telling me, 'If you want to get the money you want, you have to hold out. So I ended up holding out and going back to the Cape Cod League and playing that summer. I played 20-25 games and finally the team's scouting director came up to me and he was like, 'Alright we want to sign you, we're tired of this, what's it going to take?' And I told him. Then two days later I was in a movie and I got a call. I pressed the silent button but then my phone started blowing up and I left the movie theater. My advisor said, 'You need to get on the next flight outta Boston, you're going to Arizona to sign your contract.' It was a day or two before the signing deadline so they were trying to get it all ironed out and get the physical done before the deadline passed. That was

the start of my career." Anonymous

Similarly, Marc Brakeman also held out and ended up doing better than he expected.

"I went into the year expecting to be a pretty high pick and then came down with an injury, so that was not very appealing to all the teams. One thing led to another and I ended up falling quite a bit. I went in the 16th round and I was very disappointed. I didn't know I was drafted until I got a couple of texts and then the Red Sox scout called me and said, 'We just picked you.' I didn't think there was any chance that I would get any kind of money but luckily my advisor was able to draw something up to where I was satisfied leaving school and I ended up signing. I signed on the last day. My negotiating was definitely a process because I had to wait for the top ten picks to sign before they could figure out how much money they had left for the 16th rounder. I was pretty dead set on not going back to school but I had to convince them that I was ready to go back to school and let them negotiate against themselves. They started off pretty low and then I didn't exactly kill it but I ended up doing a lot better than where we started." Marc Brakeman, drafted in the 16th round by the Boston Red Sox, 2015. Signed for $225,000.

****

"Going back to school for my senior year was more valuable to me than signing."

Not everyone signs. In 2018, across all 40 rounds, 866 of the 1214 draftees (71%) signed. But if you look at the top ten rounds, that number is much higher. In 2018, all but four of the 314 draftees in the top ten rounds signed, and they were all high school seniors who presumably decided to go on to college.

That means 100% of the college players drafted in the top ten rounds in 2018 signed to play pro ball. That was not true back in 2012 when Mark Appel was drafted as a junior by the Pittsburgh Pirates. That year, he was the only first

2018 Draft

	All Rounds	Top 10 Rounds
Drafted	1214	314
Signed	866	310
% Signed	71%	99%

rounder not to sign and one of eight players in the top ten rounds who did not sign.[2]

"I remember the nerves going into that weekend. My advisor and the scouting directors and the general managers had given me the expectation that I would be one of the first three players picked. When the first three picks happened and I wasn't drafted I wasn't really sure what was going on. Then my name was announced as the 8th pick by the Pirates. I had never spoken with anybody at the Pirates or hadn't gotten the phone call from them saying they were going to draft me or anything like that, they just picked me. My advisor called me and he told me that because of the new collective bargaining agreement there were some things that were happening in the draft that made it very unpredictable and that me 'falling' to 8th was a result of that, a byproduct of the new draft rules." Mark Appel, drafted #8 overall by the Pittsburgh Pirates, 2012. Did not sign that year.

Not signing was a tough decision for Mark.

"We really made every effort over the next couple of weeks to talk with the front office. It was hard to negotiate because I think that if there was a free market negotiation like they

---

[2] As related earlier, Mark Appel was re-drafted as the first selection in the 2013 draft and signed with the Houston Astros.

had in the past, I would've signed with the Pittsburgh Pirates. The issue turned out to be with the new collective bargaining agreement. Their hand was forced in how much they could spend in the draft. So they offered basically as much as they could without losing a draft pick the following year. I had to lean on the advice of my baseball advisor, I leaned on the advice of my parents, my brother, other influential people, my coaches at Stanford, my private coaches from back home, people that I really looked up to and respected and I knew would give me their honest opinion. I got a lot of mixed responses from people. Some people said, 'This is a great opportunity, it's a lot of money, you should sign.' Other people, like my advisor, said, 'The offer is not what you're worth, your value is a whole lot more than that. You never know what will happen in your future, so to protect yourself as much as you can now, you want to be principled in signing for what your value is.' Then there were other people who put money aside and said, 'What are your goals, what do you want to do?' Regardless of the money, my goal was to to get better to be a major league player. And so going back to school for my senior year was an opportunity not only to possibly do better financially, but there were so many other things that I was looking at, things that you can't really put a value on, like being able to graduate in four years from Stanford, and start my pro career with a degree in my pocket. We never got to go to the College World Series, so getting to go back to college for my senior year was giving me another chance to go to the College World Series, which was really valuable to me. There were a lot of things that, money aside, I had to figure out whether what the Pirates were offering me was worth the alternative and I came to the decision that it wasn't. I valued my senior year at Stanford and everything that it entailed more than what the Pirates were able to offer in the draft. A lot of people have told me that I'm crazy for that, but I have a different value system than a lot of people. I just stuck to my guns and I did what I knew was right and went back to school for my senior year. The thing is, the Pirates didn't do anything wrong, I mean getting drafted in the first round is unbelievable. But going back to school for my senior year was more valuable to me than signing in 2012." Mark

> "Then there were other people who put money aside and said, 'What are your goals, what do you want to do?' Regardless of the money, my goal was to get better to be a major league player."

****

*"Baseball doesn't last forever. It is nice to have that
safety net of the college degree."*

High school players are less likely to sign than college players. In 2018, high schoolers comprised a quarter of the players drafted. Less than half of them (44%) signed. The other 56% presumably went on to college. A club generally retains the rights to sign a selected player until the signing deadline or until the player enters, or returns to, a four-year college on a full-time basis.

2018 Draft

	High School	College
Drafted	303	911
Signed	134	732
% Signed	44%	80%

Many of the players who played at Stanford were previously drafted out of high school and chose not to sign. For some, it was an easy decision and they were subsequently drafted three years later.

"My senior year in high school there was a decent amount of professional interest and I had scouts coming over to my house. It was always something that was interesting to me but definitely my parents did not want me to go the professional route right out of high school. It was an attractive offer for a 17-year-old to put money in front of his face but it was not the right decision and I'm very glad I had people around me to steer me in the correct direction. I valued a Stanford education much higher than any reasonable amount of money that I would have been given in the draft." Chris Viall, drafted in the

39th round by the San Francisco Giants, 2013. Did not sign that year.

For some, it was a little more difficult.

"That was a fun time. We had several discussions with teams about signability and all that stuff. The Angels called me and said they picked me in the 15th round. So I thought about that the whole summer. Ultimately we didn't come to terms, but that was a really cool experience." Dominic Jose, drafted in the 15th round by the Los Angeles Angels, 2011. Did not sign that year.

And for some, like Jake Stewart, it was an agonizing decision.

"I got drafted out of high school in the 14th round by the Phillies. That was a long summer. You had the old draft rules back then when slot money didn't matter as much and there was a lot more flexibility on what they could offer. That was back when you had 50 rounds. It was a whole different ball game back then. We had been talking to the local Phillies' scout a bunch before the draft. My dad was acting as my agent and we had told them from the beginning what we were willing to take. They came to my house a few days after the draft and said, 'This is what we think we're going to offer you.' We went back to them and said, 'The number that it's going to take is a million dollars, that's our number, so if it's anything less than a million we're not going to take it.' They said, 'We've still got some guys that we drafted that we're trying to save some money for, so we don't think we're going to be able to meet that million dollar number for you, have fun in college, get better and hopefully we can talk again in three years.' We left it like that in June." Jake

That doesn't sound like a long and agonizing summer.

"The signing deadline back then was August 15th, and I remember sometime in late July he called me back and said, 'Some things have changed, we didn't get a few guys that we thought we were going to get, we want to talk to you again, we think we can make

something happen.' So then I was thinking, 'Oh wait, they're back in the mix.' I had kinda put that out of my mind for the last month and a half, I was 100% set on going to college, so it was a shock to say the least, but it was an exciting shock. Around the first of August the Phillies came to play the Rockies in Denver, so the Phillies GM Ruben Amaro invited me down to meet him and talk to him and I sat at the Rockies game with him. He obviously gave me his pitch for professional baseball, and that got me really excited about professional baseball. And then this is where it starts to get really interesting and nerve-wracking. It was early August, maybe a week before the signing deadline of August 15th, they came back and they offered me $800,000 this time. So it was closer but still not quite the number. So we said, 'No, that's not the number, we said a million.' They were like, 'Alright, alright give us a day, give us a day.' So the next day they came back to the house again and they had $900,000 and they had allotted something for school money, something that took it over a million. We said, 'Oh my gosh, give us a second.' We talked, and we went back to them and said, 'We said a million from the beginning, this is still not a million.' And they were like, 'Alright, alright, give us a day, give us a day.' And then the next day they came back and this time they said, 'We think we've got something you're going to like.' I remember sitting at the dining room table at my house, we were eating breakfast with them, and they slid the piece of paper across the table and it was for a million dollars. So they had finally met the number. I was like, 'Oh crap! What just happened? This is crazy.' So they left my house around lunchtime, they had given me the million dollar offer. I immediately called the Stanford coach and said, 'Hey Nine, the Phillies just came and they offered me a million dollars. I'm really thinking of taking this, I just wanted to talk to you first, because I'm either coming to you or I'm signing to play pro ball.' And he said, 'Hold tight I'll be there in the morning.' So now this is three days before the signing deadline, and the next morning he got on the first flight out of San Jose and he was in our kitchen having breakfast with us. He gave me his pitch for why I should go to college and come

> "I lay face down on my basement floor for 48 hours straight. I did not get up, I did not get into my bed, I slept on the floor in the basement. I didn't know what to do."

to Stanford and then he left. For the next two days — this is actually a true story — I lay face down on my basement floor for 48 hours straight. I did not get up, I did not get into my bed, I slept on the floor in the basement. I didn't know what to do. I kept asking my dad, 'You've been here, tell me what to do, tell me what to do.' At the moment I hated him for it but now I'm very thankful he did it, he said, 'Son, this is your decision, I can't tell you what to do. You've got great options, either way you really can't go wrong. There are two great things that are in front of you and either way, great things will happen.' At the time I was thinking, 'C'mon, just tell me what to do.' So I lay on the floor for those 48 hours and finally came to the conclusion that I was going to go to Stanford. It was an unbelievably tough decision for me but I'm happy I made it." Jake Stewart, drafted in the 14th round by the Philadelphia Phillies, 2009. Did not sign that year.

Did he ever figure out what his dad's preference was?

"He had a great poker face, which just killed me and tied me up because I was trying to ask him all these questions, trying to get it out of him. He went through it. He played all four years at Virginia Tech and his senior year he hit like 380, had 25 home runs or something, he was a First Team All-American. Every major league team wanted him really bad but his dad told them all that he wanted to be an engineer and so that kind of slid his stock down, and he was a late round pick because of it. He was a less money guy, so he got treated like a less money guy than a bonus baby going into the minor leagues, so it didn't work out for him there. So he kinda had been through the process and seen minor league baseball and seen the politics of minor league baseball and everything that goes with it. I was grilling him with questions, asking him so many different things, and everything I could think of just to try and get a reaction out of him so I could see which one he thought was the better decision but he never gave it to me." Jake

Jake passed up $1 million to go to college, but that college was Stanford. He got significantly less when he was drafted again as junior in 2012.

Once a player indicates they're most likely going to college, they often drop into a lower round than what was possible because the teams don't want to waste a draft pick on someone who is unlikely to sign. Given that only 11% of the high school draftees in rounds 31-40 signed in 2018, it's surprising that the clubs still draft players they don't expect to sign. The reasons for this are varied. The clubs typically have more draft spots than players they need, so they may use the later round picks to establish a relationship with a player whom they hope to draft in the future.

> "Once I knew that Stanford was going to be an option for college, the draft for me was going to be more of an honor than anything. I think the Atlanta Braves knew that when they took me. It was a later round and I think they had an understanding that I wasn't going to sign. They said, 'Hey, we just want to let you know that we're really interested in you, we understand you have a firm commitment to Stanford but we wanted to show you that we think you're going to turn into one hell of a player.' It was so cool at the time." Jack Klein, drafted in the 32rd round by the Atlanta Braves, 2013. Did not sign that year.

Sometimes the player has a prior relationship with someone in the organization, such as a scout or a coach.

> "I was drafted out of high school by Oakland in the 38th round. I pretty much knew I was going to college. It was just a courtesy thing from them. I played for their Area Code team and I knew the scouts pretty well. I don't think they drafted me with any intent of actually signing me." Alex Blandino, drafted in the 38th round by the Oakland Athletics, 2011. Did not sign that year.

Sometimes a team will want to recognize or honor a local player.

> "In high school I got drafted in a round that no longer exists — it was the 47th round. That's pretty funny. All the teams I talked to knew I was pretty set on going to Stanford and at the time the class above me had turned down some pretty good money to go to school so I don't think there was any shot for me, there was no way. It was the Cardinals that drafted me, the hometown team. While it was really cool and really exciting I don't

think it was anything that was incredibly serious." David Schmidt, drafted in the 47th round by the St. Louis Cardinals, 2011. Did not sign that year.

And sometimes a team comes close but doesn't end up drafting the player at all.

"It was my senior year in high school and the Orioles' scout came to our home. We cooked up a few snacks and we sat down and he talked us through the minor league process and what to expect as a high school draftee. He emphasized the difference between taking the extra four years and maturing in a team atmosphere, to grow independently in a safe space, on a college team, on a college campus, and the assurance of having a college degree. It was the first time it was drilled into me that baseball doesn't last forever. It is nice to have that safety net of the college degree. I had heard that before, I'd heard it spoken by coaches and my parents and whatnot, but to really hear that come from a baseball guy who'd been deep in the system, who'd been around baseball, that was really important to me. So when it came down to the wire and ultimately I had my commitment to Stanford, I pretty much outright said I was going to school and it would take a really high dollar amount to get me out of my college commitment. Once you announce that, it kinda takes you off the radar." Alex Dunlap

****

"I'm totally convinced that I made the right decision going to college."

Many high school guys pass up a lot of money and in some cases they either don't get drafted or don't get offered as much money the next time around. When asked if they had any regrets, the players certainly mention the difficulty of turning down the money.

"Looking back, knowing what I know now, it was a ton of money and I'm glad that I was ignorant back then because it didn't seem like as much back then as it seems like now. It wasn't really enough to consider not going to college, but I was drafted higher out of high school. I was offered more money out of high school so looking back I kinda wonder. When I think about the money I think if I had taken that much money and was smart with it and didn't spend it and invested it right, that could be a lot of wealth now, six years later. It could've been a pretty good start on life." Wayne

"Turning down seven figures is never easy. I've definitely thought about how my playing career would have gone if I had signed out of high school instead. The best part about choosing to go to college is how much you learn about life and how the world works. Stanford opened my eyes to so many new things and introduced me to some really cool people. I believe I made the right decision." Dom

Some guys look back and realize they weren't ready for minor league life as an 18-year-old.

"I think about what life was like in the minor leagues as a 22-year-old, going through that, it's difficult in a lot of ways. But I can't even imagine being an 18-year-old and being thrown into the minor league lifestyle. I personally don't know how I would have handled that. I don't know if it would have been good for me, or good for my career. Having said all that, I don't really have any regrets. I'm totally convinced that I made the right decision going to college. There aren't many people who make a living playing baseball and it's good to have a degree to fall back on. Like my coach Dean Stotz used to always say, choosing a college is a 40-year decision, not a 4-year decision. The

> "I'm totally convinced that I made the right decision going to college. There aren't many people who make a living playing baseball and it's good to have a degree to fall back on."

same can be said about choosing to go pro or go to college out of high school, it's really a 40-year decision, not a 4-5-10 year decision. The relationships that I've made with people at Stanford that are already starting to do really cool things, you can't really get that without making the decision I made." Wayne

"I looked at myself as a person holistically and was not ready to make the jump to being a professional baseball player directly out of high school. A lot of it is because my entire life I'd grown up just assuming I would go on to college, especially during high school I was planning on having those additional years to learn and grow and mature. I had the opportunity to go to Stanford and it didn't feel right to forego such a formative experience in pursuit of something that I knew would be available to me after those years at school." Kenny

Alex was equally happy with his decision.

"Going to Stanford was a great decision. I was very lucky to be led by some very wise guardians and coaches and other influences in my life that ultimately took me through college, and then I grew and matured so much while at school." Alex D.

And Jake, who had the most agonizing decision of all, puts it this way:

"I really do think I made the right decision. Looking back on it, I honestly think it was maybe not as good of a decision for my baseball career. I think in the long run it was the better decision for my life and my happiness and everything that goes into that outside of baseball. I don't regret my decision, I don't think I ever have. That was one of the things my dad preached to me when I was asking him all those questions, he said, 'Whatever one you go with, just stick to it and don't look back, and take on that decision 100%.' So as soon as I made it, I definitely felt a lot of relief. More when I made the decision than when I called the Phillies, that was obviously one of the more difficult phone calls I've made. I mean, the signing deadline was August 15th at midnight and I think I called them

August 15th at 7:00 PM or something. I was holding on as long as I could, trying to make sure I made the right decision. But I think after I got off the phone with them, as difficult as that decision was, then I felt very relieved. I had a direction, I knew what I was going to do and I felt great about it. I have not regretted it or looked back ever since." Jake

****

A few guys mentioned the difficulty of the minor league lifestyle and looking back, they don't know how they would have "handled it" as an 18-year-old out of high school. How bad can it be?

Chapter 3
Put Me In, Coach

It's safe to say that minor league baseball is unlike anything that most players have experienced before. After dreaming about it for so many years and working hard to get there every player is immediately surprised in some way with something or someone they encounter. The enormity of the minor league system becomes a reality when players show up and realize they're starting at the bottom of the system and have a long way to go to make it to the Major Leagues. The new personalities in the locker room and the ethnic diversity of the teams provide an entertaining and eye-opening experience. On top of all that, the level of play is higher and the day-to-day routine of baseball in the minor leagues is different than what they've been doing their entire lives. And they're doing all of it for less than the minimum wage.

****

"That first summer was an eye-opening experience, definitely."

The road to the Major Leagues goes through the minor leagues. Each of the 30 major league organizations has a tiered system of minor league teams that is designed to improve the skills of the players as they move up the ladder. In total, the minor league system in the US is comprised of over 5,500 players on 192 teams in 16 leagues scattered throughout the US.[1]

Depending on how you count, there are six levels before you get to the Major Leagues. Every organization has one team each in Class A, Class A Advanced, AA and AAA. It's not quite as simple in the Rookie and Short Season leagues. Some organizations do not have Short Season teams and some have more than one Rookie league team.

Rookie-level and Class A leagues tend to feature younger, less experienced players like recent draft picks or players with one or two years of service time. The average age of players in the Rookie leagues in 2017 was a mere 21 years. The average age rises throughout the A levels. The AA and AAA leagues typically feature more experienced and talented players, with the average age being 24.8 and 26.7 years old respectively. The average age in the Major Leagues is 28.

After signing their contracts, players start at the bottom of the minor league system and are generally assigned to one of the four Rookie leagues or one of the two Short Season A Leagues that begin play in June (as opposed to the Major Leagues and most of the minor league teams that begin their regular season games in early April). Players must make their way through this system in order to play in the big leagues. The enormity of the system can be a daunting realization for a newly drafted player.

---

[1] The Mexican League is currently a class AAA minor league with 12 teams in Mexico. While its teams are not affiliated with MLB clubs, some have signed working agreements with MLB teams. The Dominican Summer League adds another 1,540 players on 44 teams. Every MLB organization has at least one team in this league, and some of these players will "graduate" into the Rookie leagues of minor league baseball.

The Minor League Organization[2]

Triple-A

International League   Pacific Coast League

Double-A

Eastern League   Southern League   Texas League

Class A Advanced (or High A)

California League   Carolina League   Florida State League

Class A (or Low A)

Midwest League   South Atlantic League

Class A Short Season

New York-Penn League   Northwest League

Rookie

Appalachian League   Arizona League   Gulf Coast League   Pioneer League

---

[2] Source: Milb.com

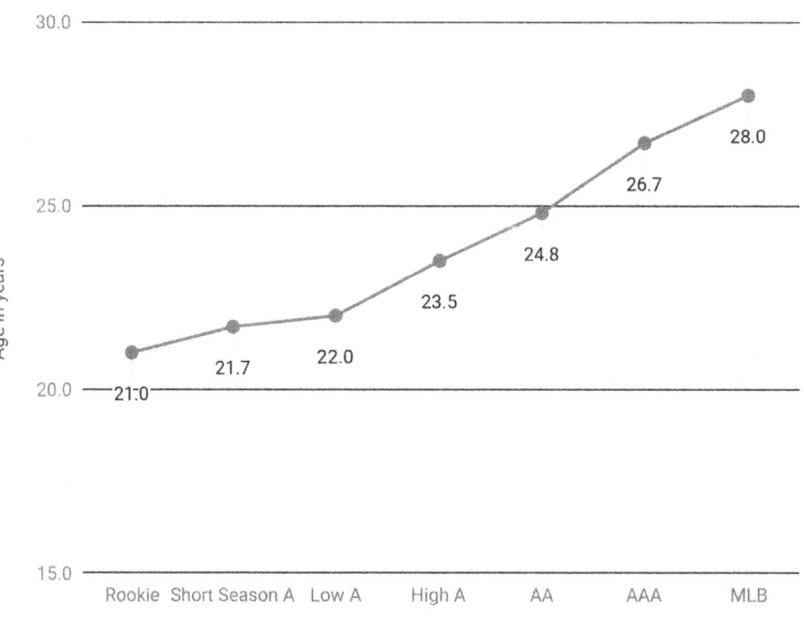

Average Age By Level

"My first summer I was on the bus and there were all these guys that had spent their entire lives playing this game. This was just one level of them and they were trying to move up, just like me. It made it more real. When you look at it from a college program you see the minor leagues as this easy hurdle you'll surpass on your way to major league greatness. But I quickly realized it's not just some elementary game that you play, the minor leagues, these are real people in it and they're all really good." Kenny

"As a recent draftee, your scope of the organization from top to bottom is so big and the big leagues seem so far away. It seems like it's almost a thing you don't even think about because it's so far away." Alex B.

No matter which league they're assigned to, most players quickly see the reality of what they've signed up for, using terms like "rude awakening," "eye-opening," and "shock" to describe their first impressions.

"You go from signing your name on this contract for all this money, you're the king of the world, every local sports reporter is writing that you're the person that's going to be the next thing there, and then the next day you're in 120 degree heat with 50-60% of the population at the camp speaking Spanish, and no one cares who you are, where you came from, and what you signed for. I'm not going to say it takes the wind out of your sails but it's a very rude awakening, we'll call it that." Anonymous

"I'm not going to say it takes the wind out of your sails but it's a very rude awakening, we'll call it that."

"That first summer was an eye-opening experience, definitely. Just playing pro ball in general was way different than college, playing every day is a whole different ball game. I was in the middle of nowhere, I didn't know anybody on the team. Trying to navigate all that stuff was a bit of a culture shock. But I got adjusted after a while, it took some time for sure." Stephen

"I reported to Lakeland, Florida, where our Tigers Spring Training stuff is. That was my first true experience because the Tigers are one of only two organizations — and this may have changed now — that in Spring Training, instructs and all that stuff, you live in dorms. I'm not talking about apartment-style dorms, it is straight bunk beds, one community bathroom, a hallway, dorms. So that was interesting coming into professional baseball and going into that. The building is actually an old hospital, and it looks like it. I mean, it's cinder block brick walls. Yeah, it was interesting." Jake

That first summer is also the first time many players get a look at the logistics of minor league baseball.

"I should have looked at the schedule before I decided when to report. I flew from California to Pittsburgh, went to a major league game there, and the next day it was a 2 1/2 hour drive to State College. I finally got there towards the end of the game. They got me in uniform and I sat there for two innings, not playing. And then they had a travel day. I hadn't even put my stuff into a house yet. All my luggage was just sitting in the locker room. And I didn't know that this was the worst travel day of the season. A 10-hour bus ride to Connecticut to begin a 7-to-10 day road trip. And I'm thinking, welcome to the minor leagues." Tyler

Walking into the locker room for the first time can be a unique experience.

"I went to the Gulf Coast League and it was so cool because with the Yankees, there was so much history and nostalgia in the locker room, everywhere you walked they put quotes from all the Yankee greats up on all the walls. There was a Joe DiMaggio quote as soon as you walked in that said, 'I want to thank the Good Lord for making me a Yankee.' It was so cool seeing all the history and knowing you're a part of something so much bigger than yourself." Dom

"It was definitely eye-opening. I was assigned to Everett, Washington and we were in a high school PE locker room. There were two sides to it, there was a girls' locker room and a boys' locker room with one main entrance. The girls were still using their side, so girls would be running in and out of our locker room — high school girls — and you'd walk right through it. The girls were there probably for a couple weeks, it must have been a summer camp or something. Yeah, we said to ourselves, 'Are you kidding me? We're in pro baseball and we're sharing a PE locker room with high school girls?' " Drew

*"I went to Scottsdale to sign my contract and was there for about a week. That was my first introduction to Latin players and that whole culture, so that was interesting. Our team there was 65-75% Latin at that point. I just remember blaring loud music. The day before I got there two or three American guys had gotten their wallets stolen so there was lot of tension in the locker room between the American guys and the Latin guys. So I came in

during a dicey time with our team. The Latin guys weren't talking to the American guys and the American guys weren't talking to the Latin guys. It was this tension-filled locker room I'd never had before. Usually I'd only ever been in locker rooms where everyone enjoyed each other's company and kind of just goofed off and shot the shit, so that was different." Anonymous

"It was odd going from a very tight-knit squad at college where you're pretty good friends with basically everyone on the team. You show up and you don't know anyone." Marc

"I didn't want to piss anyone off, I was kinda tiptoeing around. Everyone thought I was an undrafted free agent because I showed up late because of course I had to stick around for graduation. Everyone thought I was some scrub off the street, like, where'd you come from? It was interesting, there were some cliques going on at the beginning, some guys trying to fit in here and there. But I was just trying to smile and be approachable and make a good first impression." Chris C.

****

"You've got guys from really all over the world with completely different backgrounds and stories."

One of the first things the new players notice is the different personalities and backgrounds of the players they meet.

"In general what makes pro ball interesting is you're a fraternity made up of a bunch of different types of guys. There are no filters in bringing you together, like in high school or college where it was generally the same kind of people as you. In pro ball the people that come together are so vastly different, it was interesting to see how those personalities collided and came together. It was a hilarious group of people. The walks of life you share a locker room with is something you can't get again." Sam

"The cool thing about being a professional is hearing the different stories because

everyone has played baseball for a long time. Guys have played hundreds of baseball games and every guy has three or four stories about a specific game or an event that are just hilarious. And also getting to be around guys I played against for a long time and never talked to, because we were on the field. And now we were teammates. It's kind of hilarious to me I guess." Jack

"The baseball community just about wherever you go, it's got that same eclectic mix. You've got your smart alecs, you've got your knuckleheads, you've got your real baseball athletic focused guys and you've got the quirky dudes. I was one of the quirky dudes. Cliques happen more or less, you find guys that are similar to you, that's who you gravitate to in the new group." Alex D.

"In college you've got your college guys, they're your automatic friends right there. But in pro ball you've got your Latin American guys, your high school guys, your college guys, your Asian guys, your Australian guys, you've got guys from really all over the world with completely different backgrounds and stories. You play some baseball but you meet a bunch of new people too." Dom

"I found it to be a tremendous cultural experience. Some of the guys from rural parts of the country would have fun calling me a city boy. And I didn't realize there could be such heated debates about which is better, a Ford or a Chevy truck. It was something I had never thought about. Apparently Chevy is better. Ford owners are a bunch of sissies." Anonymous

As many players mention, there's also a lot of ethnic diversity. By far the largest ethnic group is Latino, especially at the lower levels of the system. In 2017, Latinos comprised 43% of Rookie-level teams. That number drops to 33% of Short Season A ball teams and continues dropping steadily to 21% of AAA players.

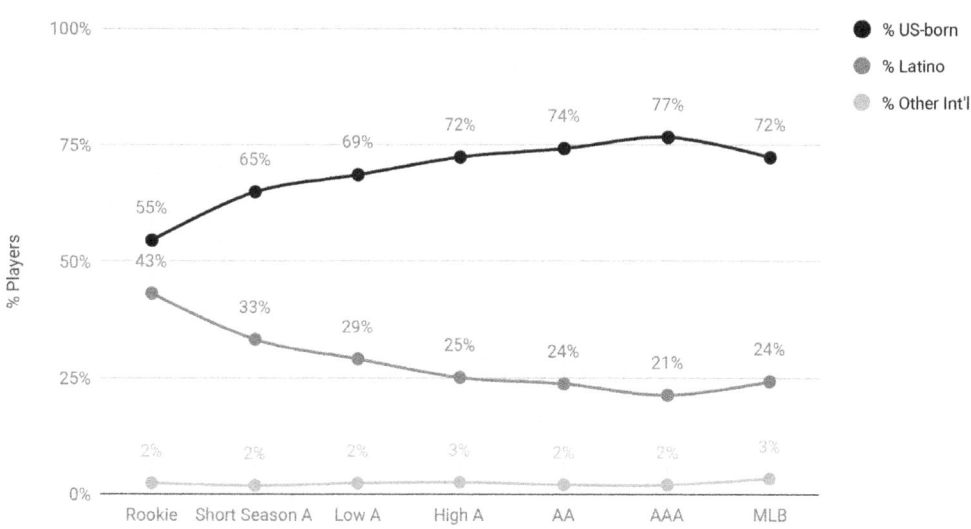

Since most of the draftees start in Rookie-level and Short Season A ball teams, this ethnic diversity is one of the first things the new players talk about.

"It was super interesting that first day when I got to Rookie ball in Arizona, there were a lot of people from the Dominican Republic, from Latin America. It's definitely a culture shock at first. I think for the most part Americans were outnumbered, there were a lot more people from Mexico and the Dominican Republic speaking Spanish. I spoke a little Spanish but they talked way too fast for me. I'm pretty sure I was one of the oldest people there. I could tell most of them were 17, 18 years old." Lonnie

"The most shocking thing was I'd been around baseball players from different parts of the country for years but that was my first time being around guys from other countries, from Venezuela and the Dominican Republic and different places. And honestly, it was

my first real exposure to anybody from other countries that were my age. In high school I remember I went on a couple trips with my church where we went and would serve in other countries but you were around either really old people or really young kids but I had never really interacted with somebody my age from a forgeign country. That was kind of cool, it was kind of interesting. Certainly a culture shock at first." Wayne

"You know that there are a lot of Latinos in baseball but you finally get to witness it firsthand. Everyone's so young, it's very cliquey, and it was cliquey right away. As soon as I walked in, I saw one group of guys together over here and all the Latinos pretty much together over there. And you have the occasional one or two Latinos that wanted to be in both, be with the Americans. They were working on their English because it was their first year trying to speak it. I loved it. I loved the melting pot." Tyler

"I would say the ethnic mix was 70/30 and I was in the minority. I spoke the best Spanish of all the gringos there. I've been taking Spanish on and off since first grade so I was able to communicate more or less. I was one of the older guys, I was Abuelito for a while (an affectionate way of calling me Grandpa). I was the gringo that knew Spanish and would dance to the songs and everything. I was just trying to keep everybody together as a unit, as a team, I knew that was going to be important. I mean, teenagers coming over from the Dominican Republic, from Venezuela, I knew they would need mentorship and I really wanted to break out. I got to try out being a leader in a new squad with a new organization. I've always loved being in that role so being one of the older guys who had some of the most experience, I was able to jump into that role and I really liked it." Alex D.

"We had 14 Latin guys on our team. I had this truck with plenty of room in the back seat and it turned into the Latin bus. Every day I would take everyone to the field in North Carolina. You can have people in the back of your truck as long as they're inside the truck bed, so I would have myself and four or five guys in the cab of my truck and five or six in the back. This is honest to God every single day, I would be taking 11 or 12 Latinos to and from the field. And the funny thing was our Latinos were all really young *and they were really high prospects and it was the most precious cargo ever. At one point I figured I probably had like $6.5 million of free agent signings in the back of my truck with no seat belts. I was always going the speed limit and they wanted me to rev and I was like, 'No, you guys don't understand, if you get hurt or something happens I get fired.' And the best part was I'd always have cops behind me running my plates, or pulling up alongside and I'd just wave at them. I don't know if they were profiling the Latins in the back of my truck. Those guys were so awesome, I freaking loved those guys so much." Colton*

With more than half of the team being Latino, the communication amongst players can obviously be difficult.

"When I first got to Arizona the two catchers that were there were both Latino and they were speaking to each other in Spanish. I had no idea what was going on and they were laughing and I was feeling totally left out." Anonymous catcher

"It was tough at first because both of our catchers were Latin, one was Venezuelan and one was Dominican. It was tough to get on the same page with them because I was the pitcher and they were my battery-mates. They were trying to call a good game for me and it was hard to communicate with them." Chris C.

"My best friend was the translator between the coach and the players and he freaking hated it. It killed him because he was 26 in Low A trying to make a name for himself. He was pitching really well, and he was constantly going into the coach's office translating these meetings for the other guys." Colton

But as the season progressed, so did the communication between players.

"We had 14 Latins on our 25-man roster and as they got to know me well they would start talking in English and really trying hard. It was super broken but they'd never tried it before. These guys would be confident enough around me to try to speak English and I would

speak back to them in Spanish, and I'd correct them and they'd correct me. By the end of the year I really caught on to a ton of Spanish, pretty much everything I needed to talk to someone new. And they bounced enough English off me that we didn't need a translator for the last 40 or 50 games of the year because they were able to comprehend enough of what coach was saying, that was an everyday lesson for both of us. Once they learned English it actually really brought us together as a team." Colton

"Even though I speak some Spanish, people from certain countries are harder to understand than others because they have different accents. Like how in the US they have a southern drawl vs. being from New York, it's similar with Spanish, being Dominican, Venezuelan, Colombian, Mexican. There's a lot of slang, you can't really get taught that." Jack

"A lot of guys can understand English pretty well but just don't speak it very well. That's kinda my situation with Spanish, I can understand much more than I can speak, and usually it's just in the short snippets and little phrases. It's interesting, whenever I'd try to speak with a Latin guy, I'd be practicing my Spanish and he'd be practicing his English and I'd be speaking to him in Spanish he'd be replying to me in English. There are just broken conversations all over the place. They usually don't pronounce their s's, it speeds things up. They're really quick talkers, usually pretty loud, they always try and talk over each other in the locker room. It's tough to understand sometimes." Alex D.

"My Spanish knowledge is very cyclical. In season it slowly gains in fluency. I'm not saying I'm ever fluent but I can somewhat converse. And then after the season it falls away and then it restarts again the next season." Chris V.

"There's one guy from Cuba I got a huge kick out of. When he came over to the US he spoke no English whatsoever. I don't know how he got around or did anything, he probably relied on other Latin guys who spoke a little bit better English. When we were in our first camp the only thing he knew how to say was, 'Group One.' That's all he would say is, 'Group One.' " Tommy

"When I was promoted to AA, that same guy started hitting a ton of home runs. When I came back down I said, 'Hey Randy, what's up? How you been?' And he pointed at himself and said, 'Me? Five home runs.' That's all he said." Danny

Most organizations offer, and in many cases require their players to enroll in Rosetta Stone, a language immersion-based software program that helps them learn English.

"I think the most significant thing that I didn't expect was how important Rosetta Stone is. With the Nationals, everybody is on a mandatory Rosetta Stone curriculum. Every now and then when a few guys at a time would graduate within a short time period of each other, they would have graduation ceremonies and they would hand out Rosetta Stone certificates to these guys. So on the last day of Spring Training, five or six of the more veteran players who had been around for four or five years, they had completed their Rosetta Stone program. They hooked up a speaker and played the classic graduation music. They called them out by name and they would come up and take a picture with their certificate. Then they'd give a short speech in English to everyone, thanking their teammates and their coaches and give a little spiel about their journey and how they're excited to be able to speak English now. It was pretty sweet." Alex D.

"The Royals offer Rosetta Stone and the Latin players have to take an English class until they pass a test. It's not like they're fluent, it's so they can get by. An American can ask for a Rosetta Stone account and get Spanish. Not many Americans do it, I would say it's majority Latins." Jack

"We're required now to take Spanish lessons once or twice a week. Starting next year everyone including the coordinators and the managers and the GM and everyone is required to take Spanish lessons. That's a new thing that Miami has implemented pretty much because we're in Miami. It's a different culture down there. Our organization is probably 50% Latins." Colton

"Over a third of our team was Latin so many of my teammates with the Cardinals had ESL classes. They'd go one or two times a week and they had a tutor that taught them English. I remember the first year these guys would come out of English class and they would walk around saying, 'How are you doing?' 'How am I doing?' 'Because why?' 'Why, because.' It was hilarious." Danny

Whether they speak Spanish or English, whether they're from the Dominican Republic or Venezuela, there's general agreement that the Latinos add buzz to the locker room, especially their music.

"What's really cool about playing with the Latin guys I think is the music. I just LOVE the Latin music. I'm Dominican and so are a lot of my good friends. Their dads played with my dad so a lot of us are friends because of that. It's just cool, we have fun together. They just have a completely different culture and passion and I love it." Dom

"There's Latin music on one side of locker room and American on the other." Drew

"I remember one guy was playing Latin music in the clubhouse and this big superman outfielder — he had already hit ten home runs, he was hitting a home run every night — he went in the locker room and he pressed the button off and said, 'This is America' and walked out. And the Latin guys were looking around at each other not knowing what to do. That was pretty funny." Danny

"It's so funny, the thing that really cracked me up about the Latin players, I don't know how they have so much energy, they're always bouncing off the walls, I don't know how, there's an excitement there." Mark

"The Dominicans are very entertaining and I was very happy I got to play with guys from Latin America. It gives you a little bit more perspective. Baseball is life for those guys." Justin

"The Latin kids are generally 17-20 years old so they're a handful. But you learn how to deal with them, and honestly learning a tiny bit of Spanish helps, but once you make a couple friends down there it's alright. A lot of the guys don't even have any plans to move up. They're so thrilled that they're staying in a hotel in America, they eat McDonald's every day, they're just so happy to be there." Marc

Despite the players' communication difficulties and the cultural differences they have to adjust to, some real friendships are made throughout the season.

"Once I got to know the Latins they got to be really awesome dudes. I got pretty close to one of the guys from the Dominican Republic on our team. He met this beautiful 20-something North Carolina girl and he wanted to take her on a date. He was going to take her out Saturday night and on the way to the game he was freaking out saying, 'I can't do it, I can't do it, I can't do it.' And I was like, 'Dude, you have to do it.' She probably thought it was really cute that he spoke only broken English but he was worried it was going to ruin it, saying, 'I'm not going to be able to talk with her.' So right before she was about to pick him up he was like, 'No, I'm telling her no.' I said, 'If anything, I'll go and translate,' and he said, 'Really, you would do that for me?' I said sure. I ended up picking her up in my truck and chauffeuring them to the place where they were going to eat. And then for their first date I sat there and translated for them. And the funny thing was she was giving me her number if she needed to ask me a question or something. I was more than just the translator, I literally went on the date with them, with an American girl while I'm single, a girl I would enjoy dating. That was probably four months ago and they saw each other every day after that and today they're still dating." Colton

"I was more than just the translator, I literally went on the date with them, with an American girl while I'm single, a girl I would enjoy dating."

"One of my favorite memories was the relationship I had with a guy from Venezuela. He was super intellectually curious. When I first met him he asked me if I went to college and

I told him I went to Stanford. He knew what Stanford was and he couldn't stop asking questions about it and what I studied. He had pretty good English but he was always trying to practice and pick up new words. We would sit together a lot in the dugouts and he would help me with Spanish and I would help him with English. That was kinda fun. It's weird because he grew up in Venezuela, his family didn't have any money, he probably grew up in a cinder block house and I grew up in total opposite circumstances. I think that's one cool thing about minor league baseball: it brings guys like him and guys like me together. On the field and around the clubhouse we're really not that different even though we come from totally drastically different circumstances." Wayne

****

"It's just all baseball and it's every single day."

It's not just the diversity of people that's different in pro ball. Playing the game itself is different than what these players have been used to. Yes, they're still playing the game they've been playing their entire lives and it's still 90 feet to first base, but there are several reasons that playing pro ball is different than college ball. One of them is that the overall level of talent in professional baseball is better.

"One of the areas where there's a big difference is the raw talent. In pro ball you have not only the best talent in the US but also the best talent from around the world. Guys are taller, they throw harder, they hit farther, they run faster, they're better fielders. The raw natural athletic abilities are definitely superior in professional baseball. And over the course of the levels the refinement and sophistication of the game improves, like how many errors are committed and how much command the pitchers have of the strike zone." Kenny

The style of the game also differs.

"The professional style game is different than college. I would say the pro game aligns itself more closely to the Latins' approach, it's very all or nothing, talent trumps any sort of strategy and fundamentals. Let's outslug everyone, let's try to throw a million fastballs by guys and let's out-talent everyone. Whereas the college game is, let's figure out how to beat this guy with a little finesse and let's try to outmaneuver your opponent." Chris C.

"For me, pro ball meant learning more baseball strategy because now I'm a starting pitcher learning how to conserve pitches, how to set people up in different counts, what pitches I can throw to get a ground ball double play. In college I was mostly a reliever and closer where I would get really pumped up and try to throw 100 mph every pitch and throw really hard sliders and get three outs and the game's over. There's not much strategy behind that." Chris V.

It can be difficult to compare the level of competition between pro ball and college ball because of where players are coming from and where they begin their careers.

"Being in the Arizona Rookie League it was a little bit of a step down compared to Pac-12 competition. You're kind of in awe and at the same time you're saying wait, this is professional baseball? Because it's usually the high school draft kids and the young Latinos and the average age is probably 19 or 20. I was 22 at the time and I had been playing in the Pac-12, which is one of the better baseball conferences." Anonymous

"I had never seen the caliber of baseball like it was in the Arizona Rookie League. It was like playing at a high school level but everyone was a big basher, everyone had the potential to hit the ball 500 feet but then you could just as easily strike everyone out. It felt like Little League, everything was a home run or a strikeout. There was no strategy, there was no approach to it." Chris C.

"To me, short season in the Northwest League was as close to college as you play, that and Low A I guess. The short season team tends to be most of the college draft players so I wouldn't say it's an All-Star college team but it would be like playing in one of the bigger conferences in college. That feels like you're right back to business. And you think it's competitive, you think it's the best baseball you've ever played, and then you realize you're the lowest on the totem pole." Cal

> "You think it's competitive, you think it's the best baseball you've ever played, and then you realize you're the lowest on the totem pole."

"I used to hear that the closest level to college ball was AA. In my experience there's no way that's true. AA was way more advanced than college because of the talent and the sophistication. The talent obviously was higher in AA and the refinement of the game was also higher. Low A is a wild level of sorts where it's the first full season for most guys. They're young, the pitchers throw hard but they generally can't throw strikes, they don't know how to throw their secondary pitches for strikes, and hitters aren't as sophisticated." Kenny

The first summer, players notice a lot of differences between college ball and pro ball, especially if they start in Rookie League.

"When I was assigned to the Arizona Rookie League I was like, 'Alright, this is interesting, it isn't really what I expected at first, but in the end I had to prove myself regardless if it was here or A ball or anywhere.' We were using wood bats, it was totally different, there was no real organization. You haven't really practiced with these guys ever, it's really every man out there for himself. Yeah, you're all on the Mariners but you're just kind of thrown right into the fire. So I went about my day to day, as I got acclimated to the coaching staff and the overall daily schedule, it was easy to get in a routine. You go there for one reason and that's just to play ball. Once you get over that little culture shock in the beginning it was like, let's get down to business." Lonnie

"Coming from college, the Rookie league was kind of a brutal spot to be. There were just some long days. We'd get to the field at noon, and we'd eat lunch, we'd hang out, we'd have extensive couple hour meetings, practice for two or three more hours, shag some balls and then around 5:00 or 6:00 PM we'd start preparing for the game, and the game went from 7:00-10:00 PM. So you're looking at 10-11 hour days in the 110-degree Arizona summer which wasn't always the most fun thing. Meetings were basic, like pitching approach for us pitchers, a lot of it was even disciplinary stuff. It was a lot of stuff that was tough to listen to coming out of college because we thought we had it all figured out and we'd been through organized competitive baseball and it was a lot of repetitive stuff. It was a little bit boring at times." Chris C.

"At the lower levels like Rookie ball it definitely still felt a little college-like with the pregame fundamentals we had every day. That got annoying because all the college guys knew exactly where to be on a ball in the gap or on bunt defense, but we had to work on it. It was more for the young guys, the 18-year-old Latins that are in Rookie ball." Drew

Some players notice the difference in team dynamics.

"You're not at college where you build relationships with your classmates or with this 35-man group of guys, where you play with them and you practice with them every day. It's much more individualized, it doesn't feel like a team, a lot of people say that about pro ball. I remember our college coach told us, 'After college you're never going to have the same team dynamic again,' and that was really really true. I think a lot of guys who've played at both levels can attest to that as well. It's like you're on the team with these guys but are you really their teammates? Do you really feel a closeness or a loyalty to these guys more than the guys in the other dugout?" Chris C.

And some notice the little things that turn out to be quite important.

"There are so many little things that you learn. In pro ball you're never ever ever allowed to say, 'Ball, ball ball!' You have to say, 'I got it, I got it, I got it' or something like that. I wasn't sure why for a long time but then we figured out it's probably because it sounds like, 'Wall, wall, wall.' This becomes a problem when two outfielders are going back for a fly ball and one outfielder needs to communicate to the other. As one outfielder is going out to catch it the other one is telling him there's a wall, there's a wall, there's a wall." Kenny

Sometimes that first game doesn't go so well.

"I remember my first game they put me at third base and I made four errors in one game. The team lost and we got back in the locker room and the manager just ripped us apart. 'Four errors! That's unacceptable!' And of course I was the one who made all the errors and I was thinking, 'Wow, what a way to start. I guess it can only go up from here.' We had a road trip the next day and the hitting coach was like, 'Are you scared? Are you scared to play? You're scared to play, you're scared.' And I remember my first at bat that road trip I hit a home run and I ran around the bases thinking, I'm not scared, screw you!" Danny

Some players comment on the different coaching styles in professional baseball.

"Coaching was different, big time. I remember getting there and I sat down in the manager's office and he was like, 'Look guys, you're in pro ball now, we're here to help you. You're professionals, we're going to treat you like professionals, go about your business. I know you guys are mature players, you went to college, so handle your business and we won't say anything.' That has kind of been my experience to date. They are a lot less hands-on. I've had a lot of guys just say be myself and trust my athleticism instead of trying to be someone else or trying to buy into one style of hitting. There's a lot of give and take and they don't hound you for not agreeing with them, they just want what feels right, as long as you perform, that's all that matters. Pro ball is an entirely new *way of going about preparing, you're your own hitting coach in pro ball." Drew*

"You could probably say college coaching is more about micromanagement and pro ball is more about letting the players find their own rhythm and figure out their own style." Kenny

"I'd say coaching in pro ball is pretty hands off compared to college ball. The thought is, 'You've done well to get to this point, continue doing the same thing because you're doing it pretty well.' They'll give you instruction and pointers if you ask them or if they think they can give you some knowledge that will help you in your career. It's more on a suggestion basis, they don't really say you have to do this or that. The only time where they could say you have to do this would be like if you're just throwing a pitch that people are hitting all over the ballpark and you continue to do it. They'd say, 'Hey, stop throwing your slider, it's not good today, throw a changeup.' " Chris V.

"In my first summer of pro ball I had a coach that basically told me that whatever worked for me in college wasn't going to work in the pros. It kind of threw me for a loop because he just was like, 'Hey, I know you were great in college but pro ball is a totally different game, you're going to have to change your routine, you're going to have to change your approach, you're going to have to change a lot of stuff.' So I kind of believed him. I had been brought up to be a coachable player and to listen to my coaches, but looking back I shouldn't have believed him, I just didn't know better. He'd probably had success with some players, saying that stuff would light a fire under them, telling them don't be content, don't be complacent, keep working hard, all that stuff, but for me it sounded like whatever you did to get here isn't going to get you to the next level. That was an interesting first introduction to pro ball." Mark

Fortunately there are takeaways from college ball that prove to be useful in pro ball.

"The further away I get from the Stanford program the more I appreciate the little things that we complained about and got used to eventually. There are things that translate really well in pro ball, like running all the time on the field. No one says anything in the minors and pro ball about always running everything out but they're taking notes and they're writing it in the report, like his effort level was not really very good today and he's not running the ball out. Or like when you're in Short Season A and you don't have the pre-game spread, it's just PB&J's and you're used to it. The short leash aspect at college was definitely indicative of how it's going to be in pro ball, especially at the upper levels. Even if you're a prospect, if you don't put up numbers in the big leagues you're gone right away. Those are the little tidbits I took away from college." Anonymous

Another difference between college ball and pro ball is the fact that players are playing it every day, which allows them to get more immersed in the game than they were used to before.

"When you play college ball there's a lot going on — you've got school, you've got your social life, you're a student athlete and you're playing once during the week and a 3-game series on the weekend. When you change over to pro ball there's no more school, it's just all baseball and it's every single day so you're constantly fine tuning and working on your craft and you're immersed in a completely different culture." Dom

"My first game in the Arizona Rookie League was so relaxed, there just wasn't as much pressure. Obviously there's pressure to develop, but relative to a college game where there are tons of people in the crowd, and scouts, and stuff like that, it felt like a little weight was lifted off your shoulders — not a huge weight — but a little bit. So it was nice to be able to get away for a little bit, and just play baseball and not have to worry about school, not have to worry about the scouts, the coaches, and stuff like that. It was almost like freedom, which was the coolest aspect of it." Lonnie

It's often said that baseball is meant to be played every day and that's exactly what they do.

"You essentially play every single day in pro ball, which means you get settled quickly into a routine. The vast majority of games were in the evening, usually at 7:00 PM. If we were at home, we'd show up around 1:00, and if we were away, the bus would leave the hotel somewhere around 2:00 or 3:00. A typical schedule for position players would start with warm up drills in the batting cages soon after we arrived. There'd be some down time before batting practice on the field with the entire team. Batting practice would last for an hour to 90 minutes. After batting practice, if we were at home, we'd have at least an hour before we'd have to suit up for the game because it'd be the visiting team's turn to take batting practice. When we were on the road, of course, we'd only have enough time to change if we needed to, grab a bite to eat and do what we needed to do to get ready for the game. Then 30 minutes before the game you'd suit up, grab your stuff and head out to the field for the most important part of your day. Depending on how long the game went we'd leave the field around 10:30 or 11:00 PM." Kenny

"In the Gulf Coast League we played a round robin each week. Every five days we'd play the Mets, the Marlins, the Astros and the Cardinals and then we would take the 5th day off and we'd just go through that cycle the whole summer. And it was at everybody's Spring Training complexes so we were all within an hour of each other. The longest drive we had to make was 2-3 hours to get to Tampa, where the Yankees complex was. Never an overnight. Everything was in the afternoon. We had the occasional rain out. When it rained it poured, and we'd get the heavy downpours and there'd be pools at second base and shortstop. At that point we'd just say, 'Ah, we're not going to pull the tarps out, let's just call it a day.' We'd head home and try again the next day. They would reschedule double headers so those were long days as well." Alex D.

"One thing that people don't realize is the schedule is very much the same every day. At 12:30 I'd take myself and my Latin buddies to get food at the local grocery store because they had a hot bar there. At 1:00 we'd get to the field, go to English class and early hitting. Then we were on the field at 2:00 for throwing, defense, and batting practice. We were off by 5:00 and there were two hours before the game. The game started at 7:00, it went until 10:00 but we were not out of there until 11:00. We'd go get *something to eat, get in bed by 1:00 or 2:00 AM, then we'd wake up at 10:00, 10:30 and do it over again."* Colton

Surprisingly, this consistent and regimented schedule creates a lot of downtime.

"There's so much downtime you just fill it with so much BS, as much BS as you can possibly think of to do. We had a ping pong table in our place and we screwed around with that." Lonnie

"You're at the field so much and there's so much downtime. Two hours between this and two hours afterwards and you just don't really know what to do. At first it really bugged me, I felt so empty and anxious and I had all this anxiety because I had all this downtime. I was thinking, shoot, I'm not doing anything right now, nothing I can do is productive, between the game and practice and afterwards. So I started reading a lot to fill that time. And now I and a friend from Vanderbilt are co-writing a research paper together on blockchain technologies, how it's going to affect local energy markets. It's something I'd never do if I had a real job, but since I have all this free time it's what I've been doing with it. The higher you move up, the more time you spend in pro ball, the more you figure out how to fill that time. Guys will play cards for three hours and be totally happy. I love doing that but I can't do it for three hours a day for 140 days straight." Colton

> **"Guys will play cards for three hours and be totally happy. I love doing that but I can't do it for three hours a day for 140 days straight."**

The reality is that players work up to 10-hour days practically every day of the season. If you look at what they're being paid, it works out to much less than the minimum wage.

****

"The lack of pay is the part that's just absolutely wild."

Some players make a lot of money in the draft and some do not. As was evident in the first chapter, signing bonuses among drafted players vary tremendously. In the 2018 draft, the first selection signed for $7.5 million while many players signed for just $1,000. Once they're in the minor league system, salaries are standardized. Until a minor league player is placed on a 40-man roster, monthly salaries are as follows:

Level	Monthly Salary	Annual Increase*
Rookie and Short Season	$1,250	$50
Low A	$1,400	$50
High A	$1,600	$50
AA	$1,800	$100
AAA	$2,250	$300

*Annual increase if repeating the same level

Players get no room and board and they owe clubhouse dues every day. Obviously, minor league players are not making much money.

"It's laughable, you just have to laugh about it. As a player it's my decision to do this, I'm the one who's accepting basically no money." Jack

"I can't imagine if I didn't have a part time job on the side. The first paycheck I got, it was cool because it was my first official paycheck, but I want to say it was $350 or something. You're just looking at that thinking, wow, that's going to last me for two weeks?" Anonymous

Hence, in February of 2014, a lawsuit known as Senne v. Office of the Commissioner of Baseball was filed by certain minor league baseball players that certain MLB Clubs failed to pay minimum wage and overtime to minor leaguers as required by the Fair Labor Standards Act ("FLSA"). The complaint was that given the salaries they are paid, and the fact that they are working 50+ hours per week, minor league players are making less than minimum wage, and in some cases fall below the federal poverty line.

"In Idaho Falls (Rookie) you're only making $500 or so every two weeks and they take $215 of each check to pay for your housing, so I was clearing a little under $300 every two weeks. Do the simple math of nine-hour days, seven days a week and I figured I was making just over $2.00 an hour. I can work a day at home doing minimum wage and if I work eight hours I'd make more in three days than I make in two weeks playing baseball." Jack

Unfortunately for minor league players there was a provision in the omnibus spending bill signed into law by President Trump in March of 2018 that classifies minor league baseball players in the same manner as some executives and administrative staff members on salaries who are exempt from minimum wage and overtime law under the Fair Labor Standards Act of 1938. That provision effectively keeps the players at the status quo.[3]

---

[3] forbes.com/sites/maurybrown/2018/03/26/the-fragile-economics-between-mlb-the-minors-and-the-minimum-wage-exemption/#74c850233c21

As you'll see in the coming chapters, many minor league players get creative with food and housing to get by, and are happy to even hover around breakeven. When one player was asked if he has any money left after paying for rent, he answered, "After I eat? No."

"Some guys had big signing bonuses so they were fine, some guys came from families who supported them, like me, my family kind of helped me out a little bit. On road trips one guy would get a loaf of bread and some peanut butter and he wouldn't go out to dinner after the games to save money. He would just eat peanut butter sandwiches. And then go to the field and eat the turkey or whatever was there." Danny

"You dip into your savings a little bit. My recurring expenses aren't very high, so I think I'm at the breakeven point to running a little bit of a negative during the season which is OK because I got a decent signing bonus. But for guys who don't have the same kind of signing bonuses it's not a good situation. I would be much more worried about my finances if I were in that situation." Chris V.

Another issue is that the minor league pay scale is the same no matter where you live. It's rare to find a business in which the pay doesn't adjust to the cost of living.

"In California, my rent was $500 more than it was in my Virginia and South Carolina leagues. So they could tailor the pay a little bit to match your living expenses. $1,400 doesn't get you that far in California. It's just not a good feeling dipping into the bank account to pay rent, then you've got car insurance, whatever other stuff, food as well." Marc

"Bradenton, Florida is not the cheapest. I basically was in the red after rent every month because you make no money." Tyler

When asked what they would change about the minor league system, the players' answers almost universally had to do with money.

"The lack of pay is the part that's just absolutely wild. The reason it's hard to ever complain is we're working at a job where you have the potential to literally make $4,000 to $5,000 a day in the big leagues. If you're making minimum $500,000 a year, and there are 160 games, you do the math, that's just an absurd amount of money. But where you pay for it is on your journey there. It's tough, it's why people fight so hard to make money in the draft and to boost their signing bonus, and to get deals, and to get sponsored by this or that, because you're just trying to cheat the system anywhere you can while you're trying to get to the top." Cal

"It wasn't something that I really had to deal with because of my signing bonus, but if there's a way that guys can have a better quality of life, that would be a whole lot better. The one glaring issue that I see with minor league baseball is that the guys don't really get paid enough to give it an honest shot. I don't know what the solution is to that." Mark

Jake has a solution.

"I would pay people more money. It's just not sustainable. We did the calculations; if they averaged $40,000 a year for all the minor league players it would only be an extra $5-10 million to the club, which to a billion dollar organization is nothing. It would give these people the ability to chase their dreams for a lot longer. Something like $20,000 in Low A, $30,000 in High A, $40,000 in AA, even if you did something like that, that's still something that you can live on, and really put your sole focus to it. If you're going to do it for a while, you've got to come back in the off-season and get a job and that's taking people's focus and energy and efforts away from being the best baseball player they could be. It would be good for the game and good for more people if they could do that so people had the ability to really put their whole power

and effort into becoming the best baseball player they could be instead of having to scrape and struggle to survive in the off-season." Jake

Jake isn't the only one who mentions that the lack of pay can affect what players do in the off-season.

"Can you make it as a 40th rounder? No doubt. I know undrafted guys who are going to play in the big leagues. If you're good enough you'll make it to the big leagues. The issue is, can you live long enough, right? Can you last on what you're making? I'm not saying that there are many guys who if they're good enough aren't going to continue to play and make it but there's definitely an advantage if you sign for a million dollars in the draft. Maybe you don't have to work in the off-season, maybe you can go live somewhere and train with a special guy who's going to up your game an extra 3% and that 3% is what gets you there. That's a very simplistic way of looking at it, it's probably not how it works, but that is the advantage of being put in a good place early on. A lot of guys, they play and they play and they play and they play, and they run out of money. It's like, I can't do this, I can't have a family. It's one thing to be a single kid, 22 years old, you can make ends meet, you can live with your family. But when you get married and you have a kid, I'm going to go out on a limb and say $8,000 a year doesn't get you very far." Anonymous

"Nobody knows what players are going through. People say you're playing the best game in the world for money but I'm like yeah, I'm making no money. I'm getting behind in a career after four years of making no money. So now I'm really behind the curve. It's a tough deal and no one understands it. If you compensated the players a little more maybe there would be better things said about it." Tyler

****

Not only is the level of pay for minor league players not adequate during the season, they are not paid at all in the off-season. They have more than five months off before they have to report for Spring Training. There are a lot of ways that they occupy their time during this period. What exactly do they do in the off-season?

Chapter 4
The "Off" Season

Minor league baseball players aren't completely "off" in the off-season. You might think they have five months free between the end of the minor league season and the beginning of Spring Training, but that's not necessarily the case. In the 2018 minor league season, all the regular season games ended by September 3rd, but teams that made the playoffs could have played as late as September 18th (if you were "lucky" enough to be in the AAA Championship game between the Pacific Coast League and the International League). After that, there are several options for players of all levels in the system, including getting called up to the Major Leagues, playing in a Fall or Winter League, going to Instructional League, going back to school, or simply going home to rest.

****

"The worst thing is to be good enough to make it to the finals and then not win."

The minor league season is long. Teams in the full season leagues that begin play at the end of Spring Training play about 140 games. Teams in the short season leagues that begin play after the June draft play about 75 games. Most of the players coming out of the draft have just finished their college or high school seasons so they've been playing games since as early as February. By the beginning of September, players are tired from the long season and don't necessarily want to make the playoffs. Some of them just want to go home.

"It's not always a bad thing for your team to be bad in the minor leagues. Everyone wants to go home by the end of August." Anonymous

"I've heard of guys rooting against their own team because they didn't want to go to the playoffs. Of course, many guys wanted to keep playing so it made for a polarizing situation. Some guys on the team didn't want to go home, the other guys did. Thankfully, as far as I know, nobody actually threw the games." Kenny

"I was always the guy that wanted to keep playing. I mean, the playoffs are only another week or two. I'd be like, 'Let's go win a championship, it's only two more weeks here guys, it's not that bad.' I never understood why when you're getting toward the end of the year, and you're one game ahead with six games to go, guys would say we should just lose. I mean c'mon. Nobody will say that officially, it's kind of under their breath, there are definitely guys like that, they're just there for their paychecks, they don't want to be there any longer than they have to be." Anonymous

"It was the last game of the year and both teams were out of playoff contention. We were all joking around and we used the same bat for every at bat, we'd leave it at home

plate. Everyone wanted to get out of there, the umpires too, everyone had flights that afternoon. During the game our outfielder dove and got a concussion. We had to wait 30 minutes for the ambulance, everyone was bummed. Guys had flights coming up that afternoon and we were thinking, this is the worst thing that can happen but we hope he's OK. They ended up carting him off the field, and he gave us the thumbs up. This guy was dying and gave us the thumbs up and both fans started clapping. And then we finished the game. The worst thing for this guy was they wanted to monitor him so they canceled his flight home that day and he had to stay for an extra week and a half because of his concussion symptoms. He was like, 'Man, I'm missing my friend's birthday party, we were going to a lake house and I'm still stuck here." Danny

"We did make the playoffs but we got knocked out on the first or second round. We didn't make it to the championship or anything. The worst thing is to be good enough to make it to the finals and then not win. So you stick around for a few extra weeks and then you don't even get a ring." Wayne

"One year we went all the way to the last possible day and lost. It's the minor leaguer's nightmare — playing until September 20th and losing. The next year we made playoffs and we basically said we had to win it all, we were going to do it. We got to the championship and we swept, we won three straight. We won the first two games in walk-offs and we should have lost those two games, the other team had them in the bag. We just clutched up in the ninth inning both times and came back to win. So then we just needed one more win to go home. We were in San Antonio and we had a rain delay of an hour, then our leadoff hitter hit a home run on the first pitch of the game. From then on we knew we were going to win. It was that double excitement of winning the championship and also being able to go home the next day. I had been in Tulsa my entire season, I had been grinding on this team the whole year and we won it all. It's already

"It's already one of the best feelings when the season is over and it's freedom when you're flying home or driving home, the off-season is upon us."

one of the best feelings when the season is over and it's freedom when you're flying home or driving home, the off-season is upon us. Then there's winning a championship and also thinking, I don't have to play baseball tomorrow, I get a break." Drew

But that's all he got. Unlike in the Major Leagues, minor league players don't get a playoff bonus.

"We just get paid our regular salary until we're finished. So I got an extra what, $400. No bonus. We got the ring the next year." Drew

Eventually the season ends whether you make the playoffs or not. The process of getting home can be an ordeal.

"The last series of the year we had a ten to eleven hour bus trip to Boise, Idaho and we had to win the last game to make the playoffs. We ended up losing the last game and didn't make the playoffs. It was a night game so we bussed back through the night into the next morning, and by the time we got back we all had plane tickets to get home. I had a little less than an hour to pack up all my stuff from the house, then I had to go back to the field, get on a shuttle, and get driven another hour and fifteen minutes up to Portland. Then I got on a plane to Atlanta and had to change planes there to my hometown. I was traveling for like 26 hours. After that, I think I slept for about three weeks. I was exhausted and tired, and I just remember feeling that whole off-season that I've gotta work harder to make sure my body's in shape to endure that grind. That last month I think I lost like 10 pounds, with the travel and the food and all of that." Anonymous

"I actually had to drive cross country because I couldn't find a shipping service for my car out of Altoona, Pennsylvania. I was on the market for two and a half weeks and nobody ever contacted me. Nobody ships a car out of Altoona, especially to California. I drove across the country as soon as the last game ended, I couldn't be ready fast enough. We went to playoffs and I think we lost two of three games and we were done. It was raining and it was cold and it was like, get us the hell out of here." Tyler

The minor league teams either directly make the players' airline reservations to their home city or give them a travel allowance to drive themselves home. Some players get creative with this.

"Everyone tries to get a little extra. What some guys would do is say they were driving home, but they would carpool with somebody and only one guy would drive, so they would get an extra allotment of gas money and they would split it." Anonymous

"Some guys would say they were driving cross country and use that money to pay for a plane flight. Or they would say their final destination was all the way across the country when they were only driving halfway across." Anonymous

"The amount of money you get goes by miles, so one year half our team said they were driving to California. One by one the players kept going into the office and saying they were going to California. Finally when the last two kids said they were going to California, the manager yelled, 'There's no way you're going to California!' " Colton

"I heard guys saying they had family in Italy so they would get a plane ticket to Italy at the end of the season." Andrew

But in at least one case, someone didn't actually want to go home.

"We had a Dominican who told the organization at the end of the season that his arm hurt so he didn't have to go back home. He got to stay in Jupiter, Florida for the off-season." Colton

****

"I had to go to Instructs and that was just a total drag after I'd finished the full season."

Once the season ends there are various scenarios for what minor league players will do next. A few players from AA and AAA might get a September call-up to the big leagues when the active rosters expand from 25-man to 40-man. This expansion allows the clubs to activate and call up any player on its 40-man roster, and most clubs use this to add at least a few players. Those minor leaguers will then finish out the season with their major league clubs, which means they could be playing all the way into the October World Series. The vast majority of minor league players, however, do not get a September call-up and are theoretically finished. Unless it's your Rookie year and you get invited to "Instructs."

"Instructional League is an extra five or six weeks you play after the season to develop your skills in a low pressure environment. Guys view it as a good thing and a bad thing. It's a good thing because if you're selected it means the organization cares about you and you get to improve your game. The bad thing is nobody wants to go because it's at the end of your season and your season is extended. You're back at the good old Comfort Inn and Suites in Surprise, Arizona and it's really hot. One game it got up to 115, maybe even 120 degrees." Kenny

"I had to go to Instructs and that was just a total drag after I'd finished the full season. It was basically just a bunch of 18-year-old kids and me, and a couple of other guys my age, but mostly just super young kids, 18-year-old Americans and 16-year-old Dominicans. There were a couple 16-year-old guys they brought over from the Dominican Republic after their season had finished. Just little boys. I don't think they can play in the regular season until they're 18, but for Instructs they bring some young kids over. I think it's good for a lot of people who didn't get a lot of at bats but I probably caught two-thirds of the games that season, so I got a lot of at bats. I wasn't super excited about being there. Maybe they just had to check the box — you gotta do it at some point." Wayne

"I went to Instructs that Fall. That was actually pretty much par for the course. A lot of baseball, living in the dorms, eating cafeteria food, all that good stuff." Jake

"It was so funny, I didn't understand pro ball really, so I asked the farm director if I could miss Instructs that year because I had to take classes, and he gave me a hard NO. 'C'mon buddy you just signed with us, you're coming.' Everyone wants to enjoy their off-season but it clearly shows they care about you if you're going there. So I went to Instructs while taking classes. I had to take a midterm in Florida, that was fun." Marc

"That first off-season I did both, I went to Instructs and went to school. The first week of school I was in Instructs and missed the first week of classes, then I was in school for the second week, and then I had surgery in the third week so I missed the entire third week of classes and then I went back to school for the rest of the quarter." Chris V.

Each organization's "Instructs" takes place in its Spring Training complex, which has multiple fields on which to play. Teams from one organization frequently scrimmage teams from other organizations throughout the camp.

"One time during Instructs there was a home plate collision on the other field. A runner was coming home and he charged the catcher. Words were exchanged but the game went on. Later somebody must have slid in hard into second base or did something stupid and the situation just erupted. There was a massive brawl, a big mosh pit in the middle of the field. We all tried to go over but our manager wouldn't let us so we just watched it all happen from our field. We saw guys throwing punches, tackling other guys, but the worse was some guy took his cleats off and was trying to hit guys with it." Kenny

In 2016, Tim Tebow, the Heisman Trophy winner and two-time national champion quarterback, was attending Instructs in Florida after signing with the Mets. He was playing his first game against the Cardinals.

"The first at bat Tebow had in Instructs he hit a home run, that was off one of my roommates. The funny part about that was after Tebow hit the home run

> "The first at bat Tebow had in Instructs he hit a home run, that was off one of my roommates."

my roommate posted on Twitter '@timtebow I thought we agreed you were taking first pitch and you hit the first pitch.' It blew up and had tons of retweets and a bunch of people saw it. Someone in the Cardinals front office texted him and told him, 'You have to take that down, you're not allowed to talk about your game like you're intending to fix it for the other team.'" Anonymous

Instructs is run like a camp, so the routine can get a little old and guys have to find a way to make it more interesting.

"We had this guy running the Instructs — his name was DJ. He was just the funniest guy. And every morning we would gather around and he would talk. He was pretty much a stand-up comedian. He would curse every other word. Mother-f this and f'ing that. It was one of the last days of Instructs, and I had been watching this guy every single day. In the training room I had started doing an impression of DJ and a couple guys thought it was really funny. And so one day one of the guys came up to me and said, 'Hey man, be ready, you're going to have to do a DJ impression, he's going to make you do an impression of him in front of everyone, so be prepared.' I was like, 'Oh dang.' I had about 10 minutes to prepare. I was thinking, what should I do, what should I say? He had a little belly so I stuffed a little shirt in my belly so I looked a little chubby. He said, 'So Ah think it's good and all that you guys are havin' a good time out here, and Ah think it's important to joke around and make fun of people. But if you're goin' to say somethin' funny, you better stand up and say it in front of everbody. So I think Diekroeger over here can do a little DJ impression. Why don't we call up Mr. Diekroeger and see what he can do?' So I stood up and revealed my pouch and everyone went, 'Oooh!' And I went through my impression and people really liked it. And then the word got out so in Spring Training the following year they made me do it again in front of the entire organization. That one actually went really well because I had time to prepare something." Danny

DJ had an epiphany that year.

"And then another day DJ was like, 'Ah'm done swearin'. Ah'm done cussin'. Neva agin.' We were wondering what happened. And he was like, 'Let me tell you somethin'. Ah've been thinkin' late at night about the words that have been comin' outta mah mouth, and Ah'm not a religious man, but for the first time Ah prayed. Ah prayed to God that if Ah'm doin' somethin' wrong, show me a sign.' So apparently what happened was the next day he was feeding the pitching machine; he would stand behind the machine every day and put the ball in the machine and it would shoot out and we'd try to hit it. Something happened where he yelled a swear word, and when he went to put the next ball in, he said, 'Ah went to put the ball in, and instead of it shootin' out, it popped back up and hit me right in the mouth. And that was the Lord speakin' to me, and that's all Ah evah needed to hear. Ah accept the Lord, Ah accept Jesus, and Ah will never cuss again!' And to his credit, I never heard him swear again. He was still funny and he was still a hilarious comedian, but he stopped swearing completely. It was a pretty crazy transformation."
Danny

Some guys unfortunately had to miss out on all the fun.

"I didn't go to Instructs. I told them when I got drafted that I was probably going to go back to Stanford in the Fall and they still invited me to Instructs. They told me it would be good for my development and yada yada and I was like, 'You know, I told you guys when you drafted me that that was what I was going to do.' It was kinda funny the next year I came into Spring Training and the first thing the field coordinator said was, 'I'm surprised to see you, I thought you didn't like baseball,' because I didn't go to Instructs."
Anonymous

****

"The competition was top notch, you could tell you were playing with potential big league guys."

Some of the top minor league prospects are chosen by their major league teams to play in the Arizona Fall League. This league consists of six teams that play for six weeks from early October until mid-November in various Spring Training stadiums located in the Phoenix area. Each major league team sends six top prospects to the Arizona Fall League so there are 180 players in all. Most are AA and AAA players but each club can opt to send one player considered a Class A player.

"To get invited to that is a really big deal. You show up and they have these meetings, they explain that some 70% of people that play in the Fall League end up playing in the big leagues. You knew you were in the right spot, you knew you wanted to do well. It was late in the year, so you're kinda tired and you're just grinding and trying to give it all you got. It sure makes for a short off-season. But it was a lot of fun. I really liked the schedule there, you didn't have games on Sunday so you had built-in off days right around the corner, and you didn't play every single game which was good because you were dead tired at the end of the year. I got to meet a lot of cool guys on my team and on other teams. A lot of them I'm playing with now. We had a good team, a good group of guys. We played in the Salt River complex, which is beautiful. I enjoyed it. The competition was top notch, you could tell you were playing with potential big league guys. Any time you get tested like that it's a big deal to perform and give yourself confidence that you can do it. I was fortunate to have a really good Fall League. That right there, I think, is what gave me confidence that I could really do this. I could be a legitimate big league player." Stephen

According to MLB, "Given the top prospects who play here, every game in the Arizona Fall League is like a future All-Star Game."[1]

"I really enjoyed it. We had a really good group of guys. It's six teams comprised of five different teams' prospects. It's the top prospects because they want them to get a look at a competitive league, or guys to get more at bats, more innings, things like that. Sometimes

---

[1] mlb.mlb.com/mlb/events/winterleagues/about/?league=119&id=history

you'll see guys that made their debuts the season before, but they got hurt or didn't play a lot at the big league level so they'll go down and play a little extra. It's a more controlled environment than winter ball, going down to the Dominican Republic, for example. It's pretty much only scouts in the stands but it's a great way to meet other players and other organizations and get extra work in at the end of the season." Austin S.

"I played in the Arizona Fall League. It was cool, but it was really hard. The pitching is really good and it's different because you're facing a new pitcher every at bat. It's a different style of ball, if you're not hot in those five weeks then it's really hard to get out of a slump because you play every other day. It's hard to get in a groove. It is so hard to hit in that league, it was tough. And you're playing til mid-November and all your friends are back home enjoying the off-season. You're thinking, I just played 140 games and I'm playing 40 more, this is exhausting. But I had a good time. I met a lot of really good guys, a lot of guys who are now in the big leagues playing every day. You get treated like a big leaguer, you get all the gear, you have a cook, it's awesome. It's an honor." Drew

In addition to the Arizona Fall League, there are a handful of international leagues throughout the Caribbean and one in Australia. One player who was fortunate to get invited to the Dominican League had this to say about who gets invited to these leagues:

"It varies team to team. Some teams really try to stress to their young guys that they want them to go down and play in a more energy-filled environment because as far as the stadium noise it's very similar to a high pressure big league game, that aspect is really cool. The fans are standing the entire game and they're playing drums and they have cheerleaders and things like that which makes it fun and a different environment." Anonymous

... and the level of play....

"I would say the Dominican and Venezuelan winter leagues are closer to AAA. Towards the end of their season, they get a number of their own players that play in the big leagues to play in those leagues. I would say probably the Dominican is the best winter league, somewhere between AAA and the big leagues. Mexico is probably a AAish winter league, Puerto Rico is probably A ball, and I would say the Australian League is a mess around league, Low A if anything." Anonymous

...and how much money they get paid...

"You can make some serious dough in the Dominican and Venezuelan leagues. Even though the countries are poor the people still pay to go to baseball games. I think that year I made just as much or more in the first two weeks than I did all of the minor league season. They put us up in a really nice resort and they treated us really well, but then you leave the resort and it's very much a third world country. The reason they can do that is because the Venezuelan-born players have their rights in Venezuela owned by their local teams and the same is true for the Dominicans. Those guys make essentially what we make in the minors here or even less. So they have all this money to go sign foreign players. Their stadiums are pretty packed — they're probably seating 5,000-10,000 per game, and they don't have to pay their players anything so pretty much all that money goes to international players. It's the reverse when they come and play over here." Anonymous

> **"You can make some serious dough in the Dominican and Venezuelan leagues...I think that year I made just as much or more in the first two weeks than I did all of the minor league season."**

****

*"I felt great going into Spring Training, definitely
the best shape I've ever been in."*

Finally, when Instructs and Fall Leagues are over, players do have time off before Spring Training. Most of them take a little break to recover and then get back to preparing themselves for the next season.

"I went to Instructionals so I got back super late. I took some time off from baseball, tried to stop thinking about baseball. I basically stepped away from it. I took an internship and then once Christmas came around I started focusing again and really got back into it." Jack

"I worked out with Coach D at the Stanford facilities and I actually got a little internship in Condoleezza Rice's office to help pass my time." Wayne

"I came back and finished my degree so that was awesome, I was fortunate to do that. I was able to get ahead academically and take more units while I was at Stanford so I only had to go back for one quarter, which was huge. One of my close friends that I played minor league ball with still had a year left, and he's just graduating next month. I'm not sure if I had to finish if I'd still be in school right now. It was kind of cool to just go to school in the off-season, that was pretty clutch to be honest." Lonnie

"After Instructs I just had a really nice relaxing Fall. I'd wake up at like 11:00 AM, work out, play catch, and chill the rest of the day." David

The off-season can be relaxing unless you're Tyler Gaffney, and you played three years of both baseball and football at Stanford before being drafted by the Pirates.

"I had a really good first season with the State College Spikes. I hit .297, I had a phenomenal on-base percentage, they were loving me. They brought me to Instructs through the end of October and I was one of the captains. They asked me my opinion on certain things, they liked the leadership I was showing, I was cruising with the Pirates. But then I saw an opportunity when Stanford was going to the Rose Bowl to play Wisconsin. I knew this was going to be Stefan's last year playing so there was going to be an opening spot at running back.[2] I decided, you know what, I'm going to play a year of football and then I'll go back to baseball and all will be well. I'll get another year of my academics under me, I'll be done and almost ready to graduate. So I presented that to the Pirates and they were all for it. I was going to miss one season, it wasn't going to be a big deal. I had not played baseball half a year every year and it didn't really matter. So after Instructs I started training for football on my own.[3]" Tyler

For everyone else, players have a responsibility to prepare themselves for the baseball season that lies ahead. That includes hitting, throwing, fielding and conditioning.

"In the off-seasons I devoted my attention and effort to my swing, my workouts, dieting, and getting my body in the best shape it could be for a 140-game season." Austin W.

---

[2] Stefan Taylor became Stanford football's all-time career leader in rushing yards and touchdowns during the 2012 season. He was drafted by the Arizona Cardinals in the fifth round of the 2013 NFL Draft.

[3] Tyler had an outstanding year at Stanford in 2013. He started in 14 games, finishing with 330 rushing attempts, 1709 rushing yards, and 21 rushing touchdowns. He was drafted in the 6th round by the Carolina Panthers in the 2014 NFL draft. He also played for the New England Patriots and the Jacksonville Jaguars before an injury led to his retirement in 2017. He resumed his professional baseball career in 2018.

"I emphasized getting my body strong, running and doing conditioning, making sure I had enough cage time. I didn't hit too much until January and February. It was mainly hanging out in the gym and running and conditioning. But then making sure my arm was ready and my bat was ready as soon as I came in, that's what I focused on in the two months leading up to Spring Training. I was actually in great shape." Alex D.

"With hitting, it is not sufficient to just hit off the tee or to do soft toss or have someone throw batting practice casually to you, it takes some getting used to, to hit a live baseball traveling 90 mph going every which way. So it's always a challenge for players during the off-season because they're not in a concentrated setting of players to see that live pitching on a regular basis. Some players are just stuck, there really isn't much they can do to prepare better. Guys will counter that by intentionally living with teammates or friends who are also pro players not only for the friendship but also because it helps from a baseball standpoint. Another part is throwing of course, you can't just all of a sudden start throwing every day at the intensity that's required in pro ball. You have to warm up your arm every day for a couple of weeks going into it. Guys will get creative about where they throw. I remember Cole Hamels asked me to play catch with him while we were on vacation in Hawaii. I was still in college and had my glove with me so I got to play catch with an MLB All-Star." Kenny

"Guys will get creative about where they throw. I remember Cole Hamels asked me to play catch with him while we were on vacation in Hawaii."

"Going into Spring Training, it was exciting to see how much I had developed strength-wise. I was basically able to dedicate from nine to five and focus on things I needed to develop. I weighed the most I've ever weighed in my life, like close to 180. I was just fully developed, my athleticism was top notch, I was stronger than I'd ever been, so I felt great going into Spring Training, definitely the best shape I've ever been in." Lonnie

****

As the season approaches, it's not just the fans who are getting excited for the start of the baseball season. The players have had enough time off and are excited to get back to the game they love. It's time to report to Spring Training.

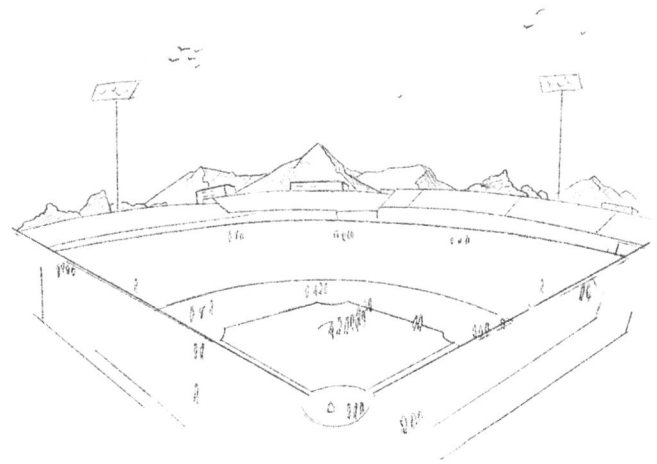

Chapter 5
Play Ball!

Spring Training is that optimistic time when professional baseball teams prepare for the upcoming season. For the six weeks from mid-February until the end of March, players and fans leave winter behind and travel to the warmth and sunshine of Arizona and Florida. Half of the 30 major league teams play in the Cactus League in the Phoenix area and the other half play in the Grapefruit League in Florida. According to the MLB, "Unparalleled player access, intimate ballparks with distinct personalities, and up-close encounters with veteran stars and blossoming prospects alike make it truly a unique baseball experience.... Many who have been there describe it as the best sports has to offer, the embodiment of the hope and promise of a new season."[1]

It's safe to say most of the fans are going to Spring Training to watch the major league games and get a close up view of their favorite major league players. But

---

[1] mlb.com/spring-training

the minor league players are there too, albeit hidden on the back fields where their experiences are very different than those of the major league stars.

They're not just working hard to secure a spot on the major league team, they're working hard to secure a spot on any team.

****

"There were fans and reporters all alongside the security gate entrance."

In January, players are given their report dates. Pitchers and catchers usually report in mid-February, about a week earlier than the position players. While there's a lot of excitement to get started again, it doesn't always go smoothly.

"I came down early to Spring Training with a teammate but the hotel wouldn't honor the team's rate because it was too early. It was high season down in Florida and we didn't want to pay $300 for a room, so we scrambled and got our own Airbnb. We stayed in a single mom's extra room down the road." Colton

"My first Spring Training I showed up with the pitchers and catchers but when I got there and tried to check into the hotel, they didn't have me on the list. The previous summer I was playing half outfield and half catcher, so I just figured I should show up with the pitchers and catchers but they didn't think I was supposed to be there. That was my hint that maybe I might just be an outfielder now. But they ended up letting me check into a hotel room and work out with the catchers. I ended up playing catcher almost exclusively that season, which was a bit ironic." Wayne

Whatever you do, don't arrive late.

"My first Spring Training I was driving from California to Arizona and there was a one hour time difference which I didn't account for. Luckily I left early enough so instead of arriving an hour and 15 minutes early I arrived 15 minutes early." Kenny

And beware of who might be reporting the same day as you. (Dom is part Dominican and he's been told he looks a lot like another famous player.)

"In March of 2015 my stepdad and I drove to Spring Training to report to camp. That was the same time that Alex Rodriguez was coming off his suspension and he was going to play again. As we were driving up the highway, getting close to Tampa, I got an ESPN alert on my phone that A-Rod was going to report to camp that day. I was thinking, nice, that's pretty cool. I was in the passenger seat of the car with my sunglasses on and my stepdad was driving. We pulled into the security gate and there were fans and reporters all alongside the security gate entrance because A-Rod was going to report in a matter of minutes. My stepdad rolled down the window and said to the security guard, 'We're here reporting for camp,' and some reporter shouted, 'THERE HE IS!' All the reporters mobbed the car, my stepdad yelled, 'HOLY SHIT!' and the security guard said, 'GO! GO! GO!' So we went flying through the gate and parked the car. My stepdad said, 'They think you're A-Rod!' We got out of the car and I looked over at the mob and someone yelled out, 'THAT'S NOT HIM!' I've actually been told so many times that I look like A-Rod. For a couple seconds the mob mistook me for A-Rod." Dom

> "Some reporter shouted, 'THERE HE IS!' All the reporters mobbed the car, my stepdad yelled 'HOLY SHIT!' and the security guard said, 'GO! GO! GO!'"

****

"I began to think it was not going to be as easy as I thought."

Spring Training is a mixture of optimism for the start of a new season and the realization of the grim reality of what lies ahead.

It's always fun to show up to a new locker at Spring Training. The lockers are nice, they're spacious, and they have all your fresh gear laid out. It's nice to have brand new shirts, socks, jerseys, pants, batting gloves, all that. Nice carpets, fresh cleats. Optimism." Kenny

"Spring Training was really cool because everyone shows up to watch the big league games so you're staying in a hotel and the hotel is jam packed with all kinds of fans watching the big league games." Chris C.

"It was kinda cool to be around everybody in the organization and get to be around all the coaches and coordinators and all that." Wayne

"The fun thing is you're with all your buddies, everyone in the organization is together, that's the only time that everyone is together, even the big league guys, so you're getting to meet guys from the different levels that you've never met before." Chris C.

"It was very cool. There are like 200 guys in a locker room, so it's packed. You get to see guys at the higher levels. It was fun, I had a really good time. You learn a lot." Jack

The reality is that most organizations have over 200 players, each of whom are competing for a spot on the 25-man major league roster. Those who don't make the major league roster are competing for spots on the other teams within the organization. Going into Spring Training, some players know ahead of time that they have a spot, but many don't.

"It's a farm system, so you're conscious of the fact that there are 200 guys in the organization, but it's not until you're around that many that it becomes real, and you realize it's much harder to move up. The first couple days of practice you realize how good everybody is, it's definitely different than college. You realize everybody is extremely talented. Like everybody. 80% of the people are really, really good. I began to think it was not going to be as easy as I thought it was." Kenny

"Going into Spring Training I didn't know what to expect. You kind of get there, you see the players you played with the previous year plus hundreds more. It's like OK, everyone *is out here battling for their position. It was a little intimidating at first, going into the locker room and seeing seven rows filled with lockers, top to bottom. There were lots of Dominicans, lots of people that are older than you, lots of people that have been around for years, lots of people out of college."* Lonnie

"Sometimes it can feel a little daunting because you see how many guys are fighting for the 25 major league roster spots." Jack

By the end of Spring Training, the 25-man roster will be set, along with the rosters of all the other teams in the system. Some players will be happy with their assignments, some will not. And unfortunately, many guys will get released. But we're not quite there yet. There's still some work to do, beginning with the medical evaluations.

"Oh my God, the first day you show up and you have the physicals. They line you up like cattle. You go through all these stations where they're just inspecting your body. You get a shot for this, you get a Tuberculosis shot, you get your heart rate measured, your EEG test, you get your blood drawn, everything. Some people don't do well with needles, and so every year a couple guys faint or freak out. And we're thinking, where are we and what are they doing to us? You feel like wow, I'm just a piece of meat to these guys, it's like they're breeding the best ballplayers." Danny

"I had teammates saying we're no better than a bunch of livestock with them subjecting us to all these tests. They're a grind to get through but of course they're important." Kenny

But soon enough, the fun starts.

"Finally you get to go on the field, finally you get to go hit. It's fun to get out there. They have these beautiful fields, six fields wide open, all freshly manicured with the nice dirt and the grass. And they have brand new baseballs, so you're hitting batting practice with brand new baseballs and the wind's blowing out. I loved taking ground balls and

hitting and that's pretty much all we did. And every once in a while you'd do all the other drills. It was really fun, it was a beautiful place to play." Danny

****

*"They definitely incentivize you to want to be a
part of the big league camp."*

The Spring Training complexes are designed to provide each major league organization with playing fields, training facilities and workout rooms for both their major and minor league teams. The main stadiums that host the major league games have close up seating with clear views, grass berms for relaxing, extensive concessions, party pavilions and kids' entertainment areas. Those stadiums are surrounded by smaller fields for practice and for the minor league games. Some teams share a Spring Training complex and some do not. In Florida's Grapefruit League, there are 13 complexes to accommodate the 15 teams, so only four teams share a complex. Most of them are located along the east and west coasts of Florida, and three are in the center of the state.

"I got really lucky. The Nationals and the Astros combined a few million dollars to make their new complex. We shared the main Spring Training stadium but we each had eight auxiliary fields on our own sides of the complex — it's almost a mirror image. It's all very new, very fresh, very nice." Alex D.

Across the country in the Phoenix area, there are 10 separate Spring Training complexes to accommodate the 15 teams in the Cactus League. Furthest to the west, the Kansas City Royals and the Texas Rangers share the Surprise Stadium complex while furthest to the east the Oakland Athletics alone play in the Hohokam complex in Mesa. Only 47 miles separate the furthest teams in the Cactus League, while in the Grapefruit League the furthest complexes are more than 200 miles apart.

"I lucked out with Spring Training in Arizona. The longest bus rides we had in Arizona were the shortest bus rides we had in Florida." Austin W.

Within the complexes, the major leaguers are separate from the minor leaguers. Separate locker rooms, separate schedules, separate fields.

"Big leaguers would work on the fields around us every once in a while and they would throw bullpens on the mounds that we would use to throw bullpens. If the big leaguers were doing stuff, we were not supposed to be around for the most part. I would sneak around and kind of watch what they were doing. If I kept to myself, they didn't say anything. It was cool, but at the same time, I didn't really have any meaningful interactions with any of them. They definitely incentivize you to want to be a part of the big league camp. I think that's by design if I had to guess." David

Most obvious to the players is the separate food.

"It was funny because the way the complex is set up you always walked past the big leaguers, past their cages, and you'd always walk past their breakfast, lunch, and dinner which was always five-star quality food. They have a personal chef cooking whatever they want every meal, omelets to order, freshly made this and that every day. Meanwhile you're getting rubber eggs and flimsy bacon on paper plates every day. We'd always walk right past them. You'd think, oh wow, how nice would that be if I ever make the big leagues, and then you'd just go on to the back fields." Justin

"Walking into our complex, you had to walk past the big league side to get to the minor league clubhouse. Every morning they were grilling steak outside the big league locker room. They had multiple chefs and they were doing the individualized meals. Minor league stuff was bad, every day it was scrambled eggs with potatoes and bacon or sausage. They clearly had a very limited budget because we would get the really crappy chicken thighs for pretty much every lunch, as opposed to their steak. Probably half the time, my buddies and I wouldn't even eat there, we'd go somewhere else for lunch after practice." Marc

There are even separate unwritten rules.

"In the weight room, if there's a big league guy working out, you do NOT get in his way." Marc

****

"Spring Training wore me down a little bit."

After the initial excitement wears off, the players get settled into a daily routine.

"Every morning we'd have a little meeting, the 100 or 150 of us out there, then we'd break the meeting and run to our fields and it felt like we were all a bunch of cattle, being herded around from field to field. Definitely a month of Spring Training feels like it's way longer." Wayne

"As Spring Training goes along, you get a feel for it, you get acclimated to the schedule, waking up early in the morning, practicing til late afternoon, it's really like a full time job. You manage your diet and all that stuff as best as you can. It was so cool to get back into it slowly but surely, with all the practice games, then transitioning to the simulation games, then playing different teams." Lonnie

"Spring Training felt like a lot of the same from college as far as how long the days were, it wasn't that big of an adjustment. I know a lot of the high school kids have a hard time with that but it seemed pretty standard after the 10-hour days with our college Coach Nine on the weekends." Anonymous

"I would say Spring Training was a piece of cake. I'm probably not speaking for everyone. Everyone's Spring Training is a little different but for whatever reason I thought it was too easy. Everything was early, the days did feel long because everything started so early, but coming from college our days were so packed and we started so early anyway, I

didn't think it was anything difficult or different." Chris C.

But it's not without some stress.

"There were parts of Spring Training I enjoyed and parts I didn't. It was pretty stressful going in just because we hadn't played in real games in six months. And so I was bad. And a lot of that was on me, and my preparation and not being able to face live pitching. That was tough." Justin

"After I retired from pro football, I went back to Spring Training with the Pirates. It was one of the most miserable experiences ever because it was hot and my knee was killing me from a surgery in August. I hadn't even started walking again until the end of October and I couldn't jog until January. And because my knee was hurting so bad I started to compensate and tried not to limp and so other things started to hurt. My hip started hurting, I had plantar fasciitis, all because I was changing the way I walked and ran to compensate for my knee. I was struggling, they were putting me against AA and big league guys because that was my age group and I was just getting diced up, striking out on a regular basis. I thought, whoa. For a couple days in the middle of Spring Training I didn't know if I was going to make it, I thought I might have to quit. I wasn't worried about being released, I figured that they were going to give me a chance as long as I didn't look god-awful. The first two weeks I did look pretty bad, I looked like I wasn't able to run, I wasn't running as fast as I could because of my knee, and my at bats weren't great. But I finally made it through and my second half of Spring Training was better. It was on an upward trend, they liked that I was getting better." Tyler

> **"For a couple days in the middle of Spring Training I didn't know if I was going to make it, I thought I might have to quit."**

Every organization starts Spring Training with the most amount of players they'll ever have. There might be 60 players placed at the big league level and the rest are filling spots on the minor league teams.

"You show up and immediately you're broken up into the four full season minor league teams. They literally have four columns of names posted in the locker room: AAA, AA, High A and Low A." Kenny

However, because the major league team is carrying significantly more players than the regular season maximum, minor league players typically play at one to two levels above what their regular season assignment will ultimately be.

"One of the stress points was everyone starts freaking out what team they're going to be on this year, and what team they're practicing with, the High A team, the Low A team. Some people are pissed, thinking why is this guy practicing with AA? Why am I on the AA team, I was on AA last year and did well, blah blah blah, a lot of stuff like that. It's a lot of that kind of stuff that ultimately gets in your head and brings you down. It's all mental obviously. I told myself I've worked hard all my life to get here so I'm not going to worry about trivial stuff right now. You know everyone's good, everyone's practiced, everyone's done the same thing their entire lives too, so it's a matter of how you stick out amongst the crowd and how well you perform, that's ultimately what ends up moving you up in the end anyway. That's why only the strong survive." Lonnie

"I don't know if that stress hit me as close to home as a lot of other people because for catchers there are only 18 of them and they have to go across six teams. I guess you don't feel as lost as some of the other positions, like infielders or outfielders where you might have 40 or 50 of those. I think it was just because of my position I never really felt that stress. Yeah, it's a lot of people but for me it felt like I was competing against two or three guys rather than 15 or 20." Anonymous catcher

In addition to the stress of where they're assigned and how well they're playing, for some guys Spring Training just gets tiring.

"Spring Training wore me down a little bit. In the off-season I was used to getting 9-10 hours of sleep a day. I'd wake up, get a good full breakfast, go work out on my time,

drink lots of water, eat lots of food, everything was on my schedule. Then you get down to Spring Training and it's not your schedule anymore, so you have to adapt. I didn't really have a system prepared to adapt like that, long days with not as many full meals in between. I could eat, don't get me wrong, they made very good meals at the complex. We had an awesome breakfast, and really it was a full lunch. But it was the constant work and then not doing the heavy lifting because I didn't want to be weak for the next day's workout. It was every day for a full month. I was on a catcher's schedule, I was on a pitcher's schedule, I was on a game schedule, I was always doing something." Alex D.

"I was a little bit thrown off by how generally pissed off the older AA and AAA guys were. I didn't understand that they'd endured a few minor league seasons and had to grind through all this. They were very judgmental about all the younger guys, they got upset, couldn't wait to go home at the end of the day. A few had had big league time and they had that saltiness because they had a legitimate chance to make the big league team but got sent down. It's different between the older guys and the new young guys. We were all excited but the older guys were like, 'Oh God, another day getting up at 6:30 AM.' " Marc.

To make matters worse, players don't get a paycheck because nobody gets paid during Spring Training.

****

"They wanted me to sign a card? To me that's kind of funny."

The autograph seekers, also known as stalkers, are a part of every minor leaguer's experience, especially during Spring Training.

"In Spring Training there were a lot of autograph hawks, people that walked around with binders of minor league baseball cards. They were just trying to collect as many autographs as possible because hopefully a few of the players would become famous someday and then they could sell those later. It's really funny because in the minor league

camp we all had jerseys with our last names on the back, and so when we were walking out to our minor league games or practice we'd see the autograph hawks waiting on the path between the locker room and the field. We'd walk towards them and they'd be looking at us trying to figure out who everyone was, but they didn't know who we were until we'd get past them and they could see the names on our backs. So we'd be walking and they'd be looking at us and kind of avoiding contact, and we knew once we passed them they were going to ask for an autograph. So we'd pass them and sure enough they'd look at the back of our jerseys and say, 'Ah, Danny, Danny, can I get you to sign something real quick?' and you'd say, 'Yeah, sure.' Sometimes just to make it easier I would just tell them who I was, so they didn't have to wait for me to pass them." Danny

"During Spring Training we had some autograph hawks for sure, but more for the higher profile guys. They always waited until you passed. You can tell, the card guys will bring backpacks with them to the field and they'd be in the bleachers and then they'd stand at the staircase where you were entering the field and they'd just be awkwardly staring at you. You knew what they were doing, you knew they were trying to figure out who you were. You'd walk by and then some guy would be like, 'Mr. Klein?' and you'd be like, 'Yes?' And he'd say, 'Can we have your autograph?' I was a late round draft pick and they wanted me to sign a card? To me that's kind of funny. But you gotta remember you're getting asked to give your signature. I do it every time absolutely. I understand once you're a big leaguer and you're trying to have your time off the field not be baseball-related, that would be a little different being asked about your autograph. But at least now I have no problem. Most people who come to Spring Training are pretty understanding, they're polite, they're not in your face, they're not asking you to sign a hundred things while you're trying to go to practice. They have a feel for what's proper and what's the right thing to do." Jack

"We had the stalkers that were always there, the guys who had binders of cards and always knew where to be. I'd always go out of my way to sign something for a kid. But it was easy to say no to the collectors." Kenny

"They had their booklet of top draft picks, top prospects that they wanted autographs, but there are so many players that for the most part you could walk on by without being interrupted, for me at least." Lonnie

"The autograph seekers have been pretty consistent at every level. They're always there and they're always wanting cards and they're incredibly persistent. You really want to sign for the young fans and the kids and sometimes they get in their way and it's a little frustrating." Stephen

"A guy paid $160 online for a card that I had signed and I couldn't believe he paid that much because I was in Low A. I ended up meeting the guy and he was like, 'I'm the guy who bought your card,' and I was thinking dude, I could have signed it for you right here. I've never denied anybody." Colton

"Those card guys are there every day, it's kind of annoying. Someone tagged me in a photo on Instagram and it was a picture of 99 cards of me with my signature. He was like, 'I have 99 Drew Jackson cards,' and I was like, 'What? Why do you need 99 of these?' " Drew

"I got a lot of inmates sending me cards to autograph. Maybe because I played football. Nine times out of ten, everyone who sent me stuff, it was football cards, even at the stadium. I didn't have a baseball card for that year so they either had my Rookie card from State College or there were plenty of football cards out there. Yeah, inmates, I think that was so strange. They weren't from the same area nor did they have anything to do with places I had played, they just came, I don't know why. They had notes that would say they enjoyed watching me. They would tell me a little bit about themselves. Never about what happened to get them in jail but who they were. And they were hoping for an autograph because that was something they were collecting." Tyler

> "I got a lot of inmates sending me cards to autograph. Maybe because I played football."

****

"It was a nice change to have an audience and some fans cheering for that game."

One of the most exciting parts of Spring Training for the minor league players is when they get called to play in a big league game. There are several reasons why there's a need for extra players. Major leaguers don't always play the whole game, veterans sometimes don't like to travel to far-away games, and the teams play split squad games where they field two teams on the same day. Minor league players get called to fill in the gaps. Some guys are taken by surprise.

"I was in minor league camp and I got called into a big league game. I didn't know that they did that. They took me out of practice and got me in this golf cart and said, 'Hey, you're filling in at the big league game.' I was like, 'What is going on? You want me to go where? What? Huh?' I ended up not playing, just sitting on the bench, but it was cool just to be in the dugout around the guys. The atmosphere in the dugout was way more serious, you could tell this was intense, serious stuff. It was a little bit eye-opening. I got called up to a handful of other games. It's kind of cool, you get the big league meal money for the day, you can eat like a king for the day." Stephen

"One day I got to go to a big league game, it was my first Spring Training. I showed up and there was a sticky on my locker that said, '9:30 bus, big league game.' And some guy was like, 'Hey, you're going to the big league game, congratulations, just get your stuff.' There are two buses, and they tell you to go on the second bus. Make sure you go on the second bus. But you get your own two seats, everyone gets their own two seats. We drove over to the field and took batting practice with the team and took some ground balls. The guy who threw their batting practice was so good. He made me look really good. I told him afterwards, that was really nice BP, thank you. He said he can see how people hit, so he was working my swing. He would throw just on the outside corner to make sure I hit one that way, and then he would throw one a little slower, slightly in, I would pull it deep to the pull side. He just knew how to place them to make you look really good. It's always nice to have a good BP." Danny

There are definitely some perks when you get called up to a big league game.

"We got off the bus and went into the locker room. I walked into the big league clubhouse manager's office and he gave me my per diem. Minor league per diem was $30-40 per day, big leaguers got $100 or $120, something like that. Then they took me into the equipment room and there were all these bats and they said I got to choose three and I said to myself, yes please." Kenny

"I got the per diem for that night, but it was more about the experience. I did get the major league Spring Training hat, though. It was just a little bit of a different texture, a little stretchier." Alex D.

"During Spring Training it was pretty cool to be in the same dugout as household big league names. I got to pick their brains, ask for tips and advice. Growing up I put these superstar baseball players on a pedestal, then I started talking to them and realized they are just normal guys like me." Anonymous

"It was definitely a great experience getting to talk to some of the big league guys and ask what's worked for them in the past and what they're working on specifically. They were pretty open." Tommy

"I lucked out, I got to sit in the bullpen for one of the big league games and it was cool. I got to spend some time with major league pitchers, just hanging out in the bullpen. It was weird because that was the same field that we played the Arizona Rookie League games on in the summertime. I was used to that field not having any fans. No one sits out in the 100+ temperature watching the AZL games so it was a nice change to have an audience and some fans cheering for that game. I never got into the game but we played the Cubs and Schwarber and Chris Bryant and all these guys were playing there right on the same field that I was on. And they pay you the big league

"I started talking to them and realized they are just normal guys like me."

per diem, it was like $110, so it definitely was nice to have a nice little bonus." Chris C.

And there are definitely some interesting moments.

"What I remember is being on the bus ride to the away stadium and I was sitting in the back half of the bus, by myself. Of course nobody wanted to talk to me, I was just a minor leaguer. I was sitting near one of the best pitchers on the major league team, and I was just listening to his conversation. I had my headphones in but the music wasn't too loud. He was scheduled to start that day and he thought the game was an hour later than it was. Pitchers, and players in general, have a certain routine when they're getting ready for a game. And for him, it involved taking a bath, doing his arm exercises, massage, whatever, and unfortunately he showed up to the field an hour late so it all got shaken up. He was talking about it, he said, 'The trainer told me to just down a few shots of Jack, so I just took a couple shots, I'll be ready to go, it's Spring Training, it doesn't matter.' So he was sitting on the bus inebriated. That's what I remember. Of course he goes out and pitches and gets shelled but he doesn't care because it's the end of Spring Training. And he ended up carrying the team to the World Series that year." Anonymous

"My first Spring Training big league game was at the Mets, in Port St. Lucie. I played four innings at second base and got one at bat. I think we were winning like 9-1, so there wasn't too much pressure on my at bat but it was definitely pretty nerve-wracking because the stadium was really nice and there were like 7,000 fans. It was just a really cool experience. Anyway, we were against the Mets and Tim Tebow, the former pro football quarterback, was on their team. We were winning by a lot, and I remember at the bottom of the 9th inning the entire stadium started chanting, 'WE WANT TEBOW! WE WANT TEBOW!' " Tommy

"At one point they put me in because they wanted a left handed pinch hitter and I was the only one on the bench. I hit an RBI double, and I scored a run myself. I think that put us up by three runs or so, and we ended up winning by one, so it was my two runs that ended up winning the game, so that was kind of cool." Danny

"One of the cool experiences I won't forget, it was the end of Spring Training in 2013. The Dodgers were doing a three-game exhibition series against the Angels and it was a split squad game. They brought over major leaguers to play with the Rancho High A team. I was selected to play and I thought I might play a little. I ended up starting and caught Chris Reed, and he dominated. I went two for three in the game and we actually won. It was really cool." Eric

****

"The difference between big league camp and minor league camp is night and day."

Even better than being called into a big league Spring Training game is being invited to join big league camp. Big league camp is comprised of players on the 40-man major league roster and non-roster invites who are working out and playing games with the major league squad. If you're a minor leaguer who gets to experience that side of camp it means that the organization thinks highly of you, they see you in the future as a potential major leaguer and they want to give you the chance to interact with the big leaguers and see how they operate. It's an honor and it gives players a taste of what big league life is like.

"The difference between big league camp and minor league camp is night and day. It is just a whole different breed. You get treated like a big leaguer. There's media in the clubhouse, you don't put your dirty clothes on a loop, you just throw them in a bin and they end up in your locker hung up. It's just amazing. And you don't feel like you're in Spring Training at all. I don't know why you'd ever complain about Spring Training if it was like that." Cal

It would also be hard to complain about the additional money you get being in big league camp.

"I got paid really well in big league camp. I got paid over $1,000 a week in cash for meal money." Anonymous

In addition to noticing the differences in perks and pay, minor league players invited to the big league camp notice a difference in how major league players go about their day.

"In Spring Training one year I was one of the non-roster invites to big league camp. They have the 40-man guys and then they invited about 25 non-roster guys so I was one of the 25 non-roster invites. I felt like I could definitely hang with them. The talent level wasn't too much different but you see the difference with their preparation and consistency and doing all the little things right. I feel like the guys at the major league level have a much better plan for how they approach their days. They've been doing it for so long so they know exactly what works for them and what they need to be working on in order to put themselves in the best position to prepare well for the game, whereas minor league guys are almost told what to do and haven't really established a plan for themselves. Everything they do, they do with a plan. That's probably the biggest thing I've taken away from it, approaching each day with a little bit more of a set plan, being more intentional throughout my day, trying to get better and working on specific things I need to improve on." Tommy

"The biggest difference between minor league camp and big league camp is everything is shorter and more to the point on the big league side. They do the fundamentals but it's 5-10 minutes of it versus 30-45 minutes of it, because they have so much more experience and they've all played together before and little things like that. Everything on the big league side is meant to get you ready for the season versus on the minor league side it feels like they're trying to improve skills during Spring Training, use it as a time to not only get ready for the season but to improve your own ballgame." Anonymous

"Big leaguers work their butts off. The difference is they've earned the right to prepare themselves for the season the way that they need to prepare themselves for the season. There's regular practice and they're going to take you through all the stations they want to, but I think there's a little more ownership put on a big league player. You're 32 years old, you need to be ready for the season, whatever you need to do to be good, you do

that. Whether that is working out in the morning or working out at night, you do what you need to do to be prepared. Minor league is a little less on you, it's pretty much from the hours of 6:00 AM until 2:00 PM they're going to tell you where you're going to be for each one of those hours. It's OK, it's all part of it. There are a million reasons why you want to be in the big leagues and one of them is you get to start having a little more control over your life. You use it as motivation I guess." Cal

The problem for some of these players is that as the camp wears on, the roster will be shortened and guys will be sent down.

"Two to three weeks in I got told I was heading back down. I was kinda strolling into the clubhouse thinking it was going to be a regular day and my stuff wasn't there. That was a little rough, I walked in and my locker was empty. My stuff was sitting in one of those bins and the guy was rolling it over to the minor league side. That was kind of a depressing walk. To be expected I guess. It was like well, that's unfortunate, my mornings just got a lot earlier and my days just got a lot longer." Cal

"There are a million reasons why you want to be in the big leagues and one of them is you get to start having a little more control over your life."

****

"That was always my mentality, stay out of the way but still listen and try to absorb as much as I could."

It can be a thrill for minor league players to interact with major league players even if they don't get called into a game or invited to big league camp.

"In Spring Training, whenever a major league team is facing another team in their division, they sometimes won't pitch their top starters against that team because they want to hide their pitching arsenals, so they'll pitch them in the minor league Spring Training games on that day to keep them on schedule with their rotation. In my first ever Spring Training,

Felix Hernandez was pitching against us on the back fields and my first at bat he struck me out, but the second at bat I got a broken bat hit off of him and in my head I thought, 'Yes! I got a hit off the King!' " Austin W.

"The cool thing about Spring Training is I played with guys who ended up making the big leagues. My second Spring Training I played with the AA and AAA teams for the most part, and I had a lot of interaction with guys who either had been in the big leagues or eventually made it to the big leagues." Justin

"We only had one weight room and everyone shared it. When we were working out there would be Nelson Cruz or Kyle Seeger or James Paxton. It was just moments like that which are cool that you remember." Chris C.

"One day I remember it was the day Hooters had their all-you-can-eat wings for pretty cheap, so we went there in the afternoon to watch the big league game. In those early Spring Training games the big leaguers only play like two innings. So we got to Hooters in the 3rd inning and Dan Uggla was sitting at the bar. He had actually started in that game, played one inning, and by the 3rd inning he had showered and was sitting at Hooters having a beer, watching his team finish the game. It was hilarious." Jake

But whenever you get exposure to the big leaguers, it's important to know how to behave.

"My first Spring Training I just remember trying to stay out of everyone's way. I don't think I talked to anyone. I don't think I played in a single game. For me it was like, try to listen to as much as I could. You see other guys go over there and they try to talk to all these guys and they just get on peoples' nerves and then all of a sudden they stop going over to those games. It's kind of interesting to see that develop. That was always my mentality, stay out of the way but still listen and try to absorb as much as I could." Anonymous

"They had non-roster invite hazing for all the young guys who were in big league camp.

A couple of the big league guys took us to a Boot Barn and bought us all cowboy outfits, really nice cowboy boots, everything. We had to dress up like that at the field the next day and we got introduced one by one in front of the whole team. Then that night we all went to a rodeo dressed in our cowboy outfits and we got announced at the rodeo in front of everyone. It was hilarious." Anonymous

"We have such a great group of guys I don't think they treated anyone poorly. But you can just tell when guys come in loud and obnoxious, they aren't going to say anything or be jerks to them or be mean to them, they're just going to write them off and try to avoid them if they can. But if you're quiet or say something that's a good observation or just a genuine comment, they take kindly to that, they are more likely to try to get to know you and respond to that. I think that's just general locker room dynamics. You get turned off by that person who comes in loud and doesn't really read the room or know what's going on. It kind of applies to everything, but especially in baseball where you have 18- and 22-year-olds who are interacting with guys who are 35 years old who have kids and have families. That's where the locker room stuff gets a little weird, especially in baseball." Anonymous

According to Urban Dictionary, the verb to "big league" someone is to "intentionally ignore a person in order to feel superior." There's a reason they use the term "big league."

"I was in the big league dugout and one guy got an RBI groundout, and so I ran up to him and gave him a high five and he walked right by me. I was like, 'Are you serious? Really bro? I'm trying to be nice here.' I didn't know what I was supposed to do in the dugout. I was walking around on eggshells. He literally big leagued me. That was my first time actually getting big leagued." Anonymous

You could also use the term "learn your lesson."

"I had the advantage of growing up in a big league clubhouse, I knew more of the

rules than some of the guys. But I still got crushed. It was after all of our work had been done. I saw a couple guys had Chick-fil-A and lunch was bad that day so I grabbed two of my teammates — who are both big leaguers now by the way — and I was like, let's go get Chick-fil-A. So we went and got ourselves Chick-fil-A, came back and were eating it. Turns out you can't just go get food for yourself, that's not how big league camp works. We learned that the hard way. We had to take every single player's order, there were like 60 players at this time, so 60 orders, personal orders, not like regular orders, personal orders, and then the entire staff, so another 20 or 30 people. We had to go to Chick-fil-A and we spent a thousand dollars minimum. We had to take it all, put it in each guy's locker before they got to the field the next day, and then yeah, serve them, go get the sauce that they wanted. I learned my lesson. Never will I ever show up to the clubhouse empty-handed. I'll never eat it where they can see it, I promise you that. That was a learn-your-lesson, you're 21, 23 years old, you will buy food for other people. That was a tough learning experience I guess, but Chick-fil-A did good business from us." Cal

Or you could "get put in your place."

"The one time I guess I got put in my place a little bit was during live BP, this was my first big league camp. I was trying to make a name for myself, do well, all that sort of stuff. Live BP is just for the pitchers to basically throw to the hitters. There are no fielders, it's work mainly for the pitcher. One guy I will not name was pitching and for safety reasons if they're ever going to throw a fastball inside, the catcher has to tell you. I took that as an opportunity to know what was coming, to cheat and guess on a fastball inside. So he threw the fast ball in, I hit it well. I didn't hit a home run but I hit a high fly ball that landed on the warning track, which is pretty good considering it's live BP and I hadn't seen a pitch since last season. He took exception to that, and the next pitch he just drilled me right in the ass. I guess maybe I shouldn't have done that. I don't know if there's an unwritten rule there, I just know there are certain guys that take exception to that, especially when it's a Rookie doing that sort of stuff. I was a young buck, I hadn't really done anything and there I was cheating and showing him up a little bit. I learned *my lesson that way."* Stephen

And finally, there are times when you're not sure if you're being big leagued or not.

"I was in big league camp after my first full year. I had just had a cup of coffee[2] in AA pretty much and I got invited to big league camp and it was great. It was my first taste of being in a big league locker room, being around the team and I was kind of walking on eggshells a little bit. This one player, very interesting guy, very unique personality, he's one of the best players on the team, he thought my name was Tony for some reason. Even though it's on my locker every day, he was calling me Tony during camp and I wasn't really correcting him, I was just dealing with it. Eventually I got around to telling him my name was Alex, and he was like, 'Oh sorry I just thought your name was Tony for some reason.' So he started calling me Alex. And then this Spring Training he was calling me Tony again. I mean, I was in AAA, I was feeling a lot more like I was a part of the team, part of the plan, I almost made the team and he was calling me Tony again. I didn't know if he was doing it to mess with me or if he actually thought my name was Tony so I was just rolling with it. One day I was working one on one with him and one of the Latin infielders and at the end he said, 'Great job Tony, great stuff out there, thanks for working with me, really nice.' And the Latin guy was like, 'Who's Tony?' And this guy looked at me and he was like, 'Oh my God, your name's not Tony is it?' And I was like, ah well, I was just basically, like, damn. I was riding in the car with him to a game and this was happening, him figuring out my name was not Tony. He felt really bad, he was apologetic. The Latin guy thought it was hilarious." Alex B.

****

"There was actually one guy we called the Grim Reaper."

---

[2] A sports idiom meaning that he only spent a short time there.

The problem is, there are too many players. There are over 200 guys competing for the 25 spots on the major league roster and for the 100 spots on the Low A, High A, AA and AAA rosters. As the weeks go by, the extra guys from the big league camp get sent down to the minor league teams so the organization has to make room for them down below. And that's why guys get released.

"This is one of the defining aspects of Spring Training for sure. Releases start maybe halfway through. After the first Spring Training we knew what was in store. We had a term for it: 'judgment day.' It's when many of the cuts happen. The truth is, it's not really one day, but we still called it judgment day. Of course with little else to talk about we knew this part of Spring Training was looming because only 25 guys could end up on each team and there were 30-something on each minor league team. So guys were playing their hardest knowing that they might be released in a couple days and they never knew when." Kenny

"You're always looking at the rosters because you're still divided into levels in Spring Training but everything's a little off because the big league team is carrying an extra whole roster of 15-20 extra players. So all the top players are up with the big league camp. But you can kinda see who you're playing with, and you start to try to figure out how many cuts are left, what positions are available, what team you might be on. In the mornings you take a bus from the hotel and you walk into the clubhouse and this administrative manager would just be standing there in the hallway, and every morning one or two guys, some days three or more, would get released. So you just walk through and try to survive. A lot of people knew they were safe but there were always a few people on the edge. For my last year I could feel I was on the edge, so every time I'd walk in I was just waiting for the guy to say, 'Hey, come to the office,' and you just knew you were done. That's how a lot of guys' careers ended, they'd just pack up their stuff. Everyone else would be getting dressed to go out to the field and these guys would be in their street clothes, packing their lockers, with a flight home booked already. Alright, see ya man." Danny

"I think different regimes do their releases different. I remember my first Spring Training, if you showed up to the field and there was a little sticky note on your locker that said 'come see me' or whatever, you knew you were getting released. They would actually clean out your locker and put a little sticky note on it. So if you showed up to the field and you had an empty locker with a sticky note on it, you were getting the axe. But the next Spring Training we had a new staff and there was actually one guy we called the Grim Reaper because he would show up and tap somebody on the shoulder and pull him out of the lunch room or whatever, and they'd go back into some office and you wouldn't see him again. So we called him the Grim Reaper." Wayne

"The Royals didn't clean out your locker. The Royals pride themselves on having more integrity, that's not how it was with them." Kenny

"In Spring Training, every Sunday or Monday, depending on the organization, is cut day. Those are some anxious eyes. That's really sad, not a fun two hours. You kinda know what day it is because you roll into the field and there are pieces of paper on certain people's lockers saying 'come to the office.' You know that's not a good sign because you're not moving up from Spring Training." Cal

"So if you showed up to the field and you had an empty locker with a sticky note on it, you were getting the axe."

"It's interesting to see the dynamic. You see people walk up to their locker and go, 'Oh shit.' That feeling sucks, it's like damn, this guy got released. It's surprising too, there are a couple guys that you don't think they're going to get released and they do and you're like dude, what the hell, he got released, like no way, he was really good." Lonnie

"At the Angels there was one low level intern who they made come into the locker room and pick guys out and say, 'You gotta go to the office.' " Marc

"At Spring Training a guy will be there one day and the next morning he'll be gone. And you'd see his locker empty and then everyone knew and it'd be like, oh man. There are definitely people that you recognize in the organization that you're hopefully not going to hear from during Spring Training. You see that guy walk into the cafeteria during breakfast and you really hope he doesn't come up and talk to you. You definitely don't forget the business side of it." Jack

"At Spring Training we knew who the guy was who came to cut people, it's one of the training staff. He'd be like, 'Hey, the skipper wants to see you in his office,' and you'd know you were going to get cut. So you're on edge, you're not hiding but you're trying not to make eye contact with him when he walks by. Those are some of the stressful moments. People would joke that they would never hang out in the locker room and they would hide as much as possible. But they definitely find you for sure." Alex B.

Sometimes you make it but your friends don't.

"One morning I remember walking up to one of my teammates and he was crying. And he didn't get released but one of our good buddies did. It's tough. The releases in Spring Training happen behind the scenes and these guys oftentimes disappear and it's the last you hear of them." Kenny

"Guys handle it differently. Some guys were kinda happy about being done. Other guys were really bitter and did not want to say bye to anybody. I mean understandably, some guys were pretty upset." Danny

"There were some guys who were very good and I'm shocked they got released. They were instantly picked up. One kid got released in his second Spring Training after posting a sub-4 ERA his first year. He was really upset about that, didn't see it coming. He immediately got picked up by the Diamondbacks and he's in High A now." Marc

****

*"You would end up eventually where you
were supposed to end up."*

Finally, it's the end of Spring Training and the players who've survived until the end get assigned to a team somewhere in the organization. Because the extra players from the big league roster are being sent down until the last day, most players end up getting pushed down a level or two below where they were playing throughout Spring Training.

"The minor league rosters can't be set until the major league roster is set. There are always a few guys on the cusp of the major league roster, so when they get sent to AAA, someone on the AAA roster will go down to AA, etc. That creates a trickle-down effect throughout the system." Danny

"They had us slotted to different teams and then they started sending the big guys down and then everybody gets pushed down. The first half I was switching back and forth between AA and AAA, as backup bullpen catcher for those guys. With about a week and a half left, that's when I jumped down to the Low A team." Alex D.

Sometimes guys will get pushed down so far that there isn't a spot for them on any of the four full season minor league teams. Instead of getting released, these players will end up in "extended spring training" where they're left behind to practice and play in what amounts to baseball purgatory.[3]

"After Spring Training I started out in extended spring training. They set out the rosters at the beginning of Spring Training and the way it worked they would put you at a level above where they thought you were going to start, so as the players would trickle back down from big league camp and get cut from the roster, it would create a waterfall effect and you would end up eventually where you were supposed to end up. I was on the High A roster at the time so I thought I had a pretty good chance to go to Low A. I hadn't

really done well the year before but I thought if I had a good spring I might have a shot but unfortunately I didn't make the squad so I spent a little bit of time in extended." David

"Extended" lasts for about two months, from early April when Spring Training ends until early June when the Short Season Leagues begin. And just as players aren't paid for the six weeks of Spring Training, players aren't paid for the additional two months in extended.

****

Now that we've seen the ups and downs of Spring Training, let's take a look at the fun of finding housing and food once it's all over. Where do these players go and where do they live?

---

[3] For more detailed information about extended spring training, go to springtrainingconnection.com/extended.html

Chapter 6
Safe at Home?

Spring Training is over, and for the players who made it to the end of camp it's time to report to their minor league team assignments. From their temporary accommodations in Arizona and Florida, thousands of players will fan out across the United States in a matter of days. Since the minor league rosters aren't resolved until the very end of Spring Training, there is usually less than a week between when players are told what team they're assigned to and when they start league play. In that time, they have to pack up, get their cars shipped, figure out who they want to live with and find a place to live. If you think they will then settle into their comfortable living arrangements and establish a healthy lifestyle so they can be at their best for the upcoming 140-game season, then think again. Finding housing is one of the biggest logistical challenges for minor league players. Some teams put the players up in a hotel and some don't. Some have a network of host families and some don't. Some will help you find an apartment and some won't. Some players get help with furnishings and some don't. In addition, once their housing is sorted out, players find that getting enough nutritious food requires a bit of creativity and more effort than it should.

****

"We stayed in a hotel. It was kinda fun, it felt like a dorm."

For the Rookie and Short Season Leagues, where some players can be as young as 18 years old, many minor league teams will put the entire team up in a hotel for the summer. This is by far the easiest option for newly-drafted and young players.

"In Arizona we stayed at the Comfort Inn. We knew it very well, they treated us great there. It takes that issue away of having to find housing." Jack

"In Troy, New York (Short Season A) they put the entire team in this one apartment complex/hotel type situation. I don't think the place even exists anymore. It was an interesting living situation to say the least, but it was easiest for the team to keep everybody in the same place for the most part." David

"We lived in the Red Roof Inn in Kingsport, Tennessee (Rookie). I had never lived in a hotel before so it was interesting. We spent a lot of time at the field and then we were traveling roughly 50% of the time so we really weren't there that long for me to complain about it. It was nice for them to do all that, especially after getting drafted. Having all that stuff prepared by somebody else makes it a much easier start to pro ball." Chris V.

Although it's easy for the players, it's not free. Teams usually take money out of their paychecks.

"When I was in Idaho Falls (Rookie) they said $15 a day was the deal they had set up with the team, but who knows. It's a hard number to say because each team has a very

different deal with their hotel. I believe it was a flat monthly rate because half the time we were on the road and we weren't even in the hotel. At $15 a day that's $450 per month which was a better deal than if you had to pay for housing yourself." Jack

As you might expect, the hotels are not five-star properties. Or even four. The Days Inn in Batavia, New York currently has a 1.5 star rating on Yelp.

"I was in the Days Inn in Batavia (Short Season A) for one and a half months. We didn't have host families because someone donated $30,000 for us to stay in the hotel. They told you to check for bedbugs. In 48 days we had bedbugs three different times and we had to ask for a new room each time. The last time they said all the rooms were full, so I slept in the back of my truck for the last two nights of the season." Colton

"Our living situation was a little bit cramped, we had basically a two-bedroom place and they stuck three people in it. The air conditioning didn't work because the freon was frozen in the window AC units so it was really hot all the time. Our lights didn't work in the room and we had a little tiny TV that didn't have any channels. But we spent so much time at the field and we had computers, so we didn't really need too much. Because we were in a hotel, they had this white van that took us to the field every day and we ended up fitting 17 people in it. There were three or four rows, it was a tight squeeze. I guess it was one of those things where the guy didn't necessarily want to take two trips so we all squeezed in." David

"That first summer with the Yankees I lived in a hotel and the funny thing about this hotel is that it was right next to a strip club called The Penthouse. In the Gulf Coast League you play Monday through Saturday, with Sunday off, so the joke was we were all going to the Penthouse Saturday night because it had the best steak. They advertised the best steak in town. We'd say to each other, 'Boys, let's get a win and go to the Penthouse tonight.' But we wondered if this was a test or something. Was the organization trying to weed out the guys who went to the strip club?" Dom

"We played in a really rough part of Virginia, there's really nothing there. Definitely not a place conducive for players to live with host families, so we stayed in a hotel. It was kinda fun, it felt like a dorm. We took over the top floor of one wing of the hotel. Nobody else stayed in those rooms on that floor, it was just the team." Wayne

When a bunch of young guys are living in a hotel for the entire summer, some crazy things are bound to happen.

"We lived in a hotel all summer and one day our manager called us in and said, 'Alright guys, we gotta talk. We got a report from the hotel that we have a problem.' I'm thinking it's girls, or alcohol, somebody got caught doing something, but he goes, 'There are reports and complaints of citizens walking by getting shot with BB guns and this has to stop! If you have a BB gun, Coach so-and-so will be in the hotel lobby this afternoon at 4:00 PM and you need to come down to the lobby and turn it in to him.' We had one of the coaches translating it for everybody and I was just sitting there thinking, are you kidding me? Guys shooting up random people on the street with a BB gun? This is insane! It was someone on our team." Dom

> "I was just sitting there thinking, are you kidding me? Guys shooting up random people on the street with a BB gun? This is insane! It was someone on our team."

"My first day in pro ball I got into the hotel at 2:00 AM and they put me in a room with someone but the kid wasn't there. I stayed up until 4:00 AM and the kid still wasn't there. So I went to sleep, woke up and the next day when I got to the trainers' room I said, 'Where's my roommate?' They told me the kid sleeps with the maids in the master suite. They know that because he's the happiest guy on the team, he's always smiling ear to ear." Anonymous

****

"They were the best family in the game."

Some teams have a network of host families who are willing to house players. It tends to be more of an option for the lower level players because they're typically younger, less experienced and making so little money. Unlike having to find and rent an apartment, staying with a host family doesn't cost much, if anything, for the players and they don't have to worry about furnishings. For the most part, the players who choose to live with host families love it.

"I think host families are generally a good idea, it's nice to stay with some locals. I think it's better than staying in an apartment." Chris C.

"Having a host family that's going to help you out for minimal to no rent is amazing. You're getting fed, you can be as much a part of the family or not as much a part as you want to be. I got lucky, the Oylers in State College (Short Season A) were the best host family, no doubt about it. I ate breakfast with them every morning, I hung out with the two kids, I enjoyed being low key and hanging out with the family. They were the best family in the game. I talked to other host families and some of them were a little weird. It takes a different person to have a random college kid in your house. There are some pretty hilarious stories about host families but my family was the best." Tyler

"I stayed with the Oylers too, they were a really nice family. They lived in a nice neighborhood, about 10 minutes from the stadium. They would drive me to the field and pick me up every night. And they had two kids who were really fun to be around. I remember I had a really cool routine. I'd wake up, go downstairs, make this big smoothie, and then I would sit out on their little bench swing out in their yard. At night I would sit out there and decompress after games. It was really nice." Danny

"When I first got to Great Lakes (Low A) I was told I had a host family, but three days in a row I checked in and out of the hotel hoping for a family. Luckily one came through and I was able to stay with them both of the years I was there." Anonymous

"When I played for the Spikes (Short Season A) I lived with three other guys in the basement of a house. It had just been remodeled, it was brand new. There was a separate bedroom and separate living room area with a TV, ping pong table and pool table so it was really cool, they definitely had a pretty good setup. It was designed for either two or three people but we ended up having four people stay there, so we were all kinda crammed. The bedroom had one bed so one guy stayed there, and then out in the living area there was a little corner with two beds. There wasn't a fourth bed so one of the guys bought an air mattress and he slept on it in the corner for pretty much the whole summer. About a month in, the guy on the air mattress got sent up to Peoria so there was just three of us. Then one of our other teammates who really didn't like his host family said the place was terrible, there was no AC, they were really crammed in there, and he asked if he could come over to our place. The first teammate left the air mattress there and the new teammate came over and just assumed his place in our host family's house, and once again we were four. They try to cram people in because I think it's a little bit of a struggle for most teams to find those families who are willing to host a bunch of baseball players." Tommy

That brings up the question of why someone would host minor league players. In many cases, it's because the family is involved with the team in some capacity or they're just big baseball fans.

"My first summer in Peoria (Low A) I lived with a host family, I just moved in and took the spot of a guy who got promoted. Super nice people, they hosted every year. The mom was involved with the Chiefs in some way." Justin

"My host mom loved baseball, she was a season ticket holder, she went to every single game in Everett (Short Season A) and she even came to some of the games on the road

too. I don't think it was for the money." Chris C.

"In San Jose (High A) it was really nice to have a host family because that area is pretty expensive and the High A salaries are maybe $1,000 a month so that was great. I had host parents who had an extra pool house area. They were huge Giants fans so they would take the train up to see a bunch of Giants games and they just wanted to know players, which was fun." Austin S.

"My host dad collected memorabilia like there was no tomorrow. He had hundreds if not a thousand baseball bats signed by guys. I'd help him out by getting access to some of the guys on my team. It was fun to help with his collection." Kenny

While some families might be doing it for the money, there is some variation on whether or not the players actually pay.

"I think it's a team rule that you pay your host family whatever the amount is, like $100 per paycheck. Some host families will follow through with that and some won't even care if you pay them or you don't pay them. I think a lot of host families are just happy to be hosting some ballplayers and so they don't charge them." Chris C.

"In San Jose (High A) we didn't have to pay. In the Northwest League (Short Season A) we were supposed to pay and I paid my host parents. I would leave it on the counter and I would come back that night and it would be sitting on my bed. I think maybe the team helped them out with something, the players didn't have to pay anything." Anonymous

"We paid but it was pretty small, it would get used towards groceries, that kind of stuff. It wasn't much, maybe 100 or 200 bucks. I think my last family actually wrote us a check for all of it back at the end of the year." Jake

It's not just comfortable for players to get to live in someone's home, but the relationships they make with the host family can be special.

"I had a host family and they were great. They lived out on a farm in Salem-Keizer, Oregon. They had an extra Ford Explorer that my roommate and I would drive to the field. Our host mom worked for the supermarket so she always had fresh fruit and food and it was great. They loved baseball and I still keep in touch with them." Anonymous

"My host family was fabulous. They had a spare Jeep that they let me use. They included me in their family gatherings, right along there with grandma, grandpa and the whole gang. They often would come down to Spring Training and I would get them a 'backdoor family pass.' We still exchange holiday gifts." Brant

"I think that I'm one of the very very lucky people in any summer ball, any pro ball. I loved every single host family I had. I keep in touch with all of them still, I loved every one of them. I always somehow got picked for the great families." Jake

It can be special unless they have a cat.

"I had an allergic reaction at my host family's house in Everett (Short Season A). One night after petting their cat I started getting hives real bad. I broke out over my whole body, my stomach, my arms, my neck, everything was broken out in hives from touching this cat. This was like 10:00 or 11:00 at night, we were getting ready for bed and the family was asleep. My roommate was dozing off and I had to wake him up and say, 'Hey, I need to get allergy meds.' I was so itchy and inflamed and it was awful. So I had to run to the store and grab some Benadryl. I don't know how I was able to sleep that night but I woke up the next morning pretty much unscathed. There were no signs of this awful outbreak I had. It was so strange. It taught me that I was allergic to cats. The saving grace was it was my last night there because the next day I got the call to go play for the AAA team so I didn't say anything about it." Chris C.

"I've heard of upwards of six or seven guys in a three-bedroom."

Some guys look for apartments either because they don't want to stay with a host family or it's not an option. With only a few days notice, they use Craigslist, Zillow, and whatever local sources they can to find a place to live for as long as they're in that location, which can be anywhere from a few days to a few months to the entire season.

"You get there on April 1st and you have three nights in a hotel and you have to go find apartments, find out who's living with who, set it all up, get beds and everything, before the first game on the 4th or else you have to pay for another night in a hotel." Drew

"In Clinton, Iowa (Low A) we got three days in a crappy hotel room before we had to figure out where to live. After that we were on our own. Most people lived in apartments, and so I got an apartment with a few other guys. We actually got lucky, there was only one two-bedroom available at this complex so we were able to get it. We had five guys in a two-bedroom apartment, so it was pretty close quarters. We had two guys in one bedroom and two guys in the living room. I actually ended up with my own bedroom because I put my name down for all the bills, the utilities, and the lease so everybody agreed that it was OK that I got my own bedroom, so that was kinda nice. It wasn't furnished." Wayne

"We had five guys in a two-bedroom apartment, so it was pretty close quarters."

"My first summer there were four of us that shared a little house in Johnson City (Rookie). It was set up through the team. We basically had to decide if we wanted to live on our own or with a host family. We got down there and within the first few days we had to find a few guys that we'd do well living with, so I ended up living with a few of the other guys

who had just graduated who had gotten drafted out of college." Justin

"We were able to get a place fairly easily in Columbia, South Carolina (Low A) because the University is right there and there are a decent amount of places to rent. It's kind of like a whole team effort because once you find one area you can rent for a reasonable price everyone else wants to live there too so you'd be geographically in the same location." Chris V.

"Sometimes you have literally two days to find a place to live so you're scrambling. One year I was on Craigslist in Pensacola (AA) and I saw a house that looked OK. I called the lady and I said, 'Yeah, I'll do it, it looks good.' I got there and it was old and creaky, with old furniture. It kind of had a unique little vibe to it but it was definitely old and broken down." Alex B.

"When they sent me to Oklahoma City (AAA) I wasn't necessarily planning on getting an apartment there at first, I was going to try to hop around in Airbnb's. I did that for about a week and it was just miserable, moving in and out all the time, so I got an apartment." Anonymous

"We stayed in a dorm room because there's no place to rent in Altoona, Pennsylvania (AA). People who live there, they live there. Nobody's looking to rent in Altoona. There's not a lot going on, it's in the middle of nowhere. It's an off campus for Penn State and we were in a college dorm room. There was me, my wife and my two kids in a five-bedroom suite. It was good in that sense but we had no TV, we had no internet. We just basically hung out as a family every day. As grindy as it became, I look back on it and really appreciate it because we did so much together. That's all we had pretty much. I think we paid probably like $700-800 per month. Nobody stayed in these dorms, it was just our entire team. And so the other guys were splitting a four-bedroom dorm for that same price while I'm playing the entire thing. I'm done with roommates, I've got kids. I was done with roommates before I had kids. But definitely after." Tyler

"We lived in Section 8 housing, it was a government assisted housing complex. It was super cheap which is nice. We all moved in next to each other, we had four- and six-man apartments. It wasn't bad, we had a kitchen and a living room. I was in a four-person apartment and I think we paid $300 apiece, $1200 a month, which is more than what most people living there year round pay. I think they paid $1000 a month. It was nice because we saw every single religion and ethnicity that you could imagine, it was crazy. It always gets a bad rap, but we had a great stay there for six months. Kids would be playing out in the yard and they would bring baseballs over and knock on our door and stare at us and I was like, 'Hi, you want me to sign them for you?' and their moms would say, 'Yes,' and we'd sign them and we'd go play football with them in the street. It actually ended up being really fun." Colton

Yeah, it was really fun except for the fact that some roommates are better than others.

"There were four of us in a two-bedroom apartment but I have a really tough time sleeping. I literally can't sleep if there's a light on, I can't sleep if someone is creaking their bed, or if someone's light is on across from me. So when I moved in I told my roommate, 'You can have this room to yourself, I'll go sleep in the closet.' I could put down my full size mattress and walk next to it and I could put my clothes up on the shelves. I threw a fan in there and the mattress and I slept in that closet all six months. And you had to go through the bathroom to get to the closet, but I told my roommate, 'Listen, I'm choosing this, I don't care what you do, it's your bathroom, use it when you need to, I have the fan on, it's dark, even though I don't have a curtain over the door I'm not going to wake up, I'll be fine.' But when I said don't worry about me he took it to the next level. I would wake up every single morning and my roommate would be drinking coffee sitting on the toilet. He'd say, 'Morning Hock, how we doing?' like it was totally normal, and I'm like, 'What's up dude?' Luckily he left after a month and

> "I would wake up every single morning and my roommate would be drinking coffee sitting on the toilet."

got moved up to High A and the next guy used the bathroom downstairs so the closet and bathroom pretty much turned into my own room." Colton

"I had two roommates who really didn't like each other. It was weird because they were super cool to me but for some reason they couldn't stand each other. When one got called up to our team we had an extra room and we were paying $1,500 a month for the house so we decided to let him move in. After a few weeks of living with us, one day he just left. On an off day he called me and said, 'Hey man I just moved out, I'm moving into Torres' place, thanks for letting me live there, blah blah blah.' Literally one day notice. I gave him the whole first month free because we had already paid the rent. So he lived there for free that month and right before the next rent was due he left. I hounded him, I was like, 'Dude, that's not fair,' and he finally paid me a little bit. It was sad because I was really close with him and he burned a couple bridges with this little dispute over housing. It's really interesting because there are teams where there are guys who just don't get along and that can make housing difficult." Anonymous

The discrepancy in cost between the cities can be sizable and yet the players' salaries are standardized throughout the league.

"One year I had an apartment with three other guys, there were four of us in a three-bedroom place. One guy lived in the living room because it was a little cheaper to live in the living room. I've heard of upwards of six or seven guys in a three-bedroom, it kinda just depends on what everyone's willing to spend and where you're at. San Antonio (AA) is not the most expensive housing market, so it's pretty reasonable. Ours was $1,300 a month for a three-bedroom, it's really not bad at all. But you gotta imagine if you had a team somewhere in Northern California, I'm going to go out on a limb and say that the housing there is a little steeper, you've gotta find a different way to break it down because as I'm sure you know, our minor league every-two-week salary is not exactly huge." Cal

"Basically it's a matter of luck where you're put in the country in terms of housing and renting costs. One year I was in Bakersfield (High A) where I was paying $600 a month for a three-bedroom house with a pool, and then I was in Rancho Cucamonga (High A) and it was $2,100 for three bedrooms. At one point we had six guys in that three-bedroom place. There were two guys in the master, one guy in the master closet, one guy in the living room, I had my own room and this other guy had his own room. I had to pay $200 more per month just so I had my own room. Then I got promoted to AA and I was paying $300 a month for a master bedroom and bath in Tulsa. A lot of it is luck, you go to these cheaper areas and you can get a pretty nice place and live comfortably for nothing or you're in the California League and you're paying double that for a closet. It's kind of ridiculous but you make it work." Drew

Most apartments aren't furnished, so guys have to get creative when furnishing their places. This is especially true given that they have such a short time to get settled and they know that they might not be there very long.

"The apartments aren't furnished, of course not. I had a blow up mattress, we had some beach chairs, a couple of us had TV's but no furniture at all." Marc

"You move in and there's nothing there. My first necessity was a bed. I didn't want to be sleeping on the ground the first night. So we went to the local Walmart and I got a $150 bed in a box, one of those beds that inflates when you open it. It was actually a better option than an air mattress, most of the guys got air mattresses. A few of the guys got cheap little TV's so they could hook up their game systems but we were struggling. We didn't have a kitchen table or anything, we didn't really have much silverware, anything like that. We got a few cheap pots and pans, but other than that we slowly accumulated some things. I was digging into the savings for sure because we don't get paid in Spring Training, we just got per diem which was barely enough to eat. I needed a fair amount of cash just to get myself started. You've got to put down your first month's rent and you've got to put down the security deposit. We were lucky we had a guy with a car because if we didn't have a car I don't know what we would have done. I think we made the best of a bleak situation but it's hard not to look back on that situation and cringe a little bit." Chris C.

"Our place wasn't furnished, we all slept on air mattresses. We made a trip to Walmart and picked up some air mattresses, we had a few pots and pans and one card table and that was it. No couch. No TV. Some guys would go to Costco or Walmart where they would buy a TV. There's a 30-day or 90-day return policy and they would just go return it right before the return period was up and get a new one. So they were constantly buying new TV's and returning them. There were a couple groups that did that. They managed to get a free TV for the summer." Wayne

"In Lancaster I roomed with two other guys but none of us had furniture. There was a booster club that loved to support the players and they had a warehouse of furniture we could use. We'd throw a mattress on the floor and the living room would have folding chairs, beach chairs, it was a simple life. We had to give the stuff back, many people from the team had used this stuff over the years." Mark

"When we first got there we flew in at midnight. There was nothing in the apartment, literally nothing. The carpet on the ground and the refrigerator were the only things there. We had to find an Uber at midnight because none of us had our cars, they were being shipped. We had to get a bedsheet and a pillow to cover us for the first night. We literally all slept on one pillow and blanket on the floor together the first night. The next day the boosters brought us stuff, they helped us out, they came and pretty much supplied what we needed until our cars got there to go buy stuff. From there we furnished everything. We Ikea'd it and furnished the place with at least a couch and everyone just bought air mattresses. By the end of the year everyone's mattresses were just deflated. One of my buddies lived in the living room and I'd wake up and see he'd be engulfed by his air mattress because there was a hole in it. If you didn't wake up and fill it up, you'd wake up in the morning and you'd be flat on the floor. Guys were so cranky about it by the end of the year because they weren't getting enough sleep." Colton

Eventually Colton and his teammates found one solution to getting more sleep.

"Because the mattresses were so uncomfortable we got hooked up with a sensory deprivation tank, it was awesome. It's the art of floating, you just float and it's supposed to take all the stress away, you have no pressure points. That helped guys a lot, they'd go sit in those tanks for an hour and a half, they would feel so much better after that. It's really expensive but they offered us a free week and we promised them we'd give them any scientific info they needed because they were running studies. So they let us continue to use it. And we acted super interested about all the ways we were feeling, they were loving that information. So we just kept going as long as it was free for that month or two and it actually helped us a lot." Colton

Some players don't live in a hotel or a house or an apartment at all.

"One of my teammates decided to live in a trailer park by a big lake near the field. He was really big, he wore a lot of camouflage, he had a colored tattoo of a bald eagle with the American flag in the background. He hit the ball really far, I said there's no way this guy is natural. It turns out he got tested positive for steroids later on. I visited his trailer. He showed me his venison jerky that he made, he also showed me moonshine that he made. He showed me that the way to test if you have good moonshine is to burn it and see if it has a blue flame. A bunch of the guys on our team had gotten fishing kayaks, and in the morning they would take their kayaks over to his trailer and go in the lake and do some bass fishing. And I wanted to do that too, so I bought myself a fishing kayak and we'd go in the morning, at sunrise, and catch ourselves some bass. And later on in the day we'd go to the field. That was a lot of fun. That was Arkansas." Anonymous

"We had a landlord in Pensacola (AA) who rented us a house. But we wanted the place for five months during the season and since he would rent out his house for vacation rentals he said, 'Hey I have this booking in the middle of your season so I'll try to cancel it so you guys can have the place,' and we were like OK cool, it was a handshake agreement. But then when the time came he said, 'Actually I can't cancel it so I need you guys to move out for a week and two weekends,' which we were obviously not happy about. We debated getting someone to legally help us but then he said he had this fishing boat we could sleep on, and I was like, 'OK I'll go to the boat.' The other two people I lived with crashed at someone else's place. So I was on this boat, it was a lot smaller than I was expecting and there were cockroaches on it. I was sleeping there on this little fishing boat rocking back and forth at night for a week. No shower. There was a shower on the dock, but I would just go to the field and shower. I was literally in the harbor across the street from the field. I've never lived on a boat, it's very unique. The nights were kinda interesting. There was a warm Florida gulf breeze and I was sitting up under the moonlight on the boat enjoying things. The more I'm playing the more I enjoy living by myself because you're at the field for 10 hours a day with the same 30 guys every day. It's kinda nice to have your own space, your own little peace and quiet at the end of the day. The more I've been in this life I'm learning to accept the good and the bad and accept that every new situation you have has goods and bads and you kinda just roll with it and try to enjoy it as much as you can." Alex B.

> "I've never lived on a boat, it's very unique. The nights were kinda interesting. There was a warm Florida gulf breeze and I was sitting up under the moonlight on the boat enjoying things."

And very few players get lucky enough to stay with their own family.

"We had family friends in Richmond (AA) so I stayed at their house which was great. Up until that point I had never had to get my own apartment in the minor leagues." Austin S.

"It was a huge positive that I got assigned to Everett, Washington (Short Season A) because I got to live at home. I don't know how many people in minor league ball get to say that. I got to keep my paycheck rather than have it go to housing." Sam

****

"It was a revolving door of players coming in
and out all season long."

Another housing scramble occurs whenever players get moved around the system when they're promoted, demoted or traded. They find themselves in another city within a day or two and have nowhere to live. This not only means they have to find a new place to live but it leaves an empty spot where they were living.

"The hardest part is when you're living with a guy and you're each paying $500 and he gets called up to the next level or he gets hurt and sent to Arizona and then you're alone with the apartment. They bring someone up and he has a buddy with a different apartment and he wants to live with his friend on the team and so you're alone paying rent at your place for two people. It's just a shitshow. It's too much. Other than that, I have a good time all season, but every year the housing stuff is always kind of a nightmare." Anonymous

"You get three days in the hotel and then you either go try to find someone's couch to sleep on, or you can do an extended stay in the hotel and then just pay for the rest of the season. The hotel gives you a deal but it's still kind of expensive. When I got promoted to Springfield (AA), the guy who got sent down when I went up was living with a player whose agent happened to live 30 minutes outside of Springfield. I ended up moving into that player's room and then maybe two to three weeks after I got to Springfield, the other guy moved up to Memphis (AAA) so it was just me staying at the agent's house. They even had cars that they let us use." Tommy

"It's pretty expensive in California obviously so when I got promoted I had guys fighting to get me to live with them. That's what happens with everyone who moves there. They're trying to cram more people in. Our team was moving pitchers around like crazy. Eventually I was in a bedroom thank God, but initially I was in the living room and then someone else came in the living room with me." Marc.

"When I got to Billings, Montana (Rookie) all the host families were taken so I was just living in a hotel. They paid for the hotel room. I got moved into a host family's house a few weeks later but I only slept there one night and then got promoted." Alex B.

If a player joins a team on the road, they can just stay at the hotel with the rest of the team. If a player joins a team at their home city, they typically get three nights in a hotel and then they're on their own.

"I had an apartment in Oklahoma City (AAA) and then when I got sent to Tulsa (AA) they were on the road, so they provided a hotel. Then I got sent to Rancho (High A) and my parents live 35 minutes from there so I stayed with them. Then I got sent back to Tulsa and they were on the road again. Whenever I went to Tulsa and Rancho I just moved my stuff out of my Oklahoma City room, kept paying rent in the apartment, had somebody else use the room and just pay me on Venmo. The rooms usually get used and shuffled around." Anonymous

When they get promoted, most guys manage to get apartments with other players but some guys just live out of a hotel for a while.

"I know guys that choose to live in the hotel the whole season and those are usually guys that sign for a lot, or guys that come in late and just for a month will pay a hotel at a discounted rate." Drew

"When I got promoted to Arkansas (AA) I didn't have a place to stay. A buddy and I didn't want to look for a place so every 3-4 or 7-8 day homestand we would just rent a hotel on Hotwire. Of course to save money we'd choose two-star hotels. One of the places was a really junky motel, it was really dilapidated, the people were really sketchy. There's a good chance people were cooking meth next door." Kenny

"I got called up to AAA and it was interesting because they had a lot of guys move back and forth that year so instead of taking over one of the apartments from one of the guys getting called up and down, I ended up staying in the team hotel pretty much the beginning of June through the rest of the season through August. I was living in hotels for about three months. It was the team hotel and it was a daily rate of about $80 a night.

I would move out of the hotel when we went on the road so I was only paying for at the most 10 nights in a row. You're probably at home for half the month. It's not great but it came down to either finding my own place for three months or moving into someone's apartment that just got moved up. But when I would look at the big league roster guys coming back from injuries I'd think that guy's probably going to be back down here in two weeks and I don't want to put them out. And then I would have to move back into the hotel and it would start to become a cluster mess. I didn't have my car, I left it in Richmond (AA). The hotel was in walking distance to the field so I was just walking everywhere, Ubering when I had to move my luggage. I'd keep my luggage in the clubhouse." Anonymous

And speaking of cars, there's the added complication if a player gets moved up or down and he has a car.

"One guy got moved from Florida to Illinois, so he had to leave his car in Florida but another guy got moved from Illinois to Florida so they just used each other's cars for the rest of the season." Danny

With all this shuffling around, the guys who initially sign a lease are rarely the guys who live there at the end.

"We all got assigned to our league, so one guy signed a lease and filled the place with teammates. Two days later he got called up, so he was paying our lease, we were paying him, and he was paying another lease in AA. Then when he got sent back down, he decided to retire. It was a revolving door of players coming in and out all season long. The next year Austin and I both signed the lease and by the end of the season we were both gone." Danny

"How funny is that, both of us signed the lease and neither of us was there at the end." Austin W.

"To be honest, it was a hassle because I was moved and I was still on the lease. So whoever filled in in my apartment spot after me had to collect money from everyone and pay my lease. I would have liked not to have the responsibility of being on a lease and I think the host family situation would have been a lot easier because guys get moved around so much. By the end of the year there were four guys who had signed the lease and only one of them was left. So we were juggling all kinds of things with different guys. We had to leave the furniture we bought for the apartment there because we had no way of getting it anywhere, we didn't even want it." Chris C.

"In Palm Beach (High A), there were about 12 different people that stayed in this apartment over the course of the season. At the end of the season the four people who were still there were completely different than the original four people." Tommy

...which can lead to complications like utilities being shut off...

"I got sent to another team and drove the seven hours from Delaware to Kentucky. I wasn't playing that night, the game was at 7:00 PM and I showed up at 6:30 PM. I quickly got in my uniform and got out to the field. I didn't know where I'd be staying that night, so as guys were coming in and out during the game I'd say, 'Hey, where are you staying, can I sleep on your couch?' And during this process I came across a Latino who I knew, and he was like, 'Yeah, I've got an open apartment and you can sleep there but the problem is we haven't been there in a while.' And I was like, 'What do you mean?' and he said they all moved out. And I asked, 'Aren't you still on the lease? Are you paying rent?' And he said they just weren't paying anymore. The way it worked was there were four Latinos in the apartment — three bedrooms and someone on the couch. One of them got promoted and one of them got hurt, so there were two left and they didn't have anyone to fill the spots. So one of them, this young guy, just said, 'Screw it, I don't want to have to pay this rent, I'm going to leave,' so he left to live with somebody else. And the last guy said, 'I'm not staying here, I'm just going to move out too.' So he moved out into a host family's house but they were still technically on the lease for this place. And because they weren't paying, the utilities got shut off. Of course, electricity powers the fridge. I *remember going to the place with my buddy Carlos who used to live there. We got to the apartment and we opened up the fridge and it was probably the most disgusting thing I'd ever seen in my life. There were thousands of maggots everywhere in the fridge, there was this dark liquid everywhere, it absolutely reeked. I didn't end up dealing with it. One of the assistant coaches who had been a major league player for 10 years ended up going there and helping him clean it up." Kenny*

... and credit problems...

"I mean there was some scrambling but I felt like I had it under control. The most I moved was in 2013, I started in High A and moved to AA within three months of that season. I had a lease, I had opened up the apartment and was leaving but had to keep it open for my other roommates. I had to work out a little agreement where they made sure to pay the bills and that sorta stuff but I just kept it and closed it out at the end of the year. It ended up hurting my credit rating. Sometimes bills just don't get paid because it's either on you or on your roommates who you trusted to pay the bill and make sure it was closed out. My dang credit report — it was always some utility charge that popped up. It's so hard to orchestrate, when you have to set up four or five different accounts, electric, cable, whatever, doing it at each level on a monthly basis. It wasn't surprising that a couple of those things got missed." Stephen

You can't help but wonder why the teams don't take a more active role in finding stable housing for the players.

"The teams need to find a way to make the whole housing system better. They need a better format on having apartments ready, having things ready for the team when they get into a city. I've actually thought about ideas, creating something that can organize that across the country but I don't know how profitable that would be or if teams would want to do that." Drew

"My idea was always that the team could go to an apartment complex and say they

want to lease 10 rooms from April until September. The leases could be owned by the team and they can take the money out of the paychecks of whichever players opt in. When a player moves and another one comes in, they can just take their spot, there's no changing of the lease, the team owns the lease. I don't know why that hasn't been done yet. I could see that happening one day. Our team was feeding people PB&J and then Gabe Kapler came to the Dodgers and said, 'No, we're going to spend $1 million on food a year, and everybody's going to eat well.' And now other teams are starting to follow suit. I could see the next thing being housing, where one person comes in and says, 'You know, we're going to get housing for these guys,' and the other teams say they can do that too." Anonymous*

Sounds like a great idea. It certainly would help out the players.[1] But what's this about being fed PB&J's?

****

"A lot of PB&J's early on."

The options for food are as haphazard as the housing situation for minor league players. When players are in their home affiliate, for the most part they're on their own for breakfast and lunch, while dinner is usually served at the field. It can be particularly challenging for those living in hotels.

"Our hotel didn't provide any food, which was a big bummer. No food for breakfast. Sometimes there'd be an early bus and they'd drive us to Subway before the game, which a lot of guys did. It was tough because we were across the freeway from a little shopping center that had a Wendy's and a gas station and a Walmart and that was really it. Those were our food options. We had to cross the freeway to get there which didn't really feel safe. We couldn't do any cooking at the hotel. Our clubhouse manager

---

[1] For more information about what one team is doing, see Chapter Six Notes.

would usually put together some food for us after the games. Unfortunately a lot of times it was just leftovers from the concession stand, their leftover hot dogs. The food situation was not very good that year." Wayne

"I just tried to eat at the field as often as possible. It's different than Spring Training where you're out of there by 3:00 PM and you need to get dinner for yourself. During the season you're waking up at 11:00 AM and you're at the field at 1:00 PM, so I would just eat a granola bar at home and then eat at the field. Sometimes I would walk to Publix, the grocery store, which was like a mile away. Have you ever been to a Publix? It's the best, it is absolutely the best — I pretty much lived off their Pub Subs the first year. You should go there the next time you're in the South." Marc

"Right next to our hotel my options were either the Chick-fil-A, the Golden Corral or the Steak 'n Shake. Or the Hooters. I'd make breakfast in my hotel room every morning because the breakfast they provided us was very poor. I bought an electric skillet and a little toaster from Walmart and I would make myself these awesome scrambled eggs, toast, and avocado every morning in the hotel room. Of course there are no garbage disposals in the sink, and they're really small, so I became a pro at cooking in the 'kitchen bathroom.' It was great. I actually had a little gas camping stove and there was this one time when I was playing around with my wok on the floor of my bathroom, and it started smoking. It was smoking so bad I had to put a towel under the door so it wouldn't get out into the room. I was cranking the fan, it was a really bad smell and the smell stuck with the room. Luckily I was able to clean up the bathroom so there was no trace but it really stunk. I definitely damaged the hotel room there." Anonymous

> **"I became a pro at cooking in the 'kitchen bathroom.' It was great."**

It's a little easier if you're in an apartment and can cook for yourself in a real kitchen.

"We had a kitchen in our little apartment, we cooked for the most part, we tried to keep

our diet as good as we could. When you're on the road and traveling to different places you can't cook for yourselves, so when we were home we tried to do what we could." Lonnie

"The Hispanics were always cooking. When we were in Lexington (Low A) I learned how to make their chicken, rice and beans, it was fun. Their technique to make the rice and beans was to boil the water, add the rice, and once the rice had absorbed the water, for the last stage of cooking you covered it. But they didn't cover it with the lid of the pan, they covered it with a Walmart plastic bag which had no seal. They just took a Walmart bag and they covered this steaming hot pile of rice." Kenny

"The crunchy rice at the bottom of the pan was a delicacy. They'd call it 'concon.' After they'd scoop out all the rice they'd take a metal spatula and scrape off what was on the bottom. The sound of the spatula on the pan was like 'con con.' The problem was some of my teammates would scrape so hard they'd scrape off all the cheap non-stick coating of their Walmart pans. They'd just scrape it all off. Once I went to their room to eat some food and I saw their pan and there were all these streak lines of pure metal. I guess extra minerals are healthy?" Kenny

Most minor league games are at night, so for dinner the players usually rely on the clubhouse manager or "clubbie" to provide a post-game meal. Like everything else, these meals aren't free. The players pay clubhouse dues to cover the cost of the pre- and post-game food. Depending on the player's level, clubhouse dues can be as low as $4 per day, although it's generally in the $6-8 per day range. For $9-10 players are getting good food and good spreads, and $11-12 and higher is like AAA premier service.

"The food in the clubhouse after the games in Clinton (Low A) was a little bit better than my first season in Virginia (Rookie). There were some local restaurants that would bring in food for us after the games occasionally which was kinda nice. Overall it was definitely a better situation than living in a hotel and eating Wendy's three meals a day." Wayne

"You had your typical spread before and after the games like peanut butter sandwiches and stuff like that. Concession stand food was pretty much it." Lonnie

"In Troy (Short Season A) we were served food at the field, it was a lot of good stuff and a lot of not-so-good stuff. It was a lot of concession stand food they had left over. They catered food a good amount, but there were some nights where you definitely got hot dogs and like, pretzels." David

"There's this meat that has cheese inside the meat, that stuff,[2] that was our pre-game meal in Short Season A." Danny

"The cheapest things they could buy, that's what was provided. You were getting wonder bread, you were getting peanut butter and jelly, the cheapest kind. Or you were getting catered from the company that sponsors the minor league team that you're at because that's the best deal you're going to get. Our meals never got better no matter what our dues were." Tyler

"A lot of PB&Js early on. I got used to that in college so it wasn't a real shock." Austin S.

If the clubhouse doesn't provide the meal, players have to go out on their own.

"I don't remember getting post-game meals, only before travel. We were in Utah and a lot of things closed down early. I can't tell you how many times I had to go to Denny's, it was the only thing open on the side of town where I lived. They found out I was playing baseball so every night they just asked if I wanted the usual. It was two eggs, toast and fruit. Every once in a while I would throw in bacon. I tried to find something that wasn't horrible, because I ate out every night at a fast food restaurant." Eric

---

[2] It's called Mortadella.

Regardless of how good the food is, it's important to treat the clubbies well.

"The clubbie might say you owe $30 for two weeks but most of the clubbies are your favorite people, so you tip them. Those are the guys that are doing your uniforms after every game. Some clubbies will supply sunflower seeds and gum and they don't have to do that. It's the least glamorous job because they're always in the clubhouse and they don't really get the respect. That's part of what we learned at Stanford, love them or hate them, Coach Nine made sure that we always remembered everybody. In baseball there are so many people that go into it you have to at least be a human and say hello and know their names. You're with them every single day for months." Jack

****

"We'd always have dinner but it certainly wasn't steak night every night."

Given the variability of pre- and post-game spreads, it's a big treat when big leaguers get temporarily assigned to a minor league team for injury rehabilitation, which is referred to as a rehab assignment. These big leaguers are generally expected to provide the team with something more than the usual meal.

"I think generally the rule of thumb is they'll get one spread while they're down. If they have 13 years of big league time or something crazy, they'll hook you up with three or four different spreads, they're pretty good about it. If you're in the big leagues you're probably not short on cash. We don't eat the best in the minor leagues so they tend to hook us up with a steak, or something nicer than our regular grub." Cal

"My first year in Peoria (Low A) we had John Jay come rehab with us. Super nice guy, very helpful, he wasn't like a big leaguer at all. He talked to everyone, he interacted with us, he was really down to earth. I think he bought us Chipotle all three days for lunch and then steak dinners after the games which was awesome. Depending on your clubhouse manager you didn't even really get lunch a lot of times. They would have some food like peanut butter and jelly or whatever. We'd always have dinner but it certainly wasn't steak night every night." Justin

"When I was in Corpus Christi (AA), we had Evan Gattis and Carlos Gomez doing rehab assignments. I heard they actually bought pretty nice spreads on their last nights but unfortunately I wasn't around for either of those last few nights." David

"We'd get Fleming's and PF Chang's when big leaguers would treat. I remember Joc Pederson got everyone smoothies before a game." Drew

"When I was rehabbing in Arizona, my buddy and I were going to get dinner and a beer at this country bar place and I remember walking out and Chad Billingsley was walking in. He recognized us and he said, 'You guys aren't going anywhere, drinks are on me,' and we ended up going out and having drinks with him. It was really funny, we were wondering if he could tell that we were in the same organization or did he think we were just miserable rehabbing guys? Either one would be a great reason to take us out for drinks." Eric

"One time Adrian Gonzalez was in Rancho (High A) and he got us Jersey Mike's subs. Sometimes we'd get Outback Steakhouse. We'd have Olive Garden leftovers for days. In Oklahoma City (AAA) Scott Kazmir got us Texas Roadhouse and Brandon McCarthy got us Chick-fil-A sandwiches. Anytime we got anything not organic it was like a godsend." Anonymous

Wait, what's wrong with organic food?

"The Dodgers were on an organic food program, they invested $1 million a year on the minor league, $1,000 per day per team. The only requirement was that it was organic. The caterers thought we wanted weird healthy dishes when in fact, we just wanted healthy normal meals made with organic ingredients. While some of it was good, a lot of it was downright awful and many times undercooked or overcooked. They thought they were catering to 35 people, not 35 athletes, so there was NEVER enough food. In Midland

(Low A), I would eat at the field and then stop by Taco Bell every single night, because I still had to get something else to fill me up and that was the only place open that late." Anonymous

"I had friends on the Dodgers and they said a lot of the players hated the catered organic food. They were upset they couldn't have their fast food." Kenny

The good news is the minor league teams are beginning to realize the importance of, and investing money in, proper nutrition for their players.

"I will say that they've done a great job of trying to get better with nutrition. The Dodgers started a trend a couple years ago improving the food in minor leagues and it's started to trickle down to other organizations because they've gotten such good results from it. As far as organizations go, the Giants usually don't cut corners. From my time in Short Season and the Arizona League to now, they've really stepped it up as far as trying to have healthier options pre-game and post-game in the minor leagues. It depends on the team you're with, but each level gets a little bit better and a little bit better and a little bit better until you're in the big leagues and they have three personal chefs on staff that cook every meal for you. That's part of the allure and part of the motivation to get up there, definitely." Anonymous

"It wasn't until my third year that the Reds actually started realizing that nutrition was important. I think they invested $1,000 more on the meals per team, they started focusing on nutrition, they hired a nutritionist who traveled to all of the affiliates to make sure the food was good and healthy. I was happy with that change because as a young guy at least my first years I kinda had to make do with what they had, lots of cold cuts and PB&J's." Alex B.

The teams are also investing resources in educating the players.

"We had a nutrition lady come in twice this past summer, mainly because the Latino guys have never really heard that much about nutrition. I've taken guys home from the field and on the way home they'd ask if we can stop at McDonald's. I'd say yeah sure, guys are hungry after a long day. We'd get there and they'd ask me to order eight McChickens, and I'd be like, 'Excuse me, you want what?' There was one time when I ordered two and this guy got mad at me. He actually wanted eight, because they were his meals for the next two days. So when he would get back to the hotel he'd have a stockpile of McChickens he could munch on. He didn't have a car and he didn't speak much English and it was hard for him to go out and get a real dinner. It was food that filled them up, food is food. So it was nice to have the nutrition lady come in and explain stuff in English and they'd have a translator as well." Alex D.

> "We'd get there and they'd ask me to order eight McChickens, and I'd be like, 'Excuse me, you want what?' "

"One day we had this nutritionist come in to talk to everyone on our team. We were all gathered around in the locker room and she was saying, 'I know your options are limited in the minor league so let's talk about Chipotle, what should you get at Chipotle? You should get a bowl, and you should get double chicken or double meat, whatever meat you prefer,' and everyone was like OK, OK, nodding their heads. And keep in mind in the locker room several of the guys don't speak English, so those guys were gathered in a corner with a translator, who was listening to the nutritionist and translating in real time to them. So this lady is saying, 'Make sure you get double meat,' and everyone was like OK, OK, and then she said, 'but no rice and no beans.' And then there was a little delay for the translator, and he said, 'Sin arroz y sin frijoles,' and then you heard all the Latin guys get up and go, 'Oh no, no way!' And they were waving their hands, grumble grumble grumble. And we all just started laughing." Danny

Does the nutrition advice actually help?

"I would say no, most of the guys don't realize it's important. Even during big league camp we had an infielders dinner with all the infielders and something like six of them *refused to eat vegetables. These were grown men in the prime of their career and they wouldn't touch a brussel sprout. Yes it's important, this is why baseball is a very frustrating sport. You can do everything right, you can sleep, you can eat, you can feel great, and then just struggle in games and not do well. Or you can go out and drink, be hungover, and get three hits just out of nowhere. I would say in the long haul of your season and your career it's very important to be responsible and do all the things you need to do, but at least for some guys it's not critical. They're putting the longevity of their careers in jeopardy." Alex B.*

"It's tough to be told that you have to eat something you don't like, but one thing that the nutritionist did help with was the other two catchers from Venezuela were getting pretty chubby. They would routinely get the 24-packs of the little baby Gatorades and they would be sipping on those all the time which is a lot of sugar, they were constantly taking in all that sugar. She found that out and made sure they didn't do that anymore and it really helped, they look a lot more fit this year." Alex D.

"You could probably eat just about anything for the first few months but once you get into June, July, August and the heat starts picking up and you're not on your nutrition and your sleep I would say your performance starts to be affected. And then also mood and other kinds of things, weight, body, everything. They call it the 'August Ass,' everyone starts to get salty. Obviously you still like the guys in the locker room and you have fun but instead of just going about your business, a lot of times it starts turning into shit talking back and forth. In a good way, guys just giving each other more heat and that's pretty standard. You're 120 games in at that point, it's been awhile and it's hot." Anonymous

But not every organization has gotten around to improving the food.

"That's the craziest thing — our organization just lacked investment in sleep and food, I couldn't believe it. They didn't value our sleep, they didn't value what we were eating. And in a season that long, those are the two most important things that you should be getting to try to maintain yourself. I know they definitely want to change it but it was

pretty absurd." Anonymous

"The Pirates had a budget of $500 per day to feed us pre-game and post-game. That's not enough for 35 players and staff. Other teams were getting $500 a meal, which is very doable, but we were getting $500 a day. I knew this because I just asked the staff. I would always complain about the food, like, 'Yo, why aren't we getting this, why aren't we getting what other teams are getting?' and they were like, 'Oh we're only getting $500 a day.' " Tyler

"Just from a nutritional standpoint, if you're going to make the investment into these young players, the return on investment for getting them chicken all the time would be much more than you're spending." Chris V.

The food situation is yet another incentive for minor league players to rise through the system and make it to the Major Leagues.

"The difference between food in the minor leagues and major leagues, I would say it's night and day. In the big leagues, everything is made there in the kitchen that's in the locker room. That's obviously ideal. They have three chefs on staff. You have some sort of steak pretty much nightly, and if you want they have fish options. They do a good job of working with nutritionists on staff to make sure you're covering all your bases. And now they're doing blood tests on you and sweat tests, and making sure your hydration is right, making sure your supplements are right, you're getting all your vitamins and things like that, either through food or through pills. It's just another whole ballgame up there as far as keeping your body right." Anonymous

****

It's hard to "keep your body right" when you're not getting adequate sleep and nutrition, but the players still manage to get out there every day and play baseball. (Well, almost every day.) Who wants to watch some baseball?

Chapter Six Notes

I talked with Andy Shea, President and CEO of the Lexington Legends (Low A). He had a lot of good things to say about what he's doing to help his team out with housing and food.

"Being in a college town, it's tough to get a five-month lease in the price range the players are looking for. We always try to make it fair if a player gets called up, down or out, that they're not on the hook for the lease in an apartment, but it's really complex, it's a challenge. The players only get here three days before, so there are a lot of hoops. They're as excited as hell and then as soon as they get here they're like, 'Oh my God, where am I supposed to live? Do I go to a furniture store and buy a $600 couch and then how do I get it back home?' For the most part we always have a plan figured out, but it is becoming increasingly harder.

"I always joke that the '06 Legends team ruined it for all future Legends teams. They had an awesome setup: fully furnished apartments, close to the University of Kentucky campus, 10 minutes away from the stadium. But they trashed it and caused so many problems. They screwed them over so much with deposits and all that stuff that the apartment complex more or less banned the Legends. This is too small of a town for that. Word travels.

"Another thing that ended up happening was only a few years ago when we had it teed up. We talked to a landlord in November and said, 'Hey, we're the Lexington Legends and we're going to need nine different apartments.' They said, 'That's great, sounds good, we'll have them ready, we won't book them,' even though April to Labor Day cuts them off from Spring and Fall semester, but they said that's fine. The last straw was the Legends players that particular year decided not to go there and only two people used them, so then that apartment complex was pissed as hell at us, they thought we pulled one over on them. We don't have the authority to tell the players of the 2019 team, you have to live here. So we can do as much as we can on the local side so they're good to move in in April, good to move out in September, that if they're up, down or out they won't be stuck with it. But there's only so much we can do and there are things we cannot do and that backfired on us.

"So that's why I'm working with the Royals on how they would in a weird way become the guys' landlords, because then they would be able to control if a guy gets called up who takes that apartment space. They would be able to prevent the ruining of the place because their name would be on it. They would be able to control if someone screwed them over on the deposit, they could deduct it from their paycheck. That's something we've been working on to make it a lot easier for the guys so when they move here they don't have to also go house hunting or apartment hunting, it would just be there for them. We can really figure out something that's good for everyone.

"On the food, we worked with the Royals on this. We've got local relationships and it's been great for the team. They get one meal a day from Good Foods Co-op, a place like Whole Foods. For every single one of the 70 home games, we get one full meal of good food prepared and delivered for the team. One protein, two veggies. I think that was awesome and definitely a step in the right direction. As far as I know that one is free to the players. They still have their dues and the clubbie makes another meal for them, but this is the extra meal on top of that. Everyone's happy, everyone wins. Good Foods thinks it's awesome that they're feeding the Lexington Legends, it's one of the better marketing things you can do. It's a win win all around."

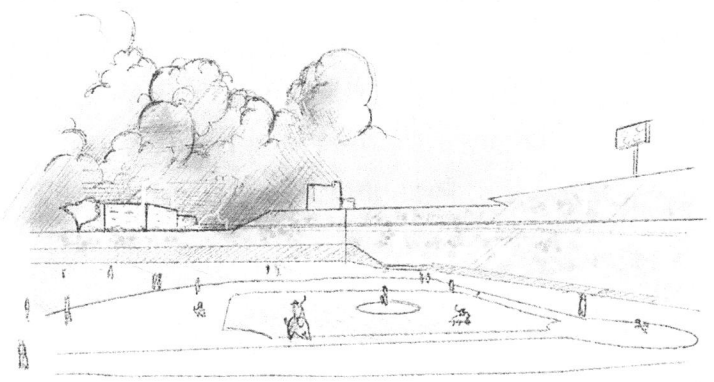

Chapter 7
Take Me Out to the Ballgame

It's finally time for the season to start. Players are (more or less) settled into their accommodations and they've had their only three days of practice all year.[1] They're anxious to get out on the field and prove themselves. They want to play baseball! But it's not quite what they imagined. They quickly learn that some team assignments are better than others. Everything from the size of the crowd to the atmosphere in the ballparks to the weather varies from team to team. There are a lot of outside elements that minor league players have to contend with. It's literally all over the map.

****

"It's just more fun when there's more people."

---

[1] Once the season starts, minor league teams don't "practice." They warm up and do drills before games, but on their very few off days they are either traveling or they're "off."

The size of the crowds and the fan support vary dramatically across the minor league system. As one would expect, the two AAA leagues bring in the most fans because they're the closest to the Major Leagues in talent. The AAA International League, with teams located up and down the east coast of the United States, averages 6,868 fans per game. On the other end of the spectrum, the Appalachian Rookie League brings in the fewest fans, averaging only 1,228 fans per game.[2]

It's obviously a lot more fun for teams to play to a big crowd.

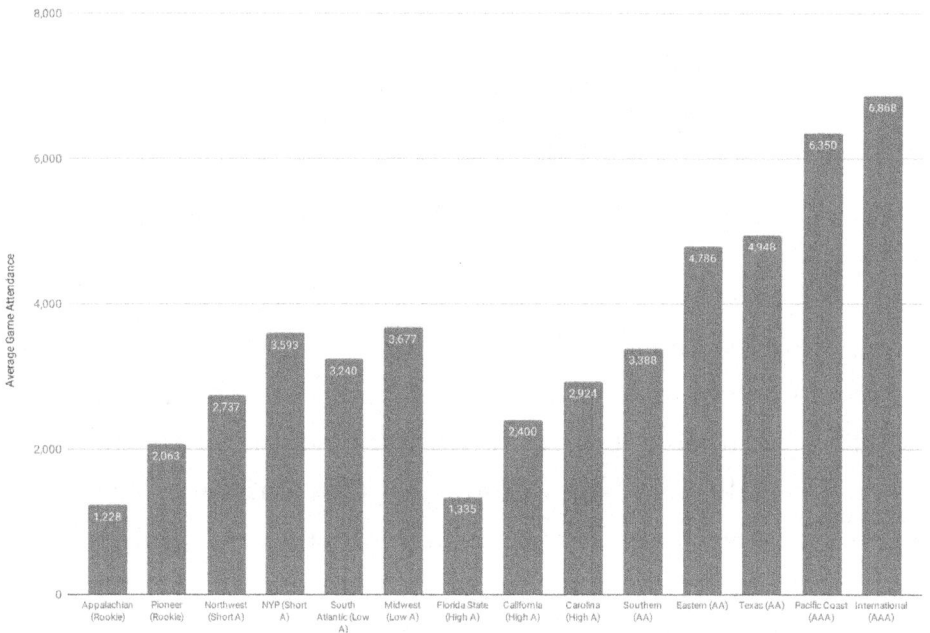

"Definitely if there's nobody in the stands the game kinda feels dead, it's more of the 'why am I out here' feeling. Yeah, we're playing baseball but it feels like we're doing this for nothing. And then when there are fans there, the excitement fuels you. When you get a

---

[2] For attendance figures for all the teams, see the Note at the end of the chapter.

base hit in the 8th inning when you're down by one and the crowd goes wild, that kind of fuels the team, fuels the dugout, it's just a different feeling. I think it helps the momentum and everything." Anonymous

"There are some teams that fans come out for every single game, and obviously everyone wants to play for those teams because it actually gives you some incentive to want to go to the ballpark and play really well. But if you're in Clinton, Iowa (Low A) there's really no drive to want to do really well and show up to the ballpark. It's like, 'Oh, we're going to have 20 fans today, it's going to be great.' There are some really cool places, even in Low A and High A that sell out every game, it's awesome, it's so much more fun." Lonnie

Surprisingly, moving up the system doesn't always result in more fans. The two Low A leagues both bring in more fans than each of the three High A leagues.

"It's hard to grind away in the Florida State League (High A) because for whatever reason that league doesn't get that many fans. Maybe it's because of the weather, maybe people are doing other things. You don't have the same small town appeal that other places have. You might have 100 or 200 fans, there's way less energy at the ballpark. It's just more fun when there's more people." Danny

Furthermore, average attendance per league doesn't tell the whole story, as attendance can vary dramatically across the teams within each league. In the Carolina League (High A), the Winston-Salem Dash average over 12 times as many fans (4,436) as the Buies Creek Astros (359). In the Midwest League (Low A), the Dayton Dragons bring in over nine times as many fans (7,868) as the Burlington Bees (859) and more than every team in every league except for some of the teams in the AAA Leagues.

Does the performance of the team drive fan attendance? Not necessarily, according to Andy Shea, President & CEO of the Lexington Legends in the South Atlantic League (Low A).

"The theory in minor league baseball is if it's one down season, no big deal, if it's two

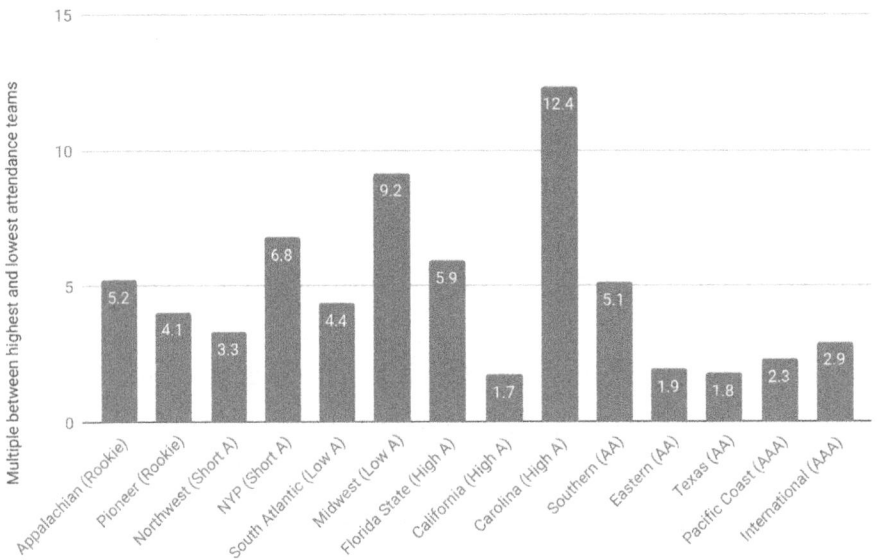

down seasons, that's fine. But once it starts to be three, four, five in a row, that's when it does start to affect your real baseball fans, the people that don't necessarily care that it's a quarter hotdog day on Tuesdays, or fireworks this night or that night, they're coming out for the actual baseball." Andy

That seems to be the case in Quad Cities.

"Quad Cities (Low A) was great, I think it's traditionally a pretty well-known team, the area and the city really rallies behind the team. It was crazy because we were the worst team in the league and we still got tons of fans every night." David

Not surprisingly, attendance also varies throughout the season. In Lexington, for example,

"Our core demographic is young families, and in April and May they still have school. And when you factor in that the weather in Lexington is so goofy, there have been opening days where it is picture perfect here and then there have been days when it's almost snowing. Another huge component of our business is group outings, whether that's a fraternity, a church, a company, Little League, a bachelor party, or just a group of buddies. It's tough for them to choose April or May over a June, July or August date." Andy

And finally, attendance varies throughout the week.

"In general, weekends are king. Saturdays in particular have been our highest average attendance for the 18 years we've been in existence. Saturdays across the board and in particular, summer Saturdays." Andy

While there's obviously not a lot a team can do about the school schedule or the weather or what day of the week it is, they can try to attract fans with promotions.

****

*"All the minor league promotional stuff is good fun,
it's pretty entertaining, it keeps people coming."*

The energy of the stadium varies dramatically from league to league and team to team and it's not just a function of the size of the crowd. Minor league stadiums are known for their zany promotions and hilarious entertainment which are all designed to not just bring in the fans but keep them cheering and engaged in the game. A look at the promotional schedules across the teams consistently reveals an abundance of fireworks nights and giveaways of Bobbleheads, t-shirts, hats and jerseys. There are always military appreciation nights and celebrity autograph nights. There are plenty of low priced food and beer nights like Kids Eat Free

Tuesdays and Thirsty Thursdays. Themes like Superhero Night and Princesses in the Park bring in a variety of ages and genders. Elvis impersonators wander around. You can even bring your dog to the "Bark in the Park" games or attend Dog Adoption Promotions Night. Pretty much any topic or theme can lend itself to a promotion. (For a preview, see announcement on next page.)

Without a doubt, fireworks nights are a big hit. Fireworks are popular to anyone and everyone almost all the time. Most teams provide them every Friday and Saturday nights, plus opening day and the 4th of July. The Greensboro Grasshoppers are one those teams.

"Greensboro (Low A) was awesome. Friday and Saturday were fireworks nights. I heard from a front office staff member that the fireworks display ranged from $30,000-40,000 every Friday and Saturday nights. It was an unbelievable display and we'd get a ton of people. It made it really fun. Our team was pretty spectacular, there weren't a lot of teams like that. Ours was what everyone wanted to be, how successful our promotions were, they ran a really good park there." Colton

One of the zaniest promotions in minor league baseball is the Cowboy Monkey Rodeo.

"One day we got to the park and I heard Cowboy Monkey Rodeo was that night. And I was like, 'What's that?' and my teammates were like, 'You'll see.' They stopped the game in the middle of the 7th inning, and they announced, 'It's time for Cowboy Monkey Rodeo!' They had these little tiny monkeys that were riding on top of dogs, and they would come out onto center field. There were probably four or five of them, and there was a guy who ran out with them, he was their big ringleader. They would run around the field, these monkeys riding on dogs, and it was Cowboy Monkey Rodeo! And then they stopped and the leader got the microphone and went out and gave a speech. He said in his southern drawl, "Ah just want to say thank you to all of you fans, if any of you have a dream, you can accomplish it. Ah had a dream for Cowboy Monkey Rodeo and bringin' all this entertainment to y'all, and now I'm livin' that dream. You can accomplish

Lexington Legends Promotions Announcement

WHITAKER BANK BALLPARK (Lexington, KY) - Lexington Legends fans can gear up for a summer of fun, new promotions, as well as classic promotional staples at Whitaker Bank Ballpark.

New for the 2019 season, the Legends welcome PJ Masks characters Catboy, Owlette and Gekko on Friday, July 12th. VIP packages will be available. To celebrate his 20th anniversary, SpongeBob Squarepants will make an appearance on Friday, August 9th. Legends players will be donning special SpongeBob jerseys. The Legends also welcome back the inflatable Zooperstars characters on Friday, July 26th.

There are multiple giveaways to highlight in the 2019 season. On Opening Day, Thursday April 4th, the first 1,000 fans through the gates will receive a 2018 Championship Replica Ring. The Legends are excited to announce a Black Panther bobblehead giveaway on Super Hero™ Day, Sunday, July 28th. There will also be a bobblehead giveaway of former Lexington Legend and multiple Silver Slugger award winner, JD Martinez on Saturday, July 13th. Back by popular demand, the Legends will be doing a Kids Jersey Giveaway on Friday, June 21st, thanks to WKYT.

Returning this season are Tuesday Night 25¢ Hot Dogs, courtesy of Kentucky Coal Association, Kids Free Ticket Sundays, with Family Play Time on the Field, along with Pepsi Bark in the Park and Kentucky Ale Thirsty Thursdays.

A Whitaker Bank Ballpark tradition, fans can look forward to 19 post-game fireworks displays including a fireworks spectacular on July 4th.

The full promotional schedule is available by visiting lexingtonlegends.com.

anythin' you set your mind to. Thank you and God bless you.' Everyone went wild. And then the cowboy monkeys ran around for another few minutes and then they left. The players were just standing there completely in awe of what just happened and then we had to finish the game. And probably most people at that point left the stadium because they had come to see Cowboy Monkey Rodeo and they walked out after that." Danny

That ringleader is probably Tim "the Wild Thang" Lepard from Tupelo, Mississippi and his Team Ghostriders. The dog and monkey pairs are actually herding rams around the field.

"The Cowboy Rodeo, that's always a fun thing. The stands would completely pack out just to watch the Cowboy Monkey Rodeo. I'm pretty sure people were there just to see that. The time they did it for us they left one of the gates open in the outfield fence and in the middle of the sixth inning there was a goat that just ran out onto the field. It somehow got out onto the field and they had to stop the game and bring that guy out and he had to usher the goat back into the pen. It was a 'Goat delay." Tommy

Unfortunately for fans of Cowboy Monkey Rodeo, the promotion is no longer making the calendar of many minor league affiliates due to the alleged cruelty to the animals involved in the activity.[3]

Another extremely popular promotion is the Human Cannonball.

"State College (Short Season A) had a Human Cannonball after the game. They set up a huge net over home plate and brought a huge cannon to the outfield beyond second base so they could shoot it from past second base all the way to home plate. They shot a guy out of the cannon and he flew through the air and landed in the net. Everyone went crazy." Tommy

"They shot a guy out of the cannon and he flew through the air and landed in the net. Everyone went crazy."

---

[3] mediapeta.com/peta/PDF/Use_Of_Animals_Statement_Final.pdf

Yes, that's David "The Bullet" Smith, the highest flying Human Cannonball in the world today. According to his website, he's been a human cannonball for over 22 years and he's performed over 8,000 cannon shots in fifteen countries.[4] (And probably every minor league ballpark.)

"I was bummed, I was promoted and missed the Human Cannonball by three days." Austin S.

When asked if those promotions bring in extra fans, Andy from the Lexington Legends acknowledged,

"Those particular acts are staples of minor league baseball for sure, but they're not cheap. The Human Cannonball was great entertainment, and it was genuinely funny to take a step back and think, 'What the heck is going on at our ballpark right now?' We have a certain budget for that added entertainment and the fun value of being out here. What I think genuinely does sell tickets are giveaways like Bobbleheads. When I first started here some people thought Bobbleheads were on the way out but I'm sorry, they're still the most popular thing we can do or give out, as long as it's a good one. You still have the avid collectors, the people who do genuinely buy tickets for that." Andy

If a fan misses one of those, there are plenty of other opportunities to be entertained.

"When I was in Lake Elsinore in the California League (High A) there was a guy who was a sprinter in college, he wore a squirrel suit, he was the World's Fastest Squirrel. We always loved it, it was hilarious." Mark

Ace, the Fastest Squirrel in the World, would streak across the outfield between

---

[4] humancannonball.us

innings, outracing the volunteers who had gotten an outrageous lead. Sadly, he hung up his cleats in August of 2017.[5] (But if you go to an Atlanta Braves game you might see a sprinter wearing ski glasses and a sleek light-blue bodysuit called The Freeze who does the same thing.)

Thirsty Thursdays or $1 Beer Nights are always a draw.

"There are four colleges in Greensboro (Low A) that are really good size. We had Thirsty Thursdays which was a huge hit with the college guys. It was really funny especially late in the game the amount of heckling they'd do to the other team was absurd and security never stopped them." Colton

While some promotions make the rounds around the entire country, some promotions are specific to only one team.

"In Lexington, Kentucky (Low A) there's an organization called Friends of Coal. They sponsored a regular promotion between innings. Of course in Kentucky, coal is part of the economy. It's coal country. There's a big billboard saying 'Friends of Coal.' During the promotion the announcer would say, 'WHO HERE IS A FRIEND OF COAL?' and everybody would start clapping and cheering. 'Coal keeps the lights on for you!' I thought to myself, I'm not in California." Kenny

"The Akron RubberDucks (AA) had a phenomenal media kit during the games. They played YouTube sensation songs, very annoyingly funny songs. They played very addictive kids songs that you couldn't get out of your head, songs that my son listens to and loves. They would play them between innings up on the board and play the music videos with them. They were the best in terms of keeping everyone entertained, they had a great PA announcer who was very hyped every day. I absolutely loved going to Akron, it was a great city." Tyler

"There was one stadium in the South Atlantic League (Low A) where they had given one

---

5 pe.com/2017/07/07/worlds-fastest-squirrel-heading-for-the-finish-line-in-lake-elsinore

of the fans a bullhorn and he was right behind home plate. It was outrageous. He was extremely loud, he was annoying everyone. It's minor league baseball so there's a little bit of weird stuff that happens, but having a guy with a bullhorn directly behind home plate is a little bit extreme." Chris V.

"There was one called Bubble-U, Bubble-U, E. Giant human bubbles. They put people in bubble suits and they would run head forward into another person in a bubble suit and just see who falls first. You would see guys get creamed, it was awesome. It was between innings and it happened to be right in front of the bullpen so we had the best seats in the house to watch the BBE go down. That was one of the more entertaining ones for sure." Chris C.

Sometimes the players themselves are part of the promotion, such as when there's a "beer batter." Before the game, the stadium will announce the name of one of the players on the visiting team as the beer batter. If that player strikes out during the game, the whole stadium gets a free beer.

"The beer batters are always fun. They'd announce the lineup and you'd wait, and when it was time for the beer batter they'd be like, 'And tonight's beer batter is ... shortstop so-and-so.' It was funny, I remember one of my buddies, every time if it was him he would be like, 'Fuuuuck!' He'd get so mad, it riled him so much. And then there was this other guy who wanted to be the beer batter and he'd be like, 'Pick me! Pick me!' Because every night he was the beer batter he'd have a good night. It was a superstition. The other guy was like, 'If I'm the beer batter tonight I'm striking out three times,' he just let it get to his head. For sure it trips people mentally. There are guys that can handle it and think it's funny, like there's nothing to lose if I do well and if I strike out all the fans are happy." Drew

> **"They'd announce the lineup and you'd wait, and when it was time for the beer batter they'd be like, 'And tonight's beer batter is'...I remember one of my buddies, every time if it was him he would be like, 'Fuuuck!' "**

"When you strike out, that's the loudest they'll ever cheer." Brant

"I actually have been the beer batter a few times in my career. One time I remember I struck out, and everyone cheered and they all got beer. And I went back and I was upset that I struck out but it was nice to know that I just got everyone a bunch of beer. That's probably why I'm not still playing." Danny

"I've definitely been the minor league beer batter, I've definitely cashed it in for the fans so it all worked out for them. It's kind of funny, you don't think about it until you have two strikes and the crowd starts really cheering. I guess maybe it's a good way to practice for a big spot when your back's against the wall. All the minor league promotional stuff is good fun, it's pretty entertaining, it keeps people coming. I was all for it." Stephen

Of course it doesn't have to be a beer promotion. It can be a Hardee's promotion.

"In Peoria (Low A) we had a Hardee's promotion where there was a Hardee's hitter, and if he struck out once, one row of the stadium would get a free Hardee's sandwich. If he struck out twice, then an entire section would get one. If he struck out a third time, the entire stadium would get a free Hardee's sandwich. One time we were winning by two runs and it was the top of the last inning and there were two outs. As the home team, we were about to win. But the Hardee's hitter was on deck and he had already struck out twice. So the fans needed the visiting guy at the plate to get on base so the Hardee's hitter could get up and strike out. So the guy drew a walk and everyone was like, 'YAY! HARDEES!' So then the Hardee's hitter came up to bat and got strike one and everyone was like, 'YAY!' And then there was strike two and everyone was even louder, 'YAY!' By this time the entire stadium was chanting 'HAR-DEES! HAR-DEES! HAR-DEES!' Then the third pitch came and the guy hit it and it was a straight pop up. So with two strikes this guy hit a pop up and everyone went, 'Awww...' because they wanted a strike out, not a pop out. Now, our catcher had struggled with these pop ups all year, and sometimes it's windy and these can be kinda difficult. So our catcher was saying, 'I got it, I got it,' and

he went to catch it and it hit off his glove and it fell on the ground and everyone in the entire stadium went 'YAY!!' That out would have won us the game but no, they wanted the Hardee's. So then this guy got back in the batter's box and got a high fastball. He swung and missed, and everyone went crazy. The announcer yelled, 'And that's the Hardee's hitter – everyone gets free Hardee's!' It was the most hilarious thing ever." Danny

It could also be Chick-fil-A.

"The funniest story was at our home field in Lexington, Kentucky (Low A), they had one of the opposing players designated the Chick-fil-A strikeout batter for one at bat. If he struck out, everybody in the stands would get free Chick-fil-A. It was funny, after they announced it, the energy of the stadium changed, everybody got more engaged and the crowd was ramped up. People started going nuts. Strike one, everybody started clapping. Strike two, he fouled a pitch off and everyone was cheering and stood up. Then a ball was thrown and the entire crowd let out a loud 'Aww...' The count eventually went to 3-2 and the batter kept fouling pitches off. It was the most intense at bat I've seen in pro ball. The entire crowd was on the edge of their seats. Finally the batter swung at a slider in the dirt. The crowd erupted. It was by far the loudest I'd ever heard that stadium. The people acted like they had just won the lottery, they were yelling and high fiving each other, and giving each other hugs. They got free Chick-fil-A." Kenny

In North Carolina, it's all about Biscuitville.

"We have Biscuitville, a chain popular in North Carolina. It has really cheap southern biscuits and breakfast food. We had the Biscuitville batter of the game. There were only two home games we did not strike him out, so imagine 68 of the 70 home games we struck out the Biscuitville batter. It definitely got into the batter's head because everyone would chant after we got a strike on him, 'Bis-cuits, Bis-cuits.' Even the PA person would chant, 'Bis-cuits, Bis-cuits.' It was absurd how many times they actually struck out. I never went there but I had a stack of these coupons. They were just handing them out every single game. You don't need to actually purchase anything, you can get two free biscuits and a drink, which is one of the options for breakfast. You would order two biscuits with sausage and gravy for free. It was actually a pretty decent deal, people would legit go and use these. People in North Carolina eat that up, literally." Colton

And in California it's In-N-Out Burger.

"Some teams will do a hometown batter instead of an away batter promotion. In Rancho Cucamonga (High A) they did the double double player of the game. In that case if the chosen hometown player got a double, everyone got a free double double certificate at In-N-Out." Brant

One problem for the players is that they have to listen to the same promotions over and over.

"When you think of games at certain fields it's like oh, that's the Chick-fil-A promotion place where they do the same thing every night and it's just in your head, you go to sleep listening to it. Like in Little Rock (AA) it was the Chick-fil-A promotion, the whole stadium chants 'EAT MORE CHICKEN! EAT MORE CHICKEN!' nonstop, 20 times over. And there's the dizzy bat thing when the guy yells, 'GO GO GO GO GO' every single night. I was talking to our radio announcer and he said there are certain fields that he just can't stand because of the promotions and he falls asleep with those sounds in his head." Drew

"The songs get annoying no matter what because you hear them too many times." Tyler

Sometimes the players themselves aren't just a part of the promotion, they ARE the promotion.

"We'd show up to the field and on the lineup card it'd say 'pre-game autographs' and it had two players' names listed. And you'd have to report out to the tunnel and this guy would pick you up and they would station you at different entrances to the stadium as *poster boys. People would walk in, get to take a picture with you and ask you to sign your autograph. So if you don't play a lot like me, you have to do it. I had to do that a few times. It was pretty funny, you feel very objectified." Danny*

Fans may not realize that a lot of the music they hear in the stadium is music that's chosen by the home team players. Most minor league players get to choose a "walk up" song to be played when they walk up to bat.

"A walk up song is supposed to be something that not just makes you comfortable when you go up to the plate, but gets you excited to hit a baseball hard. I along with many other players would have superstitions around walk up songs. If you had a certain song for a long time and you weren't doing well then you would change it. You'd choose not just the songs that you enjoyed listening to, they needed to have a good snippet that you think would resonate well in the stadium environment." Kenny

"My walk up songs were 'These Are My People' by Rodney Atkins and 'This Is How We Do It' by Montell Jordan." Justin

"The one that I used for the longest and I enjoyed the most success with was 'What I Got' by Sublime. Sublime is a Southern California ska punk band and it's played generally on the beach with the sun shining and it would bring me back to that happy place of mine. It was almost like sprinkling a little bit of California flavor onto the situation." Anonymous Californian

"This year my walkup song was 'Rich & Sad' by Post Malone. Last year it was 'Alone' by Marshmellow. I change them every year. I know a lot of guys that change it up if they're not doing well. I know some guys that change it every week. We had one guy who had a different walk up song for Friday night games, or for Monday's games. It was kind of annoying. When you hear a walk up song it's like, 'Oh, Luke's hitting,' or 'Drew's hitting,' but this guy was playing something new every time. It was like, chill out, pull it together. Guys would either walk up to a country song that all the fans would love, or a rap song

or an EDM electronic song. The country song was the safe route that a lot of guys chose even though they didn't listen to country music. One guy was not a country guy but he walked up to a country song because he wanted to be loved by the fans." Drew

"My walk up songs were 'So Fresh, So Clean' by Outkast and 'Word Up!' by Cameo. They were my favorites, I didn't care really what the fans wanted. I was doing well so I kept them, those were the only two songs I had." Tyler

"Some guys would want a different walk up song for every at bat. They'd have a sequence, first at bat they'd have one song, second at bat they'd have another song, and they would repeat the sequence each game." Kenny

"My favorite one is probably 'I Like It' by Cardi B. The crowd liked that one too. I've had several of those. I always thought it was better to pick one that the crowd liked. But you want to pick one that pumps you up too. I've tried to do a little of both. There are some guys, mostly pitchers, that will do heavy metal and you'd be like, 'What? C'mon dude.' "
Brant

"There were some guys from Texas who would enjoy playing Texas-themed songs. We couldn't get the Italian player on our team to stop singing the song 'Deep in the Heart of Texas.' He'd sing it in his Italian accent, 'The stars at night, are big and bright, deep in the heart of Texas.' " Kenny

"I went with 'Good Life' by Kanye West. I used that one the whole time." Dom

"When I was little I used to play a computer game called Backyard Baseball and my favorite player was a little kid named Pablo Sanchez. One year I used his walk up song for myself. It was funny because all the Latin guys on my team liked it because it was a Latin-themed song and all the American guys liked it because they all had played Backyard Baseball." Danny

Similar to the batters, most pitchers choose a "walk out" song to be played when they go warm up on the mound.

"I went with 'The Chain' by Fleetwood Mac. I think hitters are more superstitious about their songs than pitchers. The pitchers maybe hear it once a week, and hitters are hearing it four times a night. I think the worst thing is a lot of people use a song that has their name involved, it's just a terrible look. We had a guy who had a song with his name in it and every time you heard it, it was just brutal. Unless you're the best hitter in the world it just looks and sounds bad. For my own benefit I decided to stay clear of my own name." Jack

"My walk out song was the same one I've had since college, I used it all three years at college. It's 'Tennessee Mojo' by the Cadillac Three. I'll probably have it the rest of my life, it's pretty good." Colton

"The whole time I used Jason Aldean's 'My Kinda Party.' I guess I had some methodical reasons for picking country. I figured as a white kid from Seattle I couldn't do rap, and electronic music would be too much. I thought country was a middle of the road crowd pleaser that wouldn't raise any eyebrows. And Jason Aldean is my favorite country artist." Andrew

"I don't have one defined walk out song because I changed mine up a lot. It was a weird pitcher superstition. My first walk out song this year was 'El Chacarron.' It's not exactly the most serious song to walk out to. I guess I was too loose and messed up my shoulder. I had to change it up once I got hurt." Chris V.

"In Quad Cities (Low A), we bullpen guys would switch up our songs pretty frequently and would choose different themes. The theme that stuck around the longest was 90's throwbacks. My song during that time was 'Whoomp! (There It Is).' " David

In at least one case, the on-field entertainment took precedence over the pitcher's choice.

"Dayton (Low A) was a family oriented place as far as the on-field stuff goes, and in the 7th inning they would always play the 'Frozen' theme song. So whoever the pitcher was, it didn't matter that you usually had your own walk out song, you had to warm up to the 'Frozen' song, which was kind of a bummer. And there was an ice princess on the big screen." Alex B.

Needless to say, all this fun and games on the field can be distracting to the players.

"I was pitching in Stockton (High A) and one of my friends got into one of the promotions, he was doing Dance for Your Dinner. He pulled off his shirt and then he pulled down his pants. He was wearing an American flag Speedo under his pants. I saw him out of the corner of my eye and was trying not to laugh while I was warming up for the sixth inning." Mark

Sometimes the entertainment can stop the game entirely.

"We had a fireworks night, and obviously fireworks night is when everyone comes. I remember one night the game was going extremely long, but they couldn't blast the fireworks after 10:00 PM. Our team GM came in our dugout and said, 'Hey, we have to do the fireworks show now!' I believe it was around the 8th inning. We did the fireworks show, waited for the smoke to clear, and then finished the game. Of course, only in minor league baseball." Austin W.

"It was Superhero Night in Bakersfield (High A) so we had like 10 fans, and all the on-field crew and security guards were dressed up as superheroes. In the middle of the game all of a sudden we heard a couple gunshots go off in right field. We knew the area around the field was not great so when we heard the gunshots we were super rattled. Our right fielder was this big black guy and he came running in like you'd see in a movie, yelling, 'Hell, no, I ain't trying to get shot!' We were all in the dugout saying, 'What the heck's happening?' And then we saw someone on the light pole, a guy was up on the light pole. All of a sudden out from behind the net where you can get onto the field there were four superheroes running onto the field, running out to the outfield to save the day. Ironman and Flash and whoever. In the moment I remember thinking we shouldn't have been laughing, but we were like, 'Is this real life?' We had these dress up superheroes running after a gunman on a light pole. Luckily nothing bad happened and the cops came and that was the end of that. Then we finished the game. I'll never forget that." Drew

> "In the moment I remember thinking we shouldn't have been laughing, but we were like, 'Is this real life?'"

Although they're not promotions, the national anthems can also be a source of fun for the players.

"There were some botched national anthems, like I remember this one girl was singing it and she just stopped and freaked out. We started laughing so hard when that happened." Anonymous

"There was a marriage proposal one game in Beloit (Low A), when the guy sang the national anthem and then called his girlfriend out and she came out on the field and he proposed right there. It was really awkward. Everyone was so confused. It left us all looking around like what, did that just happen?" Justin

"We were big into standoffs after the national anthem in my first year in Greenville (Low A). You'd stand still after the national anthem with your hat over your heart, just to be a jerk, and try to outlast someone on the other team. You'd be looking at each other and people would start to cheer you on a little bit. We had some very impressive ones. My buddy and I were going up against one guy on the other team until past when the first inning started. Eventually we gave up because he was clearly not moving. The head *coach yelled at me and my buddy for that one, he said, 'Just don't do that.' It actually leads to ejections a lot of the time. We didn't deal with that luckily. It's against the rules. If you really go for it, it delays the game. Or maybe it's disrespectful to the game, I don't know." Marc*

And finally, sometimes what happens isn't a promotion at all.

"Our team owner had two bat dogs and they went out every inning and got the bats and gave the balls to the umpire. It's a huge reason people come, they've even been in Sports Illustrated. It was a really hot day, a day game, and Miss Lou Lou (Gehrig) who was the bat dog ran out there to get the bat. It was so hot she had the runs and she sat and pooped right there at home plate. Obviously the crowd went wild and the umpire faked threw her out. And then the owner went out there and tried to pick it up but it was all diarrhea, there was nothing to pick up, it was just seeping through his hands. I was dying because he loved these dogs and he was very overprotective about them, it was hilarious that this dog pooped on the field and he couldn't even pick it up. It was really funny." Anonymous

****

"I thought, this is not baseball weather."

Watching baseball can be ideal on a beautiful sunny day or a clear, warm evening. But while the fans can pick and choose which games to attend, the players are forced to play almost every single day from early April to mid-September. Wherever they are, from Midland, Michigan to San Antonio, Texas, from Vancouver, Canada to Jupiter, Florida and everywhere in between, the games must go on. The weather can have a big impact on games throughout the season. Early in the season it's cold.

"On opening day in Midland, Michigan (Low A) it was in the teens with the wind chill.

We had just come from Arizona where it was getting warm and I didn't have any cold weather clothing. We had a game postponed, it had rained a little earlier in the day and usually the box score says 'called due to rain' but the official reason was 'too cold and too windy.' I remember going outside and hitting a ball straight up and it was so windy it went 30-40 feet behind me." Eric

"The first three weeks it was either snowing or so frigid you didn't even want to go outside. It was the coldest conditions I'd ever been in. Hand warmers were a staple for the first month or so at least. If you didn't have the hand warmers you were frozen. For good. I had the long underwear, the tights, the baseball pants of course, a layer of socks underneath. I had three undershirts, a jersey, a sweatshirt, a jacket that went over it, a beanie, gloves, hand warmers in the gloves. That was the attire. I'm surprised I was able to move when I pitched. All the guys from the Midwest were like, 'Oh, you've never played in the Midwest winters before.' They knew all about the cold and we were a bunch of wussies from California, you hear it all. But it doesn't matter where you're from, you're just as cold." Chris C.

And of course there can still be snow early in the season.

"In 2016 the first game of the season was in Rochester, New York. I pitched and it was 30 degrees at game time, with snow flutters. Coming from Texas and California I thought, this is not baseball weather. And that year it was so cold in April in upstate New York and they had big snowstorms. We were supposed to play in Syracuse (AAA) but the whole field was covered in snow. So they came down to us, the Lehigh Valley IronPigs, for a 'home series' at our stadium. It was a closed game series, so there was no home field advantage. There was no one in the stadium except the staff and media and we were the visiting team. They made it as quick as possible, we had a double header and single game." Mark

"There was snow on the field for our first game in Midland, Michigan (Low A) on April 6th, but the worst place was some town in northern Wisconsin. It was the second week of

April and they weren't quite out of winter yet. It was a 7:00 PM game, it was 25 degrees and sleeting, with howling 20-30 mph winds. It was worse to not be playing. We had these giant blow torch heaters that blew hot air in the bullpen. There were about 10 guys huddled around them, they were spewing a lot of smoke. I don't know what we were inhaling. We were inhaling all sorts of things we probably shouldn't have and we started to feel lightheaded." Anonymous

> "We were inhaling all sorts of things we probably shouldn't have and we started to feel lightheaded."

"In Grand Rapids, Michigan (Low A) we got snowed out a few times at the beginning of the year. I felt like I was playing in Colorado all over again. We had a few players, it was the first time they'd ever seen snow. Some of those young kids from the Dominican Republic and Venezuela, it was the first time they'd ever seen snow." Jake

As the season continues into the summer, the cold and the snow are replaced by heat and humidity.

"We went to Augusta, Georgia (Low A) in the heat of the summer and it was 95 degrees and 100% humidity, just about as bad as it gets in the South. When you left the locker room you had to go through this long cement hallway to get to the dugout. When you started, it was still nice and cool because they were blasting the air conditioning and it was nicely insulated. But as you progressively went out it got warmer and warmer and for whatever reason there was just this wall of hot air near the entrance to the dugout. When you hit that you'd think, oh no, I'll be in this for the next couple hours in my full canvas uniform and everything's going to get soaked. But that's part of the fun of it." Anonymous

Besides the hot and cold temperatures, there are various other elements that make for some interesting conditions.

"In Bakersfield (High A) there were so many days you'd wake up and check your phone *and there'd be an air quality warning. It would say, 'Stay indoors, high temperatures, extremely low quality air, try not to exercise outside, stay indoors at all costs,' and we're in the clubhouse about to go hit BP at 3:00 PM in 112 degrees. And the dust made it hard to breathe. Literally guys would get to second base and they couldn't catch their breath. I was thinking I'm probably losing years of my life right now." Drew*

"I was in the outfield in Clinton, Iowa (Low A) towards the end of summer and I had to cover my mouth and face with my glove in between pitches because there were bugs everywhere. It looked like the plague was hitting, I can't even describe it. I wish I had a GoPro on my head." Austin W.

"I remember those gnats in Clinton, they were everywhere. We were just surrounded by these gnats, big moths, I don't know what they were. They were these giant bugs, they would come out right when the lights went on. You couldn't even see across the field there were so many of them. It was almost scary there were so many of them." Chris C.

"Probably the most notable thing in Clinton is there's a big dog food factory there. So if the wind was blowing the right direction, the whole town reeked of dog food. And it's not like dry dog food, it's the wet kind, you know the kind you open up the can and spoon it out. It smelled like that stuff, it was bad. You don't get used to it, no." Wayne

"Yeah, it was a Purina dog factory and the smell was pungent. Every day you had to smell it." Anonymous

"One of the places we played in the Florida State League was Port Charlotte, and just past the outfield there was a swamp. Our bus driver told us there were alligators in the swamp but we didn't think much of it. Sure enough, one day we saw on Instagram that the Port Charlotte game had been delayed, and we learned that it was because there was an alligator in the dugout. Literally, an alligator had wandered from the swamp onto the field and was resting in the shade in the comfort of the dugout." Danny

****

*"In the back of your mind you know it would
be nice if you had a rainout."*

More commonly, baseball teams have to deal with the rain. It can be a welcome relief from the daily grind when they're scheduled to play every day.

"When it rains it's nice because you get an off day, you get to rest, you get to eat well, off days are really nice." Danny

"There were times when we'd be playing and we'd see Armageddon on the horizon and then it would start to get really windy and the temperature would drop and you'd be thinking, here comes the rain. And sure enough you'd get destroyed and have to take cover. You'd hope it would rain so much that the field would get too soaked that you couldn't play." Anonymous

"We had a guy who was called the weatherman because he was always looking at the radar data trying to predict whether we were going to get canceled because he didn't want to play." Kenny

Merely hoping for rain doesn't always work. Sometimes it has to be helped along.

"My rain turtle actually did work, I drew one in San Antonio (AA). It was a night game and we had to bus home to Tulsa after the game. We had to drive eight hours home through the night and we'd get home at 6:00 or 7:00 AM. So it was like 2:00 in the afternoon and there was a low chance of rain but it was scattered and there was a big cell that was going to hit the field. I drew a rain turtle while the pitchers were stretching and they were like, 'What are you doing?' and I was like, 'I'm drawing a rain turtle.' There were some young guys who did not know what that was, I was like, 'How do

you not know what a rain turtle is?'[6] Everybody spit on the rain turtle and it just started dumping 20 minutes later. They canceled the game and we were able to bus home early. It was the only successful rain turtle of my career." Drew

"Doing the rain dance worked last year. We did a rain dance and we got a rainout. Just me and two other guys. One of them was like, 'Hey, who wants to go rain dance?' and I was like, 'I do, I'll go rain dance.' So we went out on the field dancing and making stupid noises, it was pretty funny and it worked." Drew

The uncertainty of whether the game is on or off can wreak havoc.

"Where we played it rained all the time. Throughout the year there was always a chance of rain and thunderstorms. It psychologically affects you, especially later on in the year when you're tired and you'd really appreciate a rain break or a canceled game so you could go back and have a free night. You look at the weather forecast and you see 80% chance of rain and it frazzles you because you have to be able to plan on playing but of course in the back of your mind you know it would be nice if you had a rainout. The problem is if it's a delay it means you'll just be playing later in the night. There's all this uncertainty as to whether you'll play or not. There are countless times when you think the game is going to get canceled and then you have to go out and play. Or the flipside, sometimes the manager would come in and say, 'Game is canceled,' and everybody would erupt in joy." Anonymous

"I was scheduled to pitch about three hours from my hometown, so my parents decided to drive up with two other couples and another kid from my high school. It was a 5:00 PM start, but the game was delayed two hours. Then they called the game off because they didn't want the players to get hurt, so it ruined my start and the seven people had to turn around and drive three hours home. I didn't pitch again for a week." Colton

---

[6] The rain turtle comes from a Native American ceremony that has the ability to bring about rain. Drew's version is that you draw a turtle in the dirt and then you spit on it.

"This happened a few times in different parks in Florida, where you get the heaviest rains ever, these unbelievable storms that would come in and just dump rain. I remember the first time our dugout flooded. We'd played six days in a row, we'd had two three-hour bus trips, everyone was hurt and tired, and we didn't really want to play this game. So the rain came. We showed up to the field and the dugout was full of water, so we figured we weren't playing that day. But the interesting thing about getting a game called off is if it's a big night, if it's Friday night or Saturday night, stadium owners go to extra lengths to make sure the game is played because of the size of the crowd. Some GM's were known for being sticklers about waiting for three to four hours to make sure we would play the game. This guy must have been super motivated to play the game because these field crew heroes came in and brought in all these different pumps and things and they took an hour and they drained the dugout and we ended up playing." Danny

"We had a tough stretch where we got rain delayed every day for a week. Two nights we were delayed so much we had an 11:30 PM start. We finally had a clear night and after the second or third inning the power went out. The entire city, grid, whatever it was. You could see the entire area was dark. Then the next day it was going to be a double header. We were going to finish the power outage game and then we were supposed to play a 7-inning game after that. But they couldn't get a hold of the umpires for the second game, so before we showed up to the field nobody knew if we were playing that day or if we were playing the second game at all. All this was happening day after day after day. And then we had a travel day. It was just pouring rain and everyone was thinking, we're not playing tomorrow. It couldn't have poured any harder and somehow they delayed the game another hour and a half after we'd traveled, got the field somewhat ready and we played. That was five days in a row just not knowing what the hell was going on. That's the epitome of minor league organizations. They only get their money from the ticket sales so whatever they can do to make sure that people aren't having to get refunds, they're going to do it." Tyler

"I remember there were a couple times in Richmond (AA) on Friday and Saturday night games, we were pretty much guaranteed to sit around and wait because they wanted

to cash in on those ticket sales and they wanted to keep people in the stadium to drink. One time they hadn't called the game yet and the dugouts were literally flooded and there was water coming into the locker room. You would wade up to your kneecaps in water in the dugout and they hadn't called the game yet. The Richmond stadium was an old stadium but the field drained really well because it rained there all the time. So the dugout was flooded and they hadn't called the game yet. And they still had people out in the stadium buying drinks and beer and food and stuff. The thought was, it'll clear up."
Anonymous

Canceling a game is a difficult decision for minor league baseball operators, as explained by Andy Shea of the Lexington Legends. It's not just about the money.

"Our rainout policy is if a game gets rained out, fans can use that ticket for any game the rest of the season, or if it's a rainout in August, they can use it for the rest of the games that season or the next season. When you look at it from a strictly money side, the people that are coming or who have bought tickets are here, they're going to come or they're not going to come. The money side doesn't mean anything. Player safety is paramount of course but then there's that classic debate of what's the difference between a little bit wet and unsafe? The rule is written that it's technically the home team's decision, but having said that, it's not a vote, it's a conversation between us, our team manager, the visiting team manager and the umpires, because theoretically they should be completely unbiased. And then there's being true and fair to the fans. I remember years ago we rained out a game and 55 minutes later it was sunny outside. I was so bent out of shape, I thought we should be playing baseball right now. That's not fair to the fans, that's not fair to anyone, we're a professional baseball team, we've got to be able to communicate and work together more rather than being really quick to call the game because the team wanted to go home. What I've seen over the last 14 years is now that everyone has the weather app on their phone, everyone thinks that they're a weatherman. A forecast on the weather app is exactly what it says, a forecast. It's not definitive. It's an educated guess and it's a great tool, of course we look at it. But the fact is, it's wrong a lot of times."
Andy

If it's raining, some people like to have a little fun with it.

"There was a rain delay and our team was getting crushed, we were down 12-1 in the fourth. So a couple of players decided to go out and do slip and slide on the tarp. The head coach came in and was just lighting the team up for that. He was ranting and raving and he threw a water bottle against the wall. And in the middle of the rant one of the players who was doing the slip and slide walked into the locker room with his clothes just completely drenched. It was not good timing." Marc

"One time we felt like we were on a sinking ship. We were cramped in this small dugout in Hagerstown, Maryland. It had cement backing, a cement roof, and sitting on the bench my head was up against the ceiling. This huge rainstorm came and I guess the drains were clogged so we had water from the infield pouring into this dugout. The dugout began filling up with water, we had to get up on the rafters. We had to cross this chasm of water to get out of the dugout so one by one we'd jump ship and run back to the clubhouse. Our hitting coach would take notes on our at bats in a notebook he always carried around and unfortunately in the bustle one of our players knocked it into the water. The player wasn't hitting well and he knew it. We joked that he tried to erase the bad notes about his at bats." Anonymous

"I remember during one of our rainouts it was pouring, like absolutely dumping, and the tarp was soaked with water, it looked like a lake. Our mascot went out onto the field with a raft and an umbrella and he sat on the raft with the umbrella over his head for about 10 minutes so the promotional guy could get a video of him doing it. The other team was in their dugout and we were in our dugout just watching the rain and everyone on both sides just started dying of laughter." Drew

Sometimes the rain delays are made worse by human error.

"There was one time where the second game of a three-game series got rained out so we were scheduled to play a doubleheader on the third day. But they didn't put the tarp

on in time so the field was soaking wet. So we got to the field the next day expecting to play the doubleheader starting at 11:00 AM and then get out of there, but when they took the tarp off the field was still soaked. What had happened was the field got wet and then they put the tarp on, so by putting the tarp on they kept the field wet instead of letting the field dry out. So we stayed there just sitting around for three or four hours with the sun out, just waiting for the sun to beat down on the field to dry it up. So instead of playing the original single game at 11:00 AM and heading home, we didn't start until 3:00 PM and we had a doubleheader. That was a particularly miserable day." Tommy

"I remember it was the middle of summer in Iowa. It was hot and humid and there had been a storm over 24 hours before a game started. We got there and there were puddles everywhere. They had to cancel the game even though it was sunny and 80 degrees out because they didn't tarp the field." Justin

And when there's rain, there are often other problems as well.

"Then there was the time we got struck by lightning. We were in the Florida State League (High A). We saw these really active clouds heading our way, straight for the field. It wasn't raining so we kept playing. I was playing third base and suddenly there was the loudest crack you could ever imagine. I felt a shock that went from my feet, up through my chest and through my head. I felt it everywhere. Everyone on the field sprinted off, it was mass panic, everyone was freaking out. I ran into the other team's dugout with the guy who was on third base, who fell down the stairs in the dugout but no one noticed because everyone was panicking. We realized the field had been struck by lightning. I was in their dugout because I was next to it, and I wanted to get back to my own dugout. I was NOT going to go across the field, so I had to go through the tunnel from their locker room and make the semi-circle under the stadium to my team's dugout. It was mass panic. I'm sure we could have seen some guy run out onto

> **"Everyone on the field sprinted off, it was mass panic, everyone was freaking out."**

the field completely naked and we wouldn't have thought anything about it because everyone was in complete panic. We ended up finishing that game because that was a Friday night and they had a lot of fans coming in, and so we waited one to two hours, went through another lightning storm where we got struck again, and we ended up going out there and playing. It was crazy. Everyone was talking about it too, the people in the bullpen all felt it. And then after that there was this one American guy on our team who only spoke English and after the lightning strike he could only speak Spanish. Just kidding, that last part didn't happen." Danny

"A lot of times I remember playing and clearly seeing lightning going on all around us. In Arizona, playing a rehab game, you know those desert storm cells, it's 120 degrees out and we're seeing lightning strike after lightning strike at night and it's just weird to see. I wasn't used to that." Eric

"I'll never forget I was at my house in Clinton, Iowa (Low A) and the sky started turning rainbow sherbet color. I heard a siren go off and my roommate said, 'That's a tornado siren' and I said, 'Excuse me?!' He said, 'Yeah, that's a tornado siren. This is the Midwest.' I replied, 'What do you mean tornado? What are we supposed to do here? I'm from California, I don't know what to possibly do in this situation.' " Austin W.

****

Rain or shine, come hell or high water, the teams eventually play their full schedule of 140 games each season, give or take a few that can't be rescheduled. Part of the fun is visiting other cities and ballparks throughout the league, but the travel is an adventure of its own. Road trip, anyone?

Chapter Seven Notes

2018 Minor League Average Fan Attendance

Pioneer League (Rookie)

Helena Brewers (MI)	840
Orem Owlz (LAA)	1345
Great Falls Voyagers (CWS)	1401
Missoula Osprey (ARI)	1883
Grand Junction Rockies (COL)	2221
Billings Mustangs (CIN)	2670
Idaho Falls Chukars (KC)	2742
Ogden Raptors (LAD)	3402
Average Pioneer League	2063

Appalachian League (Rookie)

Elizabethton Twins (MIN)	529
Bluefield Blue Jays (TOR)	646
Bristol Pirates (PIT)	708
Princeton Rays (TB)	760
Kingsport Mets (NYM)	904
Danville Braves (ATL)	1054
Burlington Royals (KC)	1142
Greeneville Astros (HOU)	1549
Johnson City Cardinals (STL)	2222
Pulaski Yankees (NYY)	2764
Average Appalachian League	1228

New York-Penn League (Short Season A)

Batavia Muckdogs (MIA)	784
Auburn Doubledays (WSH)	1204
West Virginia Black Bears (PIT)	1827
Williamsport Crosscutters (PHI)	1902
Connecticut Tigers (DET)	2049
Staten Island Yankees (NYY)	2083
Vermont Lake Monsters (OAK)	2209
Mahoning Valley Scrappers (CLE)	2700
State College Spikes (STL)	3243
Lowell Spinners (BOS)	3381
Aberdeen IronBirds (BAL)	3483
Hudson Valley Renegades (TB)	4004
Tri-City ValleyCats (HOU)	4119
Brooklyn Cyclones (NYM)	5329
Average New York-Penn League	2737

Northwest League (Short Season A)

Salem-Keizer Volcanoes (SF)	1897
Tri-City Dust Devils (SD)	2332
Everett AquaSox (SEA)	2937
Eugene Emeralds (CHC)	3315
Boise Hawks (COL)	3321
Hillsboro Hops (ARI)	3429
Spokane Indians (TEX)	5222
Vancouver Canadians (TOR)	6292
Average Northwest League	3593

Midwest League (Low A)

Team	
Burlington Bees (LAA)	859
Beloit Snappers (OAK)	1025
Clinton LumberKings (SEA)	1816
Cedar Rapids Kernels (MIN)	2355
Bowling Green Hot Rods (TB)	2702
Great Lakes Loons (LAD)	2880
Lake County Captains (CLE)	3062
Peoria Chiefs (STL)	3156
Quad Cities River Bandits (HOU)	3163
Wisconsin Timber Rattlers (MIL)	3475
Lansing Lugnuts (TOR)	4612
South Bend Cubs (CHC)	4911
Kane County Cougars (ARI)	5469
Fort Wayne TinCaps (SD)	5703
West Michigan Whitecaps (DET)	5770
Dayton Dragons (CIN)	7868
Average Midwest League	3677

South Atlantic League (Low A)

Team	
Kannapolis Intimidators (CWS)	1115
Hagerstown Suns (WSH)	1160
West Virginia Power (PIT)	1841
Hickory Crawdads (TEX)	1900
Rome Braves (ATL)	2286
Asheville Tourists (COL)	2840
Delmarva Shorebirds (BAL)	3097
Columbia Fireflies (NYM)	3755
Augusta GreenJackets (SF)	4050
Lexington Legends (KC)	4462
Charleston RiverDogs (NYY)	4486
Lakewood BlueClaws (PHI)	4657
Greenville Drive (BOS)	4823
Greensboro Grasshoppers (MIA)	4881
Average South Atlantic League	3240

Carolina League (High A)

Team	
Buies Creek Astros (HOU)	359
Down East Wood Ducks (TEX)	1770
Lynchburg Hillcats (CLE)	1781
Carolina Mudcats (MIL)	2744
Salem Red Sox (BOS)	2919
Myrtle Beach Pelicans (CHC)	3327
Potomac Nationals (WSH)	3766
Wilmington Blue Rocks (KC)	3842
Frederick Keys (BAL)	4297
Winston-Salem Dash (CWS)	4436
Average Carolina League	2924

California League (High A)

Team	
Visalia Rawhide (ARI)	1774
Modesto Nuts (SEA)	2072
San Jose Giants (SF)	2110
Lancaster JetHawks (COL)	2222
Rancho Cucamonga Quakes (LAD)	2454
Stockton Ports (OAK)	2724
Inland Empire 66ers (LAA)	2771
Lake Elsinore Storm (SD)	3071
Average California League	2400

Florida State League (High A)

Team	
Dunedin Blue Jays (TOR)	450
Florida Fire Frogs (ATL)	600
Lakeland Flying Tigers (DET)	840
Palm Beach Cardinals (STL)	1032
Jupiter Hammerheads (MIA)	1063
Tampa Tarpons (NYY)	1105
Bradenton Marauders (PIT)	1192
St. Lucie Mets (NYM)	1520
Charlotte Stone Crabs (TB)	1654
Fort Myers Miracle (MIN)	1849
Daytona Tortugas (CIN)	2046
Clearwater Threshers (PHI)	2672
Average Florida State League	1335

Eastern League (AA)

Team	Attendance
Erie SeaWolves (DET)	3204
Bowie Baysox (BAL)	3438
Binghamton Rumble Ponies (NYM)	3553
Harrisburg Senators (WSH)	3988
Altoona Curve (PIT)	4571
Akron RubberDucks (CLE)	4996
Trenton Thunder (NYY)	5019
New Hampshire Fisher Cats (TOR)	5065
Portland Sea Dogs (BOS)	5678
Reading Fightin Phils (PHI)	5713
Hartford Yard Goats (COL)	6014
Richmond Flying Squirrels (SF)	6198
Average Eastern League	4786

Southern League (AA)

Team	Attendance
Mobile BayBears (LAA)	1121
Jackson Generals (ARI)	1654
Mississippi Braves (ATL)	2259
Biloxi Shuckers (MIL)	2430
Chattanooga Lookouts (MIN)	3206
Montgomery Biscuits (TB)	3408
Pensacola Blue Wahoos (CIN)	4348
Tennessee Smokies (CHC)	4668
Jacksonville Jumbo Shrimp (MIA)	5037
Birmingham Barons (CWS)	5751
Average Southern League	3388

Texas League (AA)

Team	Attendance
Midland Rockhounds (OAK)	3868
Northwest Arkansas Naturals (KC)	4478
Arkansas Travelers (SEA)	4498
Corpus Christi Hooks (HOU)	4866
Springfield Cardinals (STL)	4871
San Antonio Missions (SD)	4885
Tulsa Drillers (LAD)	5230
Frisco RoughRiders (TEX)	6886
Average Texas League	4948

Pacific Coast League (AAA)

Team	Value
New Orleans Baby Cakes (MIA)	3827
Colorado Springs Sky Sox (MIL)	4104
Las Vegas 51s (NYM)	4746
Memphis Redbirds (STL)	5007
Reno Aces (ARI)	5019
Omaha Storm Chasers (KC)	5320
Tacoma Rainiers (SEA)	5403
Fresno Grizzlies (HOU)	6051
Oklahoma City Dodgers (LAD)	6713
Salt Lake Bees (LAA)	6921
Iowa Cubs (CHC)	7356
Sacramento River Cats (SF)	7808
El Paso Chihuahuas (SD)	7819
Albuquerque Isotopes (COL)	7948
Nashville Sounds (OAK)	8741
Round Rock Express (TEX)	8809
Average Pacific Coast League	6350

International League (AAA)

Team	Value
Gwinnett Stripers (ATL)	3062
Syracuse Chiefs (WSH)	4202
Norfolk Tides (BAL)	5334
Pawtucket Red Sox (BOS)	5982
Scranton/Wilkes-Barre RailRiders (NYY)	6140
Rochester Red Wings (MIN)	6537
Louisville Bats (CIN)	6658
Toledo Mud Hens (DET)	7362
Durham Bulls (TB)	7661
Buffalo Bisons (TOR)	8250
Lehigh Valley IronPigs (PHI)	8511
Columbus Clippers (CLE)	8633
Indianapolis Indians (PIT)	8845
Charlotte Knights (CWS)	8980
Average International League	6968

Chapter 8
On the Road (Again)

Minor league players spend about half of their time on the road. A full minor league season is 140 games, which means players spend about 70 days away from home traveling to other cities and towns throughout their league. (Short season leagues play about 70 games, half the number because their seasons don't begin until mid-June.) While it varies from league to league, a typical schedule is structured such that teams play two three-game series at home, then go on a road trip. They'll travel to an opposing team for a three-game series, and sometimes go directly to another opposing team for a three-game series. Some road trips can be as long as 10 days. After that, the team will return home for another six- to nine-day homestand. All this back and forth means a lot of hours on buses, a lot of nights in hotels, and a lot of bad food.

****

*"The bus would leave at midnight, and we'd get
home at nine in the morning."*

The total amount of time minor league teams spend on buses can vary significantly from league to league depending on the geographic dispersion of the teams in the league. Amongst the short season leagues, which begin games in mid-June and finish the first week of September, teams travel an average of about 2,100 miles in the Appalachian League to over 5,500 miles for teams in the Pioneer League over a 12-week period. Making a simple assumption that buses travel at 60 miles per hour, players in the Appalachian League can barely get through the first four seasons of Game of Thrones (38 hours) while players in the Pioneer League can easily consume all seven seasons of that series (63 hours) plus half of Breaking Bad, assuming they don't care to sleep.

"I could crush an entire TV series on one trip, and one time I spent the entire five-hour bus trip on Twitter." Colton

"It's incredible how much time you spend on buses for no compensation. For a regular business, you'd get travel fees, that's a very normal thing. If I have to be on a bus for 10 hours, part of that should be part of my salary or hourly wage." Tyler

Amongst the full season leagues, which begin games in early April and run through the first week of September, teams travel an average of 5,300 miles in the Florida State League (High A) to an average of over 10,800 miles in the Texas League (AA) over their 23-week season. That's because the Florida State League is contained to the state of Florida in which the longest bus ride is only about three hours, whereas the Texas League has teams not just in Texas, but in Arkansas, Oklahoma and Missouri. As you'll see, most of these bus rides are at night, but if players in the Texas League have trouble sleeping, they can polish off the entire 17 seasons of Family Guy (160 hours) and still have plenty of time to check Twitter and text their mothers.

"The bus rides were a good opportunity to watch movies. I watched a ton of movies." Justin

"A lot of podcasts, a lot of podcasts. I'd get enough music in the locker room so I just read the news, read up on stocks or something like that and listened to podcasts. I'd try to stay informed and just remember there's a real world out there besides minor league ball." Marc

Of course, within each league, the distance traveled by any particular team depends on where it is located within that geographic span. Teams that are located on the farther reaches of the league obviously rack up more miles than the teams located in the middle. For example, the Clinton Lumberkings in the Midwest League (Low A) only travel about 5,500 miles in a season while their rivals the Bowling Green Hot Rods travel over 12,000 miles in the same timeframe.

"On our side of the Midwest League (Low A) the bus rides from Clinton weren't bad. They'd be two to three hours pretty typically. There were a few series where we played teams on the other side of the league and I think the longest bus ride was 12 hours. It was overnight but we got lucky, on our longest bus trip we had an off day the next day so we got to recoup and didn't have to get off the bus and play a game like most people usually have to do." Wayne

"In Idaho Falls (Rookie) we didn't have it as bad. Most of our rides were four to six hours. Colorado to Idaho was the nine and a half hour ride. We'd play, get done at 11:00 PM, the bus would leave at midnight, and we'd get home at nine in the morning." Jack

There's a virtual tie for the longest single bus ride in miles between any two teams within a league. It's about 852 miles between the Great Falls Voyagers and the Grand Junction Rockies in the Pioneer League (Rookie) and also between the

Lakewood BlueClaws and the Rome Braves in the South Atlantic League (Low A), a bus ride of about 14 hours.

And finally, the team with the dubious distinction of traveling the most miles on a bus over the course of the 2018 season among all teams in all leagues was the Lakewood New Jersey BlueClaws of the South Atlantic League. They traveled over 14,600 miles, or more than 240 hours on a bus throughout the season. That's 10 full days on a bus!

****

*"Being able to sleep on the ground under
a seat was considered a hotel suite."*

The number and the types of buses that a team charters can vary from league to league and team to team. In the Rookie and A Ball leagues, the teams are generally crammed onto one bus.

"The Northwest League (Short Season A) was my first introduction to minor league travel. We had one bus and at that point we had 35 guys on the team, plus three coaches, a trainer, a strength coach and media guys so the bus was packed. You were always crammed next to someone else. We had two trips that were under an hour and a half and then all the other ones were eight hours plus." Anonymous

"We had two buses only when the ride was over six hours. Under six hours it was one bus. Then it's a battle of who's got the most time, who's the oldest and who's the most aggressive, who's willing to fight for their own seat." Cal

In AA, teams will frequently have two buses, and sometimes at least one of them is a sleeper bus if the rides are overnight.

"In the Texas League (AA), when we had 10-hour rides to Dallas, that's when we had two buses. The older guys got a nice sleeper bus. The younger guys were on the regular

charter bus, but there were maybe 10 people on the entire bus so each person had at least their own row, where you could spread out across four seats and kinda sleep. I was one of the younger guys. I never got to go on a sleeper bus but I've been inside, they're cool. There's a little hallway similar to an RV where you have a couch area, with two long couches facing each other. And then you have the bunking quarters with maybe eight bunks, probably two people high, where you can lie completely flat, and you have a little curtain, and you have a little compartment. I think guys liked it." Danny

"The Texas League (AA) had bus trips of 14 hours that were brutal but you could sleep. They had sleeper buses. It was actually kind of fun, they had two buses, you had room, you had space for card tables, you played poker or whatever." Stephen

"We were really fortunate because we were owned independently by a group other than the Marlins, so we got sleeper buses for all our trips even though we were still in Low A. The really nice thing about that was that if we wanted to we could just lie down. We had plenty of room and the bus was perfectly air conditioned." Colton

In AAA, teams generally fly between cities but surprisingly it's not always better.

"I found the sleeper buses in AA to be much more enjoyable. I didn't mind the bus trips because you could throw on some comfy clothes and hang out. When I got to AAA we were flying pretty much everywhere and it was always a 6:00 AM flight or earlier. You got up at 4:00 AM, got on the bus, got to the airport, and you were playing that night. The travel in the Pacific Coast League (AAA) was by far my least favorite of any level. That was tough, because I don't think we had a direct flight the entire season. I felt AAA was the hardest, most brutal." Stephen

"I would say I would rather do sleeper buses than the travel with AAA, because it was usually the earliest flight out in the morning on Southwest. You'd have a layover and then you'd play that night. So instead of just getting on a bus and driving right after the *game you have to wait until the next day and fly out the morning of games. But the AAA distances are longer, you couldn't do buses in AAA." Anonymous*

When not sleeping, some teams have a lot of fun together.

"A lot of us played poker and blackjack. I got really good at blackjack. We would do $1 hands and that kind of thing. There were some avid gamblers. I'm not much of a gambler, I'm pretty risk-averse compared to a lot of those other guys. But I learned my way around blackjack a little bit and that's how we'd pass our time in the middle of the night, after games, at two in the morning on the way back from wherever, whenever we found time." Chris C.

"We played so much Mafia on the bus. There was one time I remember specifically it was a three or four-hour bus ride after a game, it was kind of late. Usually after those bus rides everyone is super excited to get off the bus and head home and go to bed as soon as possible. But there was one bus trip where the Mafia game was so intense that we got back and there were three or four people left in the game so we stayed on the bus another 15-20 minutes just to finish the game. This was at 1:00 in the morning." Tommy

"We had some fun bus rides where someone brought their PlayStation with a TV and we played 'MLB the Show.' We could play as the Tulsa Drillers so we were on the TV. It was pretty funny, we would purposely have guys make errors and send the video replays to the whole team and say 'classic Drew' and just stupid stuff like that." Drew

"One summer we were in a tight playoff race all the way to the last game and if we lost and the Phillies had won then we got bounced out. So we controlled our own destiny and sure enough we did win the last game to clinch the division to get into the playoffs. As we were driving back we passed the Phillies complex and we all just started flipping them off and saying 'take that' and that sort of stuff. Then one of the Dominican guys, he was a big prospect, he got on the microphone and he started screaming something in Spanish like, 'Mi gente, te amo, mis amigos' and how proud he was of us and half the bus didn't

even understand what he was saying, it was really funny. It was the culmination of the season, it was such a joyous time." Dom

And sometimes it's not so much fun.

"We played a ton of Mafia and it really pissed off the players who were trying to sleep on the bus. And the coaches hated it too but they never stopped us because they were amused at how entertained we were from the game. There was a time when there was some pushing and shoving after a couple guys got really personal during the game. And a couple Latinos with very little English knowledge began playing and their strategy was hilarious. They'd just stare at random guys and would convince themselves that guy was in the mafia, then start yelling 'you mafia bro' and never stop." Marc

"All the Latin guys sit in the back and they'll occasionally play some Spanish music really loudly. Some guys don't have a very good concept of headphones, so they'll play it out loud instead of using headphones." Tommy

There's definitely some drinking on the buses too.

"One time after a game we stopped at a convenience store near the stadium and within ten minutes our coach had already consumed three pounder beers." Anonymous

"It was the most miserable loss ever in the championship game. We were riding back and everybody was hammered, drinking their sorrows away, and the Dominicans were really loud at 3:00 AM and one of the Americans just yelled, 'Turn the #$^** music off!'" Anonymous

"There was one particular bus ride we got completely hammered on the bus, it was like a 10-hour bus ride. Our coaches were cool with us drinking so we bought two handles of Fireball and we proceeded to get completely out of control. By the time we got to the hotel everyone was just throwing up, the coaches were laughing at us, it was so *obnoxious looking back on it."* Anonymous

Interesting things happen when you put a team of 25 guys on a bus.

"One time we were leaving for a bus trip and our catcher wasn't there. Someone called him because we realized he had been out partying the night before. He answered the phone and said he was still on his way, he had lost track of time. And in order to understand this story you have to know there was a guy named Freddy on our team who wasn't a bad looking guy but his picture was the worst picture ever and he looked pretty ugly in it. So the bus was waiting for the catcher, we were 20 minutes late. He finally got there and sat down and he was just in complete shock, his eyes wide open, looking around. We were like, 'Dude, what happened?' And he was like, 'I drank way too much last night and I woke up next to this girl and I swear it was Freddy. I just left, I just got in the car and started driving here because you guys were calling me.' " Anonymous

"I would be looking at Yelp trying to figure out where I was going to have lunch the next day. That was my Tinder."

"Anytime we would roll into a visiting team's place, players would whip out their phones and start checking in on Tinder. I would be looking at Yelp trying to figure out where I was going to have lunch the next day. That was my Tinder." Kenny

"Our trainer had this big heavy trunk that had all his supplies and equipment. It was on wheels and it took at least two people to pick it up and get it into the compartment under the bus. One time we were going around a turn on a highway and this thing shifted and went Boom! and it bust through the hatch and fell out into the road. Everyone was like, 'What was that?' We looked out and the trainer trunk was out on the highway, so they had to stop the bus, go back and get it." Danny

"On one of the bus trips the guys bet me that I couldn't do a perfect stand on the bus for nine hours from Lakewood, New Jersey to Greensboro, North Carolina. A perfect stand

is when you stay standing the entire ride, through the night. I wasn't going to sit down at all. Everyone put in money. Our team was so loaded with first and second rounders so they were putting in $50, $100. They went around the whole bus and ended up collecting $1,300, betting that I couldn't do this perfect stand. I don't know why they picked me but I was like, 'Yeah, I can absolutely do this, no problem. For $1,300 I'll definitely do this.' I ended up making it to hour six. I was doing fine, I had watched two movies, I talked on the phone, I was totally normal doing the perfect stand. I didn't have to pitch for four days so my coach was all for it at first, he was loving the idea, he thought it was hilarious. But after hour six he came back to use the restroom and said, 'I don't think you should do this, what if you get hurt?' and I said, 'Dude I'm on hour six.' Guys were monitoring me, keeping constant watch, updating every hour, sending video pictures, they couldn't believe I was doing it. So I'm two-thirds of the way done and my coach said, 'No, stop doing it,' and I was like, 'Are you serious? You were all about this.' So then I sat down and as soon as I sat down he texted me from the front of the bus, 'F-it, if you made it this far, you might as well finish it,' and I was like, 'You gotta be kidding me, I was almost done already.' At that point I felt good. So I never ended up getting the $1,300 but I did make it through hour six. I never got off my feet. It's a lot of money and of course all the other players were saying they'd do that every bus trip. I was like, I know, I was about to do it too. But looking back on it, it was a pretty stupid idea." Colton

Many of the bus rides begin at night after the last game of the series. Games typically end after 10:00 PM and by the time the team is ready to go it's closer to 11:00 PM. Some of the trips are nine and ten hours through the night, so players have to figure out interesting ways to get comfortable so they can sleep.

"A lot of people take melatonin so they can fall asleep for a couple hours, hopefully knockout for two hours, that helped." Lonnie

"Melatonin makes me really groggy the next day so if I were to be pitching the next day that wouldn't be an ideal situation." Chris V.

"In the lower leagues there'd be two people per row kicking each other. During the 10-hour bus rides in the Texas League (AA) guys would sleep in the aisles and across the seats." Drew

"My first road trip was a 12-hour bus ride from Everett, Washington to Boise, Idaho in Short Season A Ball. Guys were blowing up floaties like you put in the pool and they were sleeping on them in the back, those were their blow up mattresses. Other guys were making hammocks on the bus out of who knows what, they were sleeping on hammocks, it was a clown show. By the time we got there it was four in the morning and everyone was just beat because we had played earlier that day. We just crawled into bed at the hotel." Chris C.

"I generally get two seats to myself which is nice because nobody really wants to sit next to me, I'm really large. I guess it's hard to sit next to the 6'9" guy. Which I'm OK with." Chris V.

"You kinda slept. It wasn't extremely comfortable, you'd get an hour here or there and you'd wake back up when the bus hit a bump or something. It was not the most comfortable situation but at the time I was pretty happy to be there. It's just one of those things you do because you want to play. Some people would sleep on the ground but I couldn't bring myself to do that. Literally on the ground." David

Yes, a lot of guys do sleep on the ground.

"You should see some of the ways the guys find to sleep on buses. There are always the floor sleepers, some of these guys are just acrobats the way they sleep on a bus, it's impressive. If you can get on the floor of the aisle it's not bad. But what people forget is that a bus is carrying 10,000 pounds of people and equipment, and the engine's working and the floor of the bus is really really hot. So if you sleep on the floor, you're melting, you're sweating, so you gotta create a little clearance from the floor." Cal

"I slept on the floor many times. Yeah, you just stretch out underneath the rows and you get over the whole bus floor thing, and it's really comfortable." Danny

"This year we all got water rafts and just put them on the ground and slept on those. I can sleep fine with those things but in a chair I struggle." Drew

"On overnight bus rides I had to get creative with my sleeping situation. Unfortunately I had a lot of troubles sleeping upright. I tried sleeping on blankets on the floor but that didn't provide much cushion. Guys would bring the floaty rafts onto the bus so I got one from Walmart, blew it up, and slept on that. But it was such poor quality that it'd deflate over the course of the night and I'd wake up on a hard floor in a mess of cheap plastic. So then I upgraded. I went to the outdoor store Cabela's and got a camping sleeping mat. That did the trick. From then on, my go-to sleeping arrangement was on a camping mat on the floor of a bus, underneath the seats. To me that was luxury." Kenny

"My savvy move was I bought a camping blow up mattress and I slept on the floor of the bus. Usually there are some seats where there's one instead of two, and if I could find one of those, I would wedge my mattress under them across the aisle and not have my head hit anybody or have any feet or butts near my head. I thought it was better than being on the seat because sitting upright for nine hours, my hips couldn't do it. Most guys bring the pillow from the hotel and then just have that be the rotating pillow sheet because it's kind of gross being on the floor of the bus. The pool floaties are too thick for me, they took up too much space on the floor, I lost space for my head. The camping mat was crucial, that's what I asked for my birthday so that was my present." Jack

"I couldn't imagine being a really tall guy on a bus, they seriously must have hated life. There was no hope for those big guys. Luckily I could cram down and sleep on the ground. Being able to sleep on the ground under a seat was considered a hotel suite. It was so uncomfortable and so bad and yet that was considered royalty, like yeah, I get to sleep in the middle of the aisle. That was considered a good night if you got to lie down there." Lonnie

Unfortunately some guys can't sleep at all.

"I never could sleep on the bus. I can't sleep in a car, I can't sleep on a plane, I'm just not a very good sleeper. I haven't taken a nap in 20 years. So I and one of my buddies who also couldn't sleep, we had those little Gameboys — the Nintendo DS, I think that's what they were called — you could link those up and play with each other. So we'd play Mario Kart and Mario Party pretty much the whole bus rides, for 10 hours through the night. We would just sit there and play games together. We'd get to the hotel at 10:00 in the morning and the bus would load up and head to the field at 3:00 that afternoon." Jake

"If you don't get any sleep on those really long trips you get to the hotel at like seven in the morning and you will be able to sleep once you get there. It's just not an ideal situation because now you've flipped your whole sleep schedule from 11-7 to 7-2. I don't think I've ever pitched on a day when we showed up at seven in the morning but generally if you're that pitcher you just try to stretch as much as possible because you've been sitting for 14 hours. You try to go to sleep on the bus and once it's game time you try to be as awake as possible." Chris V.

"I can't sleep on buses at all. I hate pitching the day after a bus ride." Cal

"There was one night when we finished a game and ended up hopping on a seven-hour bus ride and got in at 8:00 in the morning the next day. We had a game that afternoon and we got beat by 15 runs by the team that had the worst record by far in the league. It wasn't even close. It had to be related to the fact that we hadn't slept." David

Whether it's a day trip or an overnight trip, there are times when it's just miserable.

"I remember a particularly miserable bus ride going from Corpus Christi to Springfield, it was 16 hours. I was pitching the next day. I had some kind of rash, I slept on the floor the whole night. The bus was freezing cold to keep the driver awake. We left at 7:00 PM and got in at 11:00 AM. I took a nap, got to the field, and actually pitched well. It was the season opener." Mark

"One time there was an accident on the highway and we were stuck going nowhere for four hours. It was right after a game and we were all really tired and we were all very not happy to be stuck in traffic and not be moving for four hours." Chris V.

"In the Florida State League (High A), the air conditioning had broken on the bus that we had. So we were driving around the summer in Florida, it was 90 plus degrees and humid and we had a bus that didn't have air conditioning." Danny

"I remember one time when the AC went out and we were on a two and a half hour bus ride. It was like 95 degrees on the bus the entire time. Literally everyone on the bus had their shirts off, everyone was sweating bullets. As soon as we got off everyone stormed outside. It was still probably 90 degrees outside but it felt so much cooler than in the bus. That was pretty miserable." Tommy

"I've definitely encountered the lack of air conditioning, the 100 degree bus. It's never fun, people with their shirts off and they're in sliding shorts on the bus." Lonnie

"There was at least one time when the bus really smelled. We were trying to figure out what the smell was and it turned out the Hispanics had left raw chicken in the top part of the bus. Just another day on the job." Kenny

Some of the bus rides are affected by the weather.

"One time we were going from Bowling Green, Kentucky back to Michigan, it was eight or nine hours. Our double header in Kentucky had been delayed because of rain, so it didn't start until late afternoon and we didn't get out of there until maybe one or two in the morning. I remember being asleep and all of a sudden the bus started shaking because of the crazy wind and rain. We veered off to the truck stop, we had no idea what was going on. We went inside the truck stop, everyone just strolled in thinking it was a break. Turns out we went there because they had a storm shelter. We didn't actually go into the storm shelter, but we found out later that there were tornadoes in the area." Eric

"We were driving from Ft. Wayne, Indiana to Bowling Green, Kentucky and it was the worst storm ever. We couldn't see outside the windows, it was the middle of the night. Everyone was getting tornado warnings on their phones saying there's a tornado within five miles of you. The warning said to pull over and seek shelter but our bus driver was still driving. Most people were sleeping except me and one other guy, we just kept looking with horror at our phones." Brant

And some are affected by wildlife.

"We were driving from Ogden, Utah to Helena, Montana, it's like a 12-hour drive. We drove all night because the next day was an off day. We were out in Montana in the middle of the night in the middle of nowhere. There were no clouds and there was a bright moon. People were sleeping and all of a sudden the bus screeched and swerved. We heard a thud but we kept going. We were like, what the heck happened? We actually hit a deer. We didn't stop, we just smoked this poor animal. One guy in the front of the bus saw what happened. We were probably going 80 mph on this bus and all the momentum just woke everyone up." Eric

> **"All of a sudden the bus screeched and swerved. We heard a thud but we kept going."**

"Our Midland bus driver drove like it was NASCAR. One night at 2:00 AM we heard a thud. The bus driver was laughing because he hit a deer. He said, 'That thing didn't even stand a chance.' The next morning we could see fur in the grill." Anonymous

By far the worst bus trips involve a breakdown.

"Every single minor league baseball player has had at least one bus breakdown. I had at least one bus breakdown in State College, maybe more." Tommy

"My first bus ride was a three-hour drive from Batavia, New York to Mahoning Valley, Ohio, which is considered a shorter ride in the New York-Penn League (Short Season A). We had a game to play that day and our bus broke down. The police showed up and it turns out the registration for the bus driver was out of order so the driver was taken away. Another bus and bus driver showed up and we got there 30 minutes before the game." Colton

"Our bus broke down in Iowa. I'm not sure what happened but it was shocking that we didn't have tools on the bus to fix it. Regardless we were stranded for three or four hours coming back from a road trip and we didn't get home to our apartment until the sun had risen. We stopped at the World's Largest Truck Stop in Iowa at 5:00 in the morning. I don't know what's being served at the Taco Bell truck stop at 5:00 in the morning but people were definitely eating. We had a game that night so we got back to our apartment at 6:30 in the morning and slept for three hours and went right back to the field and played that night." Justin

"I was on that bus. We were in the middle of the highway, in the middle of Iowa, in the middle of the night. We were making these little videos that changed your voice and we were sending them to each other saying, 'Oooh, we're going to die here! Oh my God!'" Danny

*"We had a six and a half hour bus ride to Helena and halfway there our bus blew a tire in the middle of absolute nowhere. It was a morning bus ride and on those rides we just tried to sleep because we'd get to bed so late the night before. So we were all trying to sleep and we heard this explosion and the tire blew. It was definitely scary, it sounded like a gunshot. You don't really know what's going on, you're asleep and you wake up to that. We were stuck on the side of the road in Dillon, Montana for two to three hours and the AC on the bus only works when the bus is moving. It was the middle of the day,

it was really hot. We were all pretty much wearing no shirts, no shoes, it was a mess. It's just another thing you add on to the lore of the minor league life, it's hilarious." Jack

"We had another one where the engine just shut down. We had to make two bus swaps. We started on one bus and it broke, so we went to another one and 45 minutes later that one broke. It changed a four-hour trip into an eight-hour trip." Jack

"The AAA team had a bus breakdown but I got called up the week after so I dodged the only bus breakdown that happened with the Giants in a while." Austin S.

Some bus breakdowns are really bad.

"We had a night game in Savannah, Georgia that finished around 10:00 PM. We packed up our stuff and left around 11:00 for our nine-hour overnight bus ride back to Lexington, Kentucky. About 30 minutes into the ride we were on a bridge crossing a river and I remember wondering why we started slowing down on the decline. We pulled over. Everyone was wondering what was going on. The bus driver tried to start the engine a couple of times and then he said loudly, 'Well this f---ing sucks.' We were thinking uh oh, that's not good. But pro ball instilled in us the ability to quickly accept new circumstances and that's exactly what we did. We sat on the bus. The problem was the air conditioning wasn't working. At first it was fine, but within 10 or 15 minutes it started to get a little warmer. After 30 minutes it started to get really warm and we learned we were going to have to wait there for a few hours. Guys started shedding clothes to stay cool and then we decided to use the fire escape levers on the bus windows to crack them open. You could say it was literally a breath of fresh air. But then things changed. There was a little bit of commotion and we heard slapping sounds. Then I heard a mosquito in my ear and I knew what was going on. We were parked on a road that went through a swamp! We turned on our phone flashlights and we could see mosquitoes buzzing everywhere. Guys started freaking out. We closed the windows but the damage had been done — mosquitoes were everywhere. We made progress eliminating them but there were bloodstains everywhere because they had just had a field day on us.

Eventually we mitigated the effect of the mosquitoes but it was still steamy and humid on the bus. By this time, most of the guys had their shirts off, many were in their boxers, sweating. I decided to put on my sweatpants and my sweatshirt and just go outside and cover up all my skin. It ended up being fine, I was just glad to breathe fresh air.

How long did they have to wait?

"We ended up waiting there for a couple hours and then a new bus came. We had to put all our gear on the new bus but the problem was there wasn't as much storage space on the new bus, so a lot of the bags had to go in the passenger compartment. Some of us were sitting in the aisle on bags, with more bags on top of us. But then we realized there were ants everywhere. These weren't just ants, they were fire ants. They were EVERYWHERE, we had a complete swarm of them. I've never seen grown men crack in the way they did when these ants starting biting their legs. Guys were yelping. It was complete chaos. We had already been mentally weakened by the whole thing, late at night. At this point the bus was moving and there was nothing we could do, we were putting our feet up off the ground, we just had to deal with it. It turns out someone must have stepped in an anthill while we transferring the bags and they brought it into the bus. One guy's foot and his entire leg below his knee must have had 100 red dots on it. It turned out ½ mile from where our bus broke down was a 24-hour strip club and restaurant. Maybe it's a good thing we didn't find out?" Kenny

"Guys were yelping. It was complete chaos."

****

"You checked your bed for bed bugs before you even sat on it."

Minor league teams spend a lot of nights in hotels. If a team plays half of its 140 games on the road, that means they're spending about 70 nights in a hotel. When a team travels overnight to a visiting city, they will typically check into the new hotel in the middle of the night or early the next morning, stumbling and bleary-eyed, to drop their gear and rest up before they head to the field. After the last game of a road trip, teams will bus home right after the game, unless they're in AAA, in which case the flight is the next morning. When a team buses overnight back home, players get to sleep in their own beds when they arrive home.

"In minor league baseball you don't really get the interesting or extravagant hotels that a major league baseball salary commands. More or less they're all the chain-type places on the side of the highway, they all look the same." Chris V.

Guys experience all kinds of things while staying in these hotels.

"We all got bed bugs in the Days Inn in Youngstown, Ohio. It was awful, the whole team was itchy. The Batavia hotel had bed bugs too." Andrew

"We definitely had those same experiences with the hotels in the New York-Penn League (Short Season A). I mean, I had some bed bugs, I slept with my clothes on." Justin

"The hotel in Beloit, Wisconsin had bedbugs. In that league you checked your bed for bed bugs before you even sat on it. In Appleton, Wisconsin the entire floor smelled like weed and cigarette smoke. As you went higher up, it got better." Mark

"We stayed in rooms that had only one bed and a couch, so someone always had to sleep on the couch." Drew

"The worst hotel was that Clinton, Iowa Super 8. The dog food factory smelled, the beds felt like you were sleeping on a piece of wood, there was mold on the coffee makers, and one player had bed bugs." Anonymous

"There was one that was a re-creation of the civil war, it was almost an Amish building kind of thing. I don't know exactly what it was but the inside was a wedding venue, it was very ornate, we were very confused when we showed up." Chris V.

"I was staying in the team hotel in Wilmington, Delaware. I definitely saw a real life pimp. There was a guy walking around in a flashy light blue suit in the middle of a weekday in a not-so-great part of town, I'm not kidding. He had white shoes. I have a picture of it. I later found out that that hotel had problems with prostitution." Kenny

Some are creepy.

"We stayed in a haunted hotel once in Ogden, Utah, that was kinda scary. They closed one of the floors completely because a bunch of people died on this one floor. The elevator doors would be open waiting for you to walk in. They played creepy music in the hallways. Honestly, I was on edge sleeping there." Alex B.

That Ogden hotel would be the Ben Lomond Hotel, which has a long history of paranormal activity. According to Haunted-Places-To-Go.com, a bride who was spending her honeymoon at the hotel in room 1102 drowned in the bathtub. Guests who have stayed in that room have documented many unusual events, such as the water in the tub running, attempting to fill the tub. The legend continues that shortly afterwards, the bride's son came to the hotel in order to acquire his mother's personal items and stayed in the room next door, 1101. That night he elected to take his life in an effort to join his mother.

"Of course on our first trip there everyone was reading all these articles online on the bus. When we got there they said some of the rooms had a little water issue. They didn't really tell us but half of the rooms had no water, zero. Turn the bath on, nothing. Sink, nothing. Nothing would come out of any of the faucets. We'd go down to the lobby and fill up a used water bottle for our water. So we went to the game that first night and when we came back my bathtub was blasting black water. I hoped there was a natural plumbing reason, but that combined with what we already heard about this place, I was definitely creeped out big time." Jack

Apparently many guests have had physical encounters in which it felt as if they were being physically pushed by an unseen force. There are several accounts of voices as if someone is talking, visions of physical apparitions, and even personal encounters in which visitors and staff have come face to face with these tormented souls.

"One of my teammates came back to his room and the glass desk was shattered in his room. He never knew why. And it was weird because it almost seemed like the hotel had done it and just didn't tell him about it, because they didn't make him pay for it." Jack

Interestingly, despite the fact that no one is operating the elevator, it is said that they often seem to operate on their own. This includes moving up and down the floors, and even stopping on certain floors with absolutely no direction from the living. In the night hours when staff is on duty, they will often report the elevator opening in the area of the lobby, and then traveling to the tenth floor of the structure. While there, it remains for quite a long time.[1]

"It seems like they're milking it because all the artwork is so dated and pretty creepy looking, the music is not happy, it's very closed and dark and pretty spooky. We stayed there three or four times and I think only once did I have a window in my room. There was a maintenance guy of course dressed in all black. He was very pale with long black hair, I mean it was just too perfect. I don't believe in ghosts, I just think it was very weird." Jack

Ogden isn't the only place with a creepy hotel.

"When we were in Spokane, we were going to bed and we heard a flickering. It was one of those little knob switches on the lights, that thing was making noise. My roommate was fully convinced that it was spinning and the light wasn't going on. He couldn't fall asleep and he was like, 'Dude, you can't fall asleep, you have to hang out with me.' So we went down to someone else's room and they said they were experiencing weird stuff

---

[1] haunted-places-to-go.com/ben-lomond-hotel.html

too. And we looked on Google and people had claimed that it was a haunted hotel and they had seen weird things. I never believed in ghosts or that kind of stuff but after that I was like maybe there is spooky stuff going on." Drew

"There's a haunted hotel in Oklahoma City. The team hotel is the hotel where there was a bombing and all these kids died. There are so many reports of people seeing midgets or kids running in their rooms at night. People were like, I thought there was a midget or a kid at the edge of my bed in the middle of the night. Those were all the kids who died in the bombing apparently." Alex B.

"It was my very first overnight road trip in pro ball, we were in Great Falls, Idaho in the Pioneer League. We'd been on the bus for four hours, finally we got to the hotel. The elevator barely worked, we got to the floor, there was a really long hallway, and there was one light right above us, and there was one light flickering halfway down the hall, all the other lights were out. I was thinking, 'Oh my God, we're going to get murdered,' it was straight out of a horror movie." Eric

"I was thinking, 'Oh my God, we're going to get murdered,' it was straight out of a horror movie."

"The Modesto hotel was really creepy, it was on the side of the highway. Guys were really scared, they made you hang out with them because they were so scared. My roommate and I both felt like someone was leaning up against the end of our beds, like putting pressure on it. You know when you're lying in bed and your eyes are closed and you feel a presence over you? You kind of know there's someone standing there, it was like that but someone was at the end of the bed. We opened our eyes and no one was there and we were like, 'What just happened?' " Drew

"We went to bed in Charleston like it was a normal night. The next day we found out someone was shot immediately outside the hotel while we were sleeping." Kenny

Other things can interrupt your sleep too.

"We were staying in a decent hotel in Florida. Yeah, it was a good hotel, it was a Holiday Inn. At 2:00 AM the fire alarm went off and we had to vacate the hotel and stand outside while they figured out how to turn if off. We got back in at 4:00 AM and the fire alarm went off again. So this time we didn't leave, we tried to cover the fire alarm using an ironing board with a pillow. We tried to stack the ironing board on top of my bed with the pillow so it would lean against the fire alarm and muffle the sound." Danny

"Sometimes you get bad roommates. I was rooming with a guy and he was younger, he was a top prospect, but he was totally going through a slump. Now I'm OK when guys drink or get a little buzzed, I'm pretty easygoing, but the day before I start I like to get a good night's sleep. One night at 2:00 AM he came in and he was stumbling around, making noise. I turned on the light and he was drunk. He was FaceTiming with his girlfriend and she had been trying to get him back to the room. So I made sure he got in bed, I turned off the light and 30 seconds later I heard him throwing up in his bed. He didn't even lean over. It was the most disgusting smell ever, it was alcohol and bar food. This guy was a mess. I couldn't leave him like that. I called the hotel manager and he brought towels, changed the sheets and cleaned the carpet. I pitched terribly the next day and the whole team just ripped into him." Anonymous pitcher

"Once we were sleeping and at 3:00 AM all of a sudden we heard the sound of the keycard and our door opened. We said, 'Hey' and they said, 'Oh s--t!' and they closed the door. We called the front desk and they said, 'Sorry, we made a mistake.' We shook our heads and went back to sleep." Kenny

With the amount of logistics involved in all this travel, it's not surprising that occasionally things fall through the cracks.

"We were going from Albany to Brooklyn in the middle of the night. We pulled up to the hotel at 3:00 AM only to find out they didn't book us any rooms. It was a big mistake by the ops guys. So we drove around New York City at night while they were trying to find rooms. They ended up putting us up in a place where couples go to have a one-night stand, it reeked of prostitution and bad behavior. They didn't have enough rooms for everyone to have their own beds, we had to share beds but we were so tired we went right to sleep." Andrew

"My first experience in AA, we were traveling after a game from Richmond, Virginia to New Britain, Connecticut. I want to say it was a nine-hour bus ride. We got in at 6:30 or 7:00 in the morning but our team had forgotten to book the hotel for that night. We were all sitting in the lobby, and slowly one by one people started getting rooms because they were scrambling to try to book them for that day and then the next night. I think I got into a hotel room like 10:30 or 11:00 AM and we were off to the field around 2:00 PM." Anonymous

And sometimes your teammates aren't the best roommates.

"We got in really late to some Sunset Inn or something in Jamestown, New York. We got to our room and we had a connecting room with some other players. We opened the connecting door and saw that one of the guys was Garcia, a large Venezuelan guy. As soon as the door opened he ran into our room saying, 'Hey, mi amigo, Diekroeger, mi amigo!' He belly flopped onto my bed and the bed just went crash! One of the legs just completely gave out and the bed broke. He was like, 'Oh my God, so sorry, so sorry,' and he ran out. The next day we showed up to the field and Garcia came up to me and in his broken English he said, 'Hey, Diekroeger, la cama? No es Garcia, OK? Is not me, I cannot pay.' I said 'OK OK, I won't tell them it was you.' " Danny

"I had a funny experience when I got called up to AAA. I checked into the team hotel and they told me I needed a credit card to have on the room for incidentals. So I put my card on file and went up to my room. They told me that I would have a roommate soon and I was like OK, that's fine, I can deal with anything. There were rumors that day that we signed Ernesto Frieri for $1 from the Rangers. The Rangers wanted to get rid of him, so we gave them a dollar and sent him to AAA. I thought alright, great, this is probably my roommate tonight. He was the ex-closer for the Angels two years back. I thought to myself that's incredible, I remember seeing this guy pitch on TV. Wow, I get to meet Ernesto Frieri. So he came in, he was a really nice guy from Colombia, super fun loving, we had a great time. It turns out a week or two later when I was back in A ball, I looked at my credit card statement and my credit card had like $800 worth of charges on it. I know I didn't wreck the room, I didn't throw a party in the room, that's for sure. I thought to myself what in the world, why did I get charged $800 at the team hotel? I was there for just one night. So I called them up and they said that was the charge for two nights at that hotel as well as $80 of those snacks they had in the room. I found out later that Ernesto Frieri stayed in my room for two extra nights and he took a bunch of snacks from the room just to spite the Mariners because he thought he was being treated badly by the team. He thought he was charging it to the team and he ended up charging it to my card, some dumb Rookie A-ball guy who was filling in for the day." Chris C.

In case you're wondering if he got his money back...

"At the end of the season I got sent back to AAA and he was still there. I approached him and said, 'Hey Ernesto, why did you charge so much money to my card?' and he didn't know what I was talking about. I still can't figure out what happened, I don't know why they didn't put his card on the room or how he even got a room key without putting his card on the room. I don't understand why the team's card wasn't on file. I did end up getting my money back, they did reverse the charges. But it was a big debacle because I had to talk to Human Resources and they couldn't figure out what happened. Ernesto Frieri, ex-big league closer almost cost me 800 bucks. I guess we have to work for every penny when they pay us pennies." Chris C.

****

"We ate a lot of pizza and went to lots of 24-hour diners."

It's hard to find healthy food on the road. For each road trip, players are given a per diem for food, which is about $25 per day, depending on the league and how long the road trip is. Also dependent on the league is whether the visiting clubhouse provides the visiting team with a meal after the game or not. In the Rookie leagues and Low A, the players are generally on their own for breakfast, lunch before the game and dinner after the game. In High A, AA and AAA, the clubhouse provides the visiting team with a pre-game and a post-game meal, for which the players are expected to pay to the clubhouse manager at the end of the trip.

"Let's say you're at a visiting team for three games and they provide you with three pre-game meals and three post-game meals. At the end of the trip, it'll say on the whiteboard that we owe, for example, $8 per pre-game meal and $10 per post-game meal so that comes to $54. And then you have to tip them a few bucks. That all comes out of your per diem meal money." Danny

"The best cash that I made the whole time was the per diem. Every guy was ecstatic when we went on the road for 10 days because that's the most money we were going to get in short season. It's almost the same amount of money as your paycheck. You're always losing money but at least on the road you're not losing as much. The way that I looked at my per diem money was if I were to save and not overspend and eat PB&J, then I could use that extra per diem once I got home to pay our own clubbie." Jack

> **"You're always losing money but at least on the road you're not losing as much."**

"We would get the standard $25 a day per diem. It was supposed to be for food on the road but we'd pay our clubbie for the day before the trip and the road clubbie during the trip, so the per diem was literally to pay the clubbies, we never had anything left over. The clubbies on the road and our home clubbie would provide a meal before and after most of the time, so that was what the per diem went towards, it never went towards the food that guys got at a restaurant or something on the side. No one just eats the food that the clubbie gives them and goes home, everyone goes out to eat afterwards anyways.

You don't have an option, you have to pay the clubbie whether you eat his food or not. Some people were strapped, it was tough for them to come up with it." Colton

If players aren't provided with post-game meals in the clubhouse, the bus back to the hotel might stop at a restaurant or they might go straight back to the hotel where they're on their own. If the team is busing to a new location, they usually stop at some point for a meal.

"A lot of bus rides happen after night games so we would always stop for food. Getting to and from Lexington, Kentucky, there's one interstate (64) that runs across the Appalachians that we had to take. There's one bus stop along the way that had a Subway. We became very familiar with that Subway. The problem was it only had one person working it, so we'd end up waiting for 45 minutes while everyone on the team had their sandwiches prepared." Kenny

"Sometimes it's hard to find places that are still open after the game so we ate a lot of pizza and went to lots of 24-hour diners." Mark

"It was almost always fast food because our games didn't end until 10:30-11:00 at night and it's not like we were going to major cities where there are better restaurants that are open late. So for the most part we wore out Applebee's. I'll never eat there again unless I absolutely have to. Sometimes we found some good little ones. In Beloit, Wisconsin there was a little restaurant connected to our hotel, the Road Dawg Restaurant. It was like six bucks for a humongous breakfast so we always went there, which is great when you make, like, nothing." Justin

"A LOT of Applebee's, that's where we went. On road trips after the game the bus would stop and the whole team would eat at Applebee's or Buffalo Wild Wings. I liked it, I would get the little boneless buffalo wings and a bunch of celery. It was Applebee's or Buffalo Wild Wings after every game. My coach said, 'If you don't like it, play better.' " Danny

"I don't think I can ever eat lasagna again or eat at Applebee's again. That was the kind of food we ate." Sam

"Bob Evans, that was a big one. It's a breakfast spot that is pretty much right next to every hotel we ever stayed in. There's actually a guy on the Cardinals whose name is Jacob Evans and everyone calls him Bob because of Bob Evans." Tommy

"Every hotel was next to a Bob Evans restaurant, so every single morning I went to Bob Evans and got the same thing. Around July 4th there was a 30% off coupon for a few days and I used it for the whole month and they never caught on." Colton

"Bob Evans is the one restaurant I'll probably never go to again. We were in Batavia, New York, the far western part of the state. Literally the only restaurant within two miles of our hotel was Bob Evans, it was in the parking lot of the hotel. You'd have to walk over two miles to get to any McDonald's, Wendy's or any other restaurant, so we ate a lot of Bob Evans." Jake

"On the road, Applebee's was definitely one of the places we went to. I haven't been to Bob Evans, that's a new one, I should definitely try that out." Lonnie

"I mean, granted, when you're in season there are some times when you have to eat like shit. But when I could, I tried to eat as healthy as possible." Anonymous

In order to eat healthy, players have to get creative.

"Eating is probably the hardest when you're on the road because you don't have many options. You try to eat healthy but it can be rough at times when there are four McDonald's in a .1 mile radius and the only healthy food is four miles away. I guess you just learn how to eat decently well within your limitations. You have the option to cook your own food and then bring it on the road, but that's a lot more preparation and foresight than I normally have." Chris V.

"I saw a door wide open in the hallway of our hotel and inside I saw one of my Latin teammates. So I walked in and I said, 'Hey what's up?' He was at his sink washing what I first thought was chicken or sausages, but no, it was hot dogs. He was cleaning hot dogs and slicing them up to put into a rice dish. The Hispanics would always bring their own little Walmart skillets with rice and beans and they would just make it on the road because it's the cheapest way to eat. Their dish that day was just hot dogs and rice."
Kenny

"I'm on a Paleo diet, so on the road I would go to Walmart and the best thing I found was to get a pack of cold cooked chicken sausages and a bag of spinach, it was the most nutritious and the cheapest. Usually I would cook a few meals before the road trip and bring them with me." Andrew

"We were in Corpus Christi and we stayed in a hotel right across from the water. There was a little marina right there and the boats were selling shrimp and crab. We knew the clubhouse had a stove so we said screw it, why not? We cooked some of the shrimp before the game and to this day, it was some of the best shrimp I've ever had. I ended up packing the blue crab into the team cooler on the bus ride back. My host family and I had an epic crab boil." Kenny

****

All this travel and bad food can take a toll on the players and affect their stamina and performance throughout the season. This can lead to all sorts of interesting behavior both on and off the field, most of which the fans never see. What's really going on out there?

Chapter 9
Just a Bit Outside

While the crowd is enjoying the ballpark experience, there's a lot happening on and off the field. The fans may be aware that there's a pitching change but they might not know why. They may see a brawl but they probably don't know exactly what caused it. They may see the coaches interacting with the players but they don't know what's really going on between them. They might see a player get hurt and leave the game but they don't always know how serious the injury is and what happens afterwards. There's a whole world of things happening out there that most people aren't aware of. Here's a look at some of them.

****

*"The benches cleared and
everybody ran onto the field."*

Pitching is arguably the most important part of the game. Every play starts with the pitcher throwing the ball and he's the one who in the end gets the win or the loss. But pitchers can also be the source of much of the drama on the field. Many of the incidents that happen during the game involve pitching in some way. The guy on the mound is the one who controls the game. Or not.

"We had this Latin pitcher, he was kinda chubby. It was one of his first appearances, he had just come up from the Rookie ball team and he was pitching well. Whenever there's a ground ball to the first baseman, the pitcher has to sprint over to first base so the first baseman can throw it to him and he'll catch it for the out. And so this happens. There was a ground ball to the first baseman and our pitcher ran over, caught it, and stepped on the base for the out. But as he started slowly walking back to the mound, he stopped and bent over. Everyone was like, oh no! The trainer ran out, the manager ran out, we all gathered around him to see if he was OK. Everyone was asking, 'Are you OK? Is it your arm?' and he was like, 'No, no.' 'Is it your leg?' 'No, no' and then he goes, 'I am tired from the sprint.' The trainer was like, 'What?' He repeated 'the sprint' and the trainer said, 'Oh.' And then the pitcher walked back to the pitching mound, threw a practice pitch and said, 'I'm OK.' " Danny

"We had this top prospect who always had a huge wad of tobacco in his mouth. He was in Arizona for a rehab start and generally you let the prospects do what they want, you don't want to mess with them. But when he walked out to the mound to warm up, the umpire saw the wad and threw him out of the game. Technically the umpire did the right thing but he broke the unwritten rules. On the way out the player spit the entire wad at the umpire's feet." Anonymous

"I had just pitched an outing in AA and they sent me to Low A the next day. I got in, checked in with the manager and he said, 'Hey, I saw you pitched an inning or two last night, how are you feeling?' I was like, 'I feel fine, feeling good.' He asked, 'Do you think you can give me an inning or so if I need it?' and I said, 'Yeah if you need it I'll be good to go.' The way they organized the bullpen at that level was basically the pitchers who had thrown the most recently were put at the bottom of the list. They had a stoplight system to determine whether or not you were good to go. Green was full blown, yes you're ready to go. Yellow was emergencies only, and red was, there's no way in heck you're pitching tonight. That night I was yellow, and we had a seven inning double header. The first game went well, pretty quickly, we didn't really use any pitching. The second game we had a stud pitching but he reached his pitch count after six and two-thirds innings so he got taken out. In the minor leagues they're very strict about that so it didn't matter that he only needed one more out and that he had basically pitched his butt off the entire game. They were like alright, he needs to go, and they took him out. And the guy they put in, before he had started warming up he was doing some weird chewing tobacco mixture that one of the guys from the Dominican Republic had made, I think it included a little bit of rum and some other stuff. So he went into the game and the first pitch he threw was halfway up the backstop and the second pitch he threw probably bounced 10 feet out in front of the mound. So it was a rough one and I was sitting there in the bullpen, kind of almost checked out at this point. I've got my feet propped up on the bench, I'm just relaxing, and I see the pitching coach come out and give me the signal that I need to get going, basically the 'get going as fast as possible' signal. So I was thinking, oh my goodness. I got up and I fired like five pitches as quickly as I could and said that I was ready. So I went into the game with the bases loaded with two outs and we were up by one. I got to a 3-1 count but luckily I got the guy to ground out to second base. Yeah, that was a very interesting scenario." Anonymous pitcher

"It was a high pressure situation. The tying run was on second and our pitcher called a meeting to the mound. He was telling everyone what to do, telling our Cuban shortstop something like, 'If I open my mouth when I look at you it means break' and stuff like that. I didn't even really understand what he was saying. He was trying to put a pick sign with his mouth, but we already had pick signs, you don't make stuff up mid game. Finally the Cuban kid said, 'I NO FUCKING UNDERSTAND.' I just started dying of laughter." Drew

"One time our pitcher threw the ball over some guy's head accidentally and the guy got upset and walked towards the mound and our pitcher was like, 'Hey come get me.' They both got ejected and I had to come straight into the game with no warm up. So I took forever getting ready, just as an F-U to the umpire for tossing our guy." Marc

"In Rookie ball there was a guy on the opposing team that was arrogant and would rub our team the wrong way. One time he went over the top, and the unwritten rules of baseball kicked in. Our manager told our freshly drafted high school pitcher to drill him with a pitch the next time he came up to bat. So the guy walked up to the plate and I was at second base ready for a good show. The first pitch went up and in, he missed hitting him. The second pitch was entirely behind his back. But that was it, the poor high school pitcher wimped out. It was a failed bean attempt. I think we ended up getting him later in the game but the poor pitcher heard about that one for a long time." Kenny

Behavior like that frequently ends up causing a brawl of some sort.

"The funniest thing that happened that summer was, it wasn't a benches clearing brawl, but the benches cleared and it was very close to becoming a brawl. And the person who was responsible for starting all this was my college teammate Tyler Gaffney. He was in State College (Short Season A), and the Spikes had come to our place, so it was the first time I got to see Gaffney all summer. He got on base and got to third somehow and one of our pitchers spiked a curveball and the ball went to the backstop. Gaffney came in from third to score, our pitcher ran to cover the plate, and Gaffney beat it by a mile (we had a big backstop). But in very true to Gaffney form, he gave our pitcher a shoulder check, he just bumped him a little bit as he crossed the plate and our pitcher did NOT like that at all. And so after that, coming back into the dugout I was trying to tell our pitcher, 'Relax, it's just him, he's playing it like it's football,' but he said, 'No, no, no, no, no, no, I'm hitting him for sure next time.' He was dead set on beaning him. And Gaffney *knew it, he said he had actually bet one of his teammates $50 that he was going to get hit his next at bat. So the next time Gaffney came up, I was standing out in center field thinking, oh man, here we go. The first pitch of the at bat was like two feet behind his head, it zoomed to the backstop, everybody knew what was about to happen. The next pitch was like 96 mph right in the back and you know Gaffney, Gaffney did not care at all, he just trotted down to first base like nothing happened. The whole time our pitcher was yelling at him, their dugout started yelling at our pitcher, we started barking back, the benches cleared and everybody ran onto the field. This whole time Gaffney had just jogged down to first base, touched first base, and then jogged out to center field. He and I were standing side by side in center field while everybody else on the entire field was gathered at home plate, yelling at each other. We were the only two people not involved in that huddle, and we were standing out in center field, just talking, just laughing." Jake*

Tyler provides a few more details of the situation.

"I was having the best series of my life. I don't think I got out that series. Honestly I think I went 13 for 13, with a handful of walks and a couple hit by pitches. I was on third base and they threw a passed ball, a simple, easy passed ball. I ran in, I scored, I got to the bench. They were throwing an argument or something and time was called. I don't know exactly what the circumstance was, but they made me get off the bench, put my helmet back on, go to third base and do it again. I was kind of annoyed by that, but I went back out and I was on third base. The next pitch he threw a ball in the dirt, a passed ball. I got ¾ of the way home and I basically stopped and I walked home. I was looking at the pitcher and he was just glaring at me, like this was my fault. He was standing on the plate so I just walked in. I didn't nudge him or anything, but we were shoulder to shoulder, you could tell there was tension. I was like dude, I didn't do anything to make you throw another passed ball. So the next at bat I was up and the same pitcher was still out there. I stepped out of the box and I was doing my routine and I looked up at the umpire and the catcher and I said, 'This ball is coming at me.' I got in the box and the first pitch whizzed right by my head. I get hit by pitch all the time so it's no big deal to me. So I looked back out at him and he was just glaring at me still, so I turned back to the umpire

and the catcher and I said, 'This is going to come at me too, and we're going to have a problem here if it does.' The catcher was like, 'No no no we're not throwing at you.' And they didn't even waste a pitch, which is the gentleman's rule when you're throwing at somebody, throw it away and then throw it at him again. So he threw it and it hit me square in the back. I started walking towards the pitcher's mound and I wasn't even mad, it was so ridiculous that I was calling it as it happened. Somewhere along the lines of walking towards him I just started walking to first base because I didn't want to deal with anything. I think it's a $150 fine if you get ejected and we're not making enough money to get a fine for $150. So I ended up walking to first. Everybody on our side jumped over our bench, everybody on their side jumped over their bench. There was a lot of tension and the game paused. They threw out the pitcher. Coaches started to yell at each other, chest bumping each other. Everyone came out but there wasn't a brawl. I just walked straight to center field and stood out there with Jake Stewart. We caught up, we talked, it was good to see a familiar face, especially because he was one of my good friends." Tyler

> "There was a lot of tension and the game paused... Coaches started to yell at each other, chest bumping each other."

"I have the uncanny ability of always being in the stands charting[1] when we get into fights. But once when I was in the New York-Penn League some kid hit a walk-off grand slam against one of our pitchers. As our pitcher was walking off, some of their guys said something to him and he started saying something back. I was way down in the bullpen in right field and we were like, 'Oh wow, they're fighting.' We broke into a dead sprint. We were far too late, it had already broken up by the time we got there." Chris V.

---

[1] Chris explains, "With the Mets, two days before you pitch you have to go into the stands and chart the game. You write down the velocities, what pitches they threw in which counts and the results. It's basically a game chart with added velocities and pitch sequences. Then the day before you pitch you have to chart a spray chart of the opposing hitters, which is basically what pitch did they hit, where did they hit it, what was the result, that kind of thing. We keep the charts throughout the year and it will inform the next pitcher that's going to pitch against that team. It's good preparation."

Bench clearing brawls can result in fines whether you participate or not.

"The way it works is if you clear benches for a fight, minor league baseball will fine you $50, but if you don't go, my team will fine you $100. So either way we're going out there. One of our bench clearing brawls we thought we had to pay the $50 but our organization ended up paying it because it was against the Yankees. All of our new coordinators and staff and VPs are all from the Yankees, so they paid the fine for us. That was pretty nice, it was big deal for the guys that they did that." Anonymous

"I don't think we get fined if we don't go out but it's more like showing that you have your teammates' backs. If this guy is going to try to crush my teammate I'm going to go out there and protect him. I'll sacrifice the 25 bucks so that my teammate doesn't get bludgeoned by a baseball bat or something." Chris V.

"It's pretty much a known thing to go, everyone needs to be out there. If you're not out there you're making everyone look bad." Drew

"I don't think you get fined if you just go out and you're part of the brawl. If you're not ejected and you get a free brawl in, good for you." Tyler

Of course not every brouhaha involves the pitchers. There are plenty of other mishaps that occur on the field.

"We had a guy get thrown out of a GCL rehab game. It was a rehab game for him and he gets thrown out." Danny

"Andre Ethier was making a rehab start in Tulsa and they had the pitch clock going because it was AA. The clock wound down to zero and they called a strike on him. He'd played like 18 years in the big leagues and he was like, are you serious? Our dugout was going nuts." Drew

"One time our 19-year-old Dominican stud told the umpire, 'Fuck you.' " Anonymous

"One year they miscalculated how many games up we were on the league, so we didn't know when we clinched. They brought the sparkling cider onto the field — because everyone's young — something like three games before we actually clinched. We had a big celebration and then the next day we realized we actually hadn't clinched. Then when we clinched it we celebrated again. With sparkling cider for the young 'uns." Marc

Off the field, away from the eyes of the crowd, there are a lot of shenanigans going on.

"We had a big leaguer come down for a rehab assignment but he wasn't playing so he was in the stands. He was having a little trouble with his weight and a scout decided to have a kid deliver him some ice cream as a joke and it didn't go over well. He ended up getting really pissed off and leaving that day. I think the scout got fired." Anonymous

"In Rancho we had a Cuban pitcher who was supposed to start a 7:05 PM game and 2:00 comes around and he wasn't at the field. At 4:00 he still wasn't there. We called him at 5:00 and there was no answer, 5:30, no answer. He showed up at the field five minutes before game time. He didn't start." Anonymous

"I remember one game I was on the bench and one of the players said he needed his sunglasses and they were in his backpack in the locker room. So I went fishing through his backpack for his sunglasses and my hand came across something metal. It was very solidly built. I realized it was a gun. I paused, took my hand off it, grabbed his sunglasses and went back out to the field. Business as usual." Anonymous

> **"My hand came across something metal. It was very solidly built. I realized it was a gun."**

"We went to Kannapolis, North Carolina for a series and the dugout smelled. We noticed the bathroom that was connected to the dugout smelled too. The problem was the plumbing was messed up, so when someone flushed the toilet it caused the pipes to backfill. The only place for it to go was through the drains of the dugout. So we literally had these puddles of toilet water on the floor of the dugout. We had to jump around them in the middle of the game. Metal spikes made it easier because they raised up our shoes, but still..." Kenny

"Last year my team was up something like seven games in the first half on the second place team with ten games to go. The other team won every game and we lost like six of our games. Going into the last day we had a doubleheader and of course half our team went to the casino the night before and got three hours of sleep. Everyone was really pressing because they didn't want to give up that lead, but we lost both games and lost the first half." Marc

"We were in Hickory, North Carolina and it was really hot and humid. We finished the game, took off our sweaty clothes, put them on a loop, threw them in a bin, showered up and left. This particular locker room didn't have laundry facilities onsite so the clubbie had to take the laundry in bags and go somewhere else. When we got there the next day we learned one of the laundry packs didn't get washed. Half the team's laundry was washed and the other half's wasn't. I was in the group whose stuff didn't get washed — compression shorts, socks, sliding shorts, everything — so I had no choice but to put on my sweaty clothes. Once you put them on, you go outside, you get used to it and you forget about it. But there's that first feeling of putting on smelly, disgusting clothes, that was bad." Kenny

****

"That feud just went on and on."

Players spend so much time together throughout the season that they inevitably play pranks on each other.

"As far as funny pranks go, the average IQ of some of the people you play with is not great, so it's easy to pull fast ones on people. There was a prank where we convinced a new guy that one of the pitchers was deaf and everyone would sign to him all the time. Or we would convince people that some of the players couldn't speak English." Alex B.

"There was this one guy on our team, he was the funniest guy to be around. He would always mess with our hitting coach 'Smokey' Ramon Ortiz. We would go on bus trips and Smokey would need his neck pillow to rest. And so one day around 9:00 AM before we were about to get on the bus for a three-hour drive somewhere, Smokey came on the bus and said, 'Oye, where's my neck pee-low? Who took my neck pee-low?' All these guys were just laughing and laughing and this one guy goes, 'Neck pillow? I thought it was a toilet seat! Check the toilet seat!' And Smokey went back to the locker room and the neck pillow was on the toilet seat like a cushion. Smokey was like, 'F-you! Oye, I'm going to get you!' " Danny

"That feud just went on and on. The next road trip, this guy got Icy Hot and baby powder and put it in Smokey's underwear. Smokey was standing out there at first base and he was moving around during the game and he couldn't stand still. He was looking over at the dugout and our guys were laughing. And he was like, 'Oye, someone put the hot stuff in my underwear!' " Danny

"There was another funny guy, he was a super type-A personality from New York. One day we had sandwiches between the games of a doubleheader, it was baloney sandwiches, $3 from Walmart. You'd open them up and the baloney juice would come out, and you'd put that with some Nutella. We were making sandwiches and Smokey would come in the locker room and he would take two pieces of baloney and he'd find someone who wasn't looking and slap them in the face with the baloney and eat it right in front of them. He'd say, 'Oh yeah, this is my sandwich!' and he'd slap them with the baloney and eat it. It just became a thing. At one point Smokey put mustard and baby

powder and maybe some mayonnaise in a tortilla and before the game he went up to our catcher and smacked him in the face with it. And our catcher was like, 'Smokey, I'm literally about to go out and play and I have mustard, baby powder and mayonnaise on my face.'" Danny

Sometimes the pranks involve the fans.

"We had the son of a famous player on our team. One time as we were walking into the locker room in Charleston there was a fan who was asking every single guy on our team if he was this famous player's son, but we knew he was already in the locker room. I mean this fan was just hounding everyone and eventually we ended up throwing this player's uniform on our assistant athletic trainer. This guy had a bad body, he was clearly not an athlete, but he walked out there in full uniform and signed autographs for the fan." Marc

And speaking of fans, they provide their own stories.

"I once heard a fan in Northwest Arkansas yell, 'That was a terrible call! Stevie Wonder could've seen he was safe. And he's dead!'" Danny

"In the South Atlantic League (Low A) where all my weird experiences were, we had a family show up to our team hotel in a really nice Porsche and stand right outside our bus asking everyone on the team to sign a blank notecard. It was very sketchy. So everyone just signed it 'Babe Ruth' or 'Mickey Mouse.' I don't think anyone really signed it. That's the thing, you sign a name that's not yours when they give you a blank sheet of paper. They were clearly scammers. It was kind of terrifying." Marc

"I always do my best to be as nice as I can with all the fans, but every team has those weird fans and you've got to keep your distance. I know some people who do too much for those super fans and then the super fans adopt an obsession about a player and it can be really bad." Drew

"In Tulsa we had a girl and her mother who would come to every game and we knew that the mother was basically there pimping her daughter out to players. She was like 17, and a player asked, 'Isn't she underage?' and her mother was like, 'She'll be 18 in a week.' It was really weird." Anonymous

****

"He was a guy who was never wrong, even when he would clearly make a mistake."

The minor league coaching staff provides even more entertainment to the game, although not everyone is privy to the details. Most minor league teams have four coaches: the manager who's in charge of everything, a hitting coach, a pitching coach, and generally one other guy. These coaches more or less live the same lifestyle as the rest of the team and they spend as much, if not more time on the field as the players. They get just as tired and cranky as the players, which can lead to a lot of bizarre interactions on and off the field.

"We had this theory that sometimes the coaches were just angry, and no matter what, they'd find whatever it was to argue with the umpire. So one time it had rained and the field was a little bit wet. There was a debate over whether or not we would start the game. We were the away team and they decided to play, and our coach got really angry. He was like, 'This is unacceptable, this field is dangerous, my guys are going to get hurt, blah blah blah.' He was all riled up. So we started playing and it began to rain during the game. The outfield was getting really wet and now people were starting to slip and it was getting even more dangerous. The umpire gets to decide whether to call off the game so eventually the umpire took his mask off and said, 'That's it!' And our coach came running out yelling, 'What the hell? Are you kidding me? You started it, you finish it! You can't call this game right now!' And we were looking at each other, like he wanted us to not play and now as soon as the umpire makes a decision he flips his opinion and

is getting mad. We just were all laughing. They did call the game and we were fine with it because we got to go home early." Danny

"In Peoria (Low A) we had one umpire who was just awful. He was missing so many balls and strike calls and I think there were a couple plays at the plate that he completely missed. Our manager had already gone out to argue two calls and he looked at the group of us and said, 'Alright, next time this umpire F's something up, I'm going to go get tossed.' Later that inning there was a terrible pitch that the umpire called a strike. Our manager stormed out there and just started unloading on the umpire and letting out all these F bombs. He got rung up and he came back to the dugout and he was like, 'That's how it's done boys.' " Tommy

"I was in AA and our manager didn't understand the double switch. The double switch is a move frequently used in the national league to substitute a hitter for the pitcher and then put the next pitcher in someone else's spot. It's a complicated move. Our coach didn't know how to use the double switch and all the other managers knew it. This guy kept using it incorrectly. He would do it and mess it up and instead of saving the extra player, because that's why you do it, he would burn an extra player on the bench. And I was a victim of that a few times. He was a guy who was never wrong, even when he would clearly make a mistake. He would reason why he'd made that decision." Anonymous

The personalities and backgrounds of the coaching staff are as varied as the players they're managing and sometimes things get lost in translation.

"I remember one day we had defensive work and our coach wrote the daily schedule out on this big whiteboard and he wrote 'Defense of work.' So the whole day I was making jokes like, 'Hey, are we defending work today?' And he would ask, 'What do you mean?' " Anonymous

"One time our coach was trying to say transvestite but he kept saying 'Tra-VEST-y.' " Danny

And sometimes the coaches just want to have a little fun.

"It was literally my first day. My teammate and I were hitting off the machine and the machine was throwing pretty hard, and some people were struggling with it, especially this guy. It was his first time hitting in a while and he was really struggling to try to hit it. He would swing and miss one, and our hitting coach Smokey would say, 'Hey, what's your name? I forgot your name, is it Rachel? Ha ha ha ha!' and he would pitch another one. He would foul it off, and coach would say, 'Oh Rachel? Na na na, your name is Susie, ha ha ha ha!' and he would start laughing at him. He would try to hit another one and he'd hear 'Ah, Susie, no your name's not Susie, it's Megan ha ha ha!' Meanwhile my teammate thought he was screwing up his whole career and he had the coach just laughing at him on his first day." Danny

In addition to four main coaches, there's also a strength coach whose job is to keep the team in good shape throughout the season by creating and enforcing a lifting and conditioning program. Players can get fined if they don't show up for lift.

"The strength coaches are in a tough position because their job is to make the players healthy and strong but they don't have ultimate control over them. And some of the players never want to do anything. The strength coaches can't really do much other than communicate to the front office which players are not doing their work. Or they can tell the manager, who will fine them. But if you're a good player and you're playing well and you don't want to lift, oftentimes it'll slide. It's an interesting dynamic." Kenny

"To get out of lift, you could do Yoga class and get a free Lululemon mat. So the Latins would do yoga. They'd never done it before, they were laughing the whole time. It was like child's daycare." Drew

"We were on the road half the season and we had to maintain some consistent workout plan. Most of the time there wasn't a weight room at the visiting team's stadium so we

needed to go to a Gold's Gym or just your random gym and those are always interesting experiences. It's amazing looking back on it how many times we boarded the bus at 10:00 AM and were shipped off to some random gym. We'd wait in the lobby while the strength coach got the paperwork, then we'd sign our name on a piece of paper and go in and lift. Some teammates would be messin' around, other guys were getting after it. Then some guys needed more time, so the others had to wait around. Then we'd board the bus and go back. Needless to say, a lot of the gyms that we would go to had a lot of interesting characters." Anonymous

****

"Pain is a bad word."

All that strength training and conditioning is designed to keep the players in top shape and prevent injuries throughout the season. Players need to stay healthy because they're competing for play time and hoping to move up the system, and the last thing they need is an injury.

"One of the things the Royals talk about is called 'prehab.' Instead of doing rehab when you're hurt, you do a lot of work as prehab, to prevent the injuries. We do a ton of stuff in the training room trying to strengthen muscles that are more common for pitchers to injure." Jack

But it's a long season, muscles get sore, bodies get tired, and inevitably injuries happen. It's been said that a serious injury will send a player to rehab and he'll never be seen again. It's not a surprise that some guys avoid letting the team know something is wrong.

"I had shoulder pain one day and someone said, 'Never, ever, ever say the word pain to a trainer.' Pain is a bad word. Sore, tight, all those are fine. You say pain and you get shut down." Anonymous

"You hear 'Don't go into the training room.' " Colton

"Going into the minor leagues I heard that you don't ever want to let anyone know you're injured, but it depends on who you are. If you're a top prospect you're more open about telling them that you're injured because an injury isn't going to change your standing that much with the team. But someone who is fighting for a job would tend not to want to let them know they're injured because they want to play as much as possible and show them what they can do." Tommy

"The Dominicans would sometimes fake injuries because they didn't want to play. 'I don't feel good.' And even though the coaches and trainers knew what was going on, they didn't have a choice." Kenny

Injuries can occur at any time, even before the season starts.

"One night just before Spring Training, I woke up in the middle of the night and I felt sick and I thought it was food poisoning. Sometimes when that happens you throw up and get it out of your system and you go back to bed and you feel a little bit better. That happened but I didn't feel any better, I actually felt worse. The pain got worse where I knew my appendix was. Fortunately I was at home and I woke up my dad and I said, 'Hey I think I have appendicitis.' I ended up having an appendectomy right before Spring Training and I basically missed the whole thing. It took me a month and a half to get back to in-season form and I probably was premature in starting the season that year. I was just eager and ready to go." Mark

"During the off-season I began to feel the pain in my hip. I spent the months leading up to Spring Training feverishly looking for ways to get healthy and reduce the pain to no avail. I went into my first Spring Training knowing that I was hurting and thought I could get through it. In my first pitching appearance I topped out at 84 mph and it felt like my hip and my elbow were on fire and were just hurting way more than they should be for a normal human being. That led me to ultimately make the decision to tell someone on the Cardinals staff that I had the pain. I remember lying in my hotel room with my hip and elbow both throbbing after this outing, and thinking about how everything is going to cascade after I tell one person. It's a cascade in that you tell one trainer on the field, but they'll send you to the next trainer, and then you'll talk to the head trainer, and then you'll go to the doctors and you'll get sent to everyone and eventually they'll decide what to do. Eventually I got an MRI and they noticed in my hip there was some damage to the labrum and there was a bony protrusion that was wearing away my cartilage. They thought they could manage it with just a cortisone shot in my hip. My elbow was fine though, it was structurally intact, it was just a result of my hip being goofy." Andrew

> "I remember lying in my hotel room with my hip and elbow both throbbing ... thinking about how everything is going to cascade after I tell one person."

Many injuries occur during Spring Training.

"I broke my leg in Spring Training. Literally my first pitch, my first game in Spring Training, an intersquad. It was a guy who was an ex-big leaguer. I thought to myself, 'He doesn't know anything about me, this low level minor leaguer, he's going to want to see a few pitches first,' so I laid one over the dish and he just smoked it back at me, off my leg, broke my leg. They had me pitch a couple times after, they didn't think it was broken, and that just severely messed up my throwing motion. That year was pretty pathetic because I basically had no idea how to throw. I'm still partially messed up now but the Angels have been awesome with working with me and getting me back to my original form." Marc

"I always prided myself on my durability, like don't get injured, don't get hurt. I was really superstitious with my health. I didn't really like going into the training room because I didn't want to put medical attention on myself but unfortunately I remember like yesterday what happened. We were playing the last game of Spring Training, the last week of March and it was in Tampa. Every now and then it pours, so it poured in *the morning and we were thinking we weren't going to play, but sure enough they said we're going to play. Pro ball is all about routine and it runs like a well-oiled engine, and that threw off my whole routine. Everything from my prep work, the gym, my breakfast, everything was thrown off. So I remember being in left field, the grass was all soggy. This lefty guy hit a line drive in my direction. It was slicing to the line so I was playing the slice. I was going to play it off the hop and keep it to a single base hit, but when I went to plant, my whole body turned except for my foot. So I sprained my ankle, it ended up being a grade three sprain which is the highest one, the worst one. It was so swollen, it was really unfortunate, it sucked. It took two months to rehab. I had crutches and a boot and the whole thing." Dom*

When a player is injured during the season, he is placed on the 15-day or the 60-day Disabled List, or DL. This removes the player from the active roster and opens a spot for another player to be placed on that roster. Depending on the injury and when it happens, it can derail the player's season temporarily or end it entirely.

"I had one season when I got a broken nose and a broken wrist within a week. I was diving back to first base on a pickoff and the first baseman missed it and it bounced up and hit me in the nose. I was scheduled to get nose surgery the next Monday and take a few days off, but the Friday before that, it was the 13th, I broke my wrist. I was playing first base and there was a bunt. The catcher fielded the ball and threw it up the baseline, but as I was reaching out to catch it I collided with the baserunner and broke my wrist. I had to have wrist surgery that weekend. It was a six to eight week recovery. A week later I went in for the nose surgery." Danny

"The injury that I had I was actually not playing that day, I had a day off from catching, thank goodness. I got brought in to pinch hit in the 8th or 9th inning. So then I was catching the bottom of the 9th, we were on the road and they had the tying run on second. The ball went to our center fielder, he threw the ball in to me at the plate, and I got speared by the runner. I got him out but his helmet dropped straight into my shoulder

and I ended up with a grade two strain in my shoulder. I just wasn't feeling great so a week later they sent me back to Arizona. That side of my body was all swollen, they thought it was pushing my spine against my nerve. Once the swelling went away, I started having numbness, kind of like that feeling when your hand falls asleep, I started feeling like that. I had an epidural in my neck and a cortisone shot in my left shoulder, and they found a herniated disk in my neck. My shoulder injury was probably a three to five week injury, and the numbness in my hand knocked me out for the season. It didn't go away until late August." Eric

"I was a pitcher and they tried to switch up my arm angle, they wanted me to throw submarine style. The summer before I thought I had a really good year and everything went well, but I came back and all of a sudden in the middle of my next season they wanted to change things up. That's initially how my arm started hurting. They started trying to implement that into games and I didn't have the right technique. Being an overhand thrower my whole life, it didn't come naturally so it was difficult for me to try and implement the side arm delivery that they were telling me they wanted me to do without them teaching me how to do it. That was really frustrating. They sent me back to Arizona to work on it but at that point I didn't want to tell them I was hurt because I thought I could recover from it. I thought my arm was just giving me trouble temporarily. But eventually I found out I had an 80% tear in my rotator cuff, which is pretty significant. I think I had a fairly significant tear in my rotator cuff for a while. I'd been pitching through it through Stanford and I think even in high school the tear started to develop but it never gave me any trouble, it never gave me enough pain to where I needed to do something about it up until this point. When I started throwing the new style it irritated it and tore it more past that point where my pain threshold allowed me to continue throwing. So they said get either PRP[2] treatment or surgery. They suggested PRP treatment so I did that, did my rehab, did my throwing program, and at the end of September they let me go for the off-season." Chris C.

---

[2] Platelet-rich plasma, or PRP. Researchers have produced PRP by isolating plasma from blood and concentrating it. The idea is that injecting PRP into damaged tissues will stimulate your body to grow new, healthy cells and promote healing.

Injuries might even affect a possible promotion.

"I think the only opportunity I had of getting promoted from AA to AAA was right around when I got hit in the face. I was hitting the best I'd hit the whole year, I was crushing balls, and then I broke my face and I missed two weeks. I stayed in AA the rest of the year." Drew

Oh no, what happened?

"I was at the plate and the pitcher had just thrown a slider so it looked like it was going to hit me but it broke over the plate. Then the count was 0-2 and I thought it would be another slider but he threw a fastball up and in. I tried to stay on it but it was hard to see, the shadows were really bad. It smoked me right in the cheek. I just went down and I felt that shooting, numbing pain in your face, when something bad happens and you're like, what just happened? I don't remember it hurting, I just remember this is not good, my face is numb, my mouth is full of teeth right now. The trainer came over, I sat up and spit out the teeth. Everything was bleeding and I just remember getting up pretty quickly and walking to the clubhouse, I didn't want to be out on the field. My face swelled up like a balloon. Literally my face was so big, it was enormous. I could chew on my right side luckily, and I had to drink water through my right side because all my teeth on the left side were exposed, any temperature change was really uncomfortable. It was not fun. But people loved taking pictures of me and posting it on social media. I didn't need surgery, just three crowns on my teeth. I only missed two weeks — 14 games. I now have a face mask on my helmet and I will use one of those for the rest of my career." Drew

> "The trainer came over, I sat up and spit out the teeth."

The hard part is determining when to come back. There are pros and cons.

"I was playing second and there was a ball between me and our right fielder. He slid into my feet and took me out and I sprained my ankle. I think I was out two to three days and then I played on a sprained ankle pretty much for a whole month. I was dealing with ankle tightness and ankle soreness pretty much the rest of the season. There's a lot of social pressure to not take yourself out as far as team dynamics and things like that. I kinda learned the hard way how that can go the other way where you're playing on something that you probably shouldn't be, and then it turns into something worse. But on the other hand when you're playing through something and it hurts and you actually perform decently well, you gain respect from the clubhouse and the guys on the team. Those are the guys you want to play with." Anonymous

"I was playing for Team Nicaragua in the World Baseball Classic, which is during Spring Training, and I tore my hamstring, which was not good. I missed the first week and a half of the season. The hamstring is tough because it takes a really long time to feel 100%, so I was playing every day with burning pain. I didn't feel good at all, I literally played the whole season feeling like that. Then the MRI at the end of the year showed my hamstring was still torn. I would say that was a valuable lesson for me. I'm not going to make excuses and say I didn't play as well because of it. But when I talk to young guys now who get hurt or are rehabbing I say that in college it's different, because games matter so much more as far as winning and losing, but in the minors winning and losing matters but it's really not that important if you win or lose at the end of the day. I wanted to come back and play; I wanted to be in the lineup every day and be a leader on the team. I always tell young guys now to make sure you're 100%, it's not worth coming back and rushing it if you're not 100% and re-injuring it and setting yourself back." Alex B.

It's not just the player who decides when to come back.

"The trainer decides at the end of the day if you're good to go or not. The training staff, the medical profession sometimes. A lot of it is on you, in the sense that you're saying, 'It feels good, I can run, I'm comfortable playing 100%, I have no reservations.' I'll take ultimate responsibility for trying to get back quickly. Essentially I was a week out from *being 100% but it never got any better from that point on. It was just 80-90% all season. At the end of the year I got a PRP injection."* Alex B.

****

It's not always a player's performance that determines his career trajectory. Injuries, even minor ones, can derail a player's season or even his career. A player's behavior on and off the field can be an asset or a liability to a team. How does all this affect how a player gets moved around the system?

Chapter 10
Curveballs and Changeups

Let's not forget, every player wants to be in the Major Leagues, not the minors. With each organization having several teams in their minor league system, players get moved up and down every year. Some players get moved around several times throughout the year. At any time, players can get promoted, demoted or traded. Promotions are generally good, demotions are generally bad. Trades can be good or trades can be bad, depending on the situation. All this movement creates psychological and logistical stress not only on the players who get moved but even for those who don't.

****

"I've always thought if you perform, good things will happen and if you don't perform, they won't."

For the most part, promotions are good for minor league players because it gets them one step closer to the ultimate goal of being a major leaguer. Life generally gets better as you move up the system. Better stadiums, better locker rooms, better food, better baseball, and slightly better pay.

"It's so exciting when you hear that you're going to move up. It's hilarious, because in the minor leagues, it's not like you're getting called to the big leagues, you're just getting called to a slightly better minor league. But it's still the most exciting thing that could happen, I get to leave San Antonio and go to El Paso or whatever. That's probably the best feeling you can have. One of my closest friends on the team got called into the manager's office earlier this year in AAA, he got called up. He walked out and he was just shivering, like he was so excited, he was going to the show. I think that's something everyone looks forward to." Cal

Promotions can happen at any time during the season and it usually happens with a visit to the manager's office.

"Being called into the manager's office is like this terrifying amazing feeling. If you're doing well, you're 90% sure this is gotta be something good. But if you're struggling a little bit you're like, 'Oh no, they're going to send me down, I'm going to have to go back to wherever it is, Fort Wayne, Tri-City.' So it's like this very nerve-wracking feeling, walking into the manager's office." Cal

It can be good news or bad news, and it's usually a function of whether it's before or after a game.

"Getting called in before the game, you're not feeling as excited about that one. There are definitely times when that's a good call but most of the time it's after a game that the good news happens." Cal

If a player is going to get promoted, the manager will generally tell him after a game so he has time to pack up and catch a flight the next morning.

"The couple of times that I got called up I got called into the office right after the game and both times it was the day we were coming back from a road trip. One time the whole bus ride back I knew I was going up, but we got back pretty late. I still had to pack up all my stuff, get my place cleaned up, figure out a ride to the stadium in the morning and then a ride from the stadium to the airport. Those two days were a huge crazy whirlwind of trying to get everything figured out. I think I actually played that first day I got there." Tommy

"I had made the All-Star team in High A, which was in Rancho Cucamonga. I drove down, played in the All-Star game and drove back. When I got back to the locker room on the third day of the All-Star break I got a call from my manager, he said, 'Pack up your stuff, you're going to Richmond (AA), you have a flight tomorrow morning,' and he gave me the flight details. The next morning I flew from San Jose to Houston, then jumped on a puddle jumper from Houston to Richmond. There was really bad weather and we ended up stopping in Charlotte for an hour and a half. We had to stay on the plane, we didn't even pull into the gate. We finally got back in the air and by the time you add the three hour time difference I think I got in around 1:30 or 2:00 AM and then we had a game the next day. They had needed a second baseman for a couple of weeks before that but they wanted me to play in the All-Star game." Anonymous

Promotions can happen for a number of reasons.

"One reason that people get promoted is that someone gets hurt and they need someone to fill a spot, like if someone in the big leagues gets hurt, the AAA guy goes up, then the AA guy goes up and so on. A lot of times it's a chain affect. Another reason is in the middle of the year they do a lot of promotions based on performance. I think from a statistics standpoint they really don't look at your stats until you have about 100, 150 at bats, there has to be a sample size to judge you on your performance. At the beginning of the season there are so many fluctuations, I could be hitting .400 one day and then

go 0 for 5 and drop down to .100." Alex B.

"The last weekend of the season a few of us got sent to AAA because they did the September call-ups. They had all kinds of space on the roster and all kinds of innings that needed to be covered. So they sent me, along with a couple other players, from Everett (Short Season A) to help fill in for that weekend, which happened to be in Vegas. That was really cool because that's where my girlfriend lived and I had family there. My parents and my sister came up to see me play — that was the first time they'd ever seen me play professionally. They were out of starting pitchers, someone had been claimed off waivers, and for whatever reason they had no arms left. They said, 'Hey, you started in college, do you think you can give us a few innings?' And I said sure, and I ended up starting the last game of the season for the AAA team." Chris C.

Players don't always know when it's going to happen.

"Personally I've tried not to think about it. I find always checking box scores and keeping up with not only other players' stats but your own stats is counterproductive because you can't control what other people do, you can only control what you can do. My first full season I was that guy who was always checking box scores and looking ahead and thinking the guy at the next level ahead of me is only hitting whatever and I'm hitting this. That's counterproductive because you can't make those decisions. I've always thought if you perform, good things will happen and if you don't perform, they won't. You can force the issue by playing well. But it doesn't matter what you're doing or what they're doing if you're not playing well." Anonymous

"You don't really know when you're going to get promoted but you can talk a little bit with your manager and find out what their expectations are. You get this weird feeling in your gut when you feel like you're going to get a promotion. You're showing up at the field on edge, looking at the manager's office hoping he's going to call you in there at some point during the day." Alex B.

When you have a family, however, it's nice to have some warning.

"I was having a great season. I was hitting home runs, getting on base, getting steals. So they started hinting to me that I was going to move up. Within a two-week period all these coordinators were saying I was going to get moved up. So I just called up the minor league director of operations, I said, 'What's the deal, everyone says I'm going to move up. I have a family to think about, I need some sort of warning so I can get them situated because I can't just uproot my family.' He let me know that they were going to move me on such and such day, so I knew for four days that I was going to be moved up officially. I'm not the regular person that is on the team. I let them know that. I'm very transparent, very confrontational, if there's a problem or anything I'd come right to you and ask what's up." Tyler

Either way, when the promotion happens, it's good to know the protocol.

"When you get there the first thing you do is say 'Hi' to the manager. That's the number one rule whenever you get placed on a new team, you have to go and check in with the manager. I didn't know that at the time but they told me, 'Hey, you need to make sure when you get there you say Hi to Rodney and introduce yourself.' I'm glad they told me because I don't know if I would have otherwise. It's a big no no if you don't." David

For some guys, their first promotion is from Rookie to Low A.

"We finished our Rookie season in the GCL and we didn't make playoffs. The farm director came in and said, 'A couple of you guys are going to stick around because September call-ups are coming and we're going to start sending you up as we go into September.' So I was hitting in the cage one day and our director of baseball ops came over and said, 'Dom you're going up to Charleston (Low

"He wanted me to fly but I was like, 'No, I'll just drive.' I was so excited I wanted to make that drive."

A). He wanted me to fly but I was like, 'No, I'll just drive.' I was so excited I wanted to make that drive up I-95 from Tampa to Charleston. I drove up and it was so cool seeing Holy City, they call it Holy City. They play in a stadium called the Joe, it was right on the water in Charleston, it was a lot of fun. We were there for one game — it was when the Charleston RiverDogs broke the record of season attendance of something like 300,000. Bill Murray is the owner of the team so he gave the person who bought the 300,000th ticket a car with 300,000 miles on it. I thought that was pretty funny." Dom

"I was in Rookie ball in Billings, Montana. After a game I came in the locker room and the manager called me over and said, 'Hey, you're going to Low A in Dayton, Ohio, and your flight's tomorrow, thanks for coming.' My family was actually visiting so it was cool for them. I was definitely happy, I mean getting promoted is a very good thing. It's all so new that you're just along for the ride. I didn't know what to expect at all. I think it was because someone got hurt, they needed me to fly straight there and play. I got off the plane and went straight to the field and got there late, after the whole team, and I was in the lineup for that day." Alex B.

For some players it's from Low A to High A.

"I was playing in Low A and getting frustrated because regardless of how well I did I knew I wouldn't play every day. So I had in the back of my head that whatever I did didn't matter anyway and I got on fire. I think I hit over .400 in a month and I still wasn't playing every day, that seriously drove me insane. My manager called me into his office after a game and he was like, 'Hey man, you're going home,' and I was thinking I was going to get released. Then he said, 'Yeah, you're getting promoted to High A.' Bakersfield High A was only an hour and a half away from home, where my parents lived. But then after he said that, he continued, 'Yeah, I didn't advocate for you to get promoted, I told them you should still stay down here for a little bit longer but they didn't care, so you're moving up.' And then he said, 'That feeling you just had, I want you to remember that, it's not a good feeling to get released so play your ass off,' and I was like, 'Alright, thanks man, can I go now?' I told my teammates after and they were like *what the hell, he actually did that? I was so happy to get out of Clinton, that place was treacherous. I called my parents right after, they were stoked. But then I got there and it was another rinky dink stadium, it was super hot out, 100 plus degrees, it was in the desert. You're basically dealing with the same stuff. Same lack of amenities and all that good stuff. But it was nice to be in Southern California again."* Lonnie

The jump from High A to AA is considered to be a more significant step up in the system.

"Even though AA is only one more layer, it's a big step up. They say AA is when real baseball starts, guys just know what they're doing, there are nicer parks. It's just a more polished game, whereas Single A and below is a lot more raw and unrefined." Kenny

"One of the main differences between the low levels and the high levels like AA was we didn't do any fundamentals before games. That was what Spring Training was for, you got all your practice in then. In AA it was just BP and games, at least for the Dodgers. Apparently the Mariners still do fundamentals all the way through AA every day and it's more exhausting. I talked to guys on that team and they were like, 'Dude, I'm so jealous of you over there, we're all so wiped out because of all the fundamentals we do. It's an extra hour of practice every day before games.' For the Dodgers it's pretty much a big league pre-game process; it's BP some days but most days it's just hit in the cage and then get what you need to be ready for the game. If you want ground balls they'll go out there and give you ground balls, it's really nice. A guy like me, I feel like I perform a lot better when my pre-game is low energy and I can save it all up for the game. Nothing is worse than going into a game feeling wiped out. That was the case a lot at the lower levels and in college." Drew

"It was so structured in Rookie ball, you have your new draft guys, you have these 18-year old kids, and then you go up to AAA and we didn't even stretch as a team. They just told us to go stretch on our own, get your work done on your own, there's no one telling you to do anything. The dichotomy was very apparent for sure." Chris C.

"The Corpus Christi AA team was really good, that's where a lot of the prospects of the organization were at the time, like a couple of the pitching guys who have spent a little time in the big leagues: Musgrove, Paulino. We probably had five or six guys on that team end up in the big leagues by last season. It was definitely cool to be around that and see how they conducted themselves, how they prepared every single day. And it was good because I did halfway decently there." David

The lifestyle is generally considered to be better when you get to AA.

"AA was my first real taste of, I don't want to call it the good life, but it was definitely a step up from what I had seen before. We had two buses instead of one, they handled all of your luggage. I remember I had some laundry in my suitcase and they had taken everything out of my suitcase and organized it in my locker. I was like, 'Guys, I appreciate it but I don't need that. I don't need my laundry stuff organized in my locker.' It was really cool. The league was nice, stadiums were really nice, lots of fans, the food and the player amenities were better." David

> "I don't want to call it the good life, but it was definitely a step up from what I had seen before."

"I think when you get to AA you start to feel more like a big leaguer because they pack your bag and they handle a little bit more of the travel for you which is nice. As you go up, things do get a little better, the clubhouse is a little bit more enjoyable, there are more TVs, more video game setups. The biggest jump in food was from A ball to AA, although I'm not sure that's true for every organization. I'd say as a general rule of thumb it gets better." Stephen

"Maybe the nicest place to play in AA, maybe even in the whole country, is Springfield, Missouri (the Cardinals AA affiliate) because they have a beautiful stadium, it's a college town with tons of fans, the community really loves the team, there's a nice locker room, everything was really nice. It was a huge jump in terms of playing because it just gives you energy when you come out to the field and it's packed full of people, everyone is watching you, you can feed off of that." Danny

"By the time you get to AA you've been in the organization for a few years and there's a solid core of guys that you're with. There are cliques I guess, certain groups hang out with certain groups, but you know who your best friends are in the organization. You're united in the sense that everyone's in the common struggle, trying to make it. You're doing something that you enjoy that's incredibly difficult and you're all struggling to do it. Being in that fight you have that camaraderie, it's special. I don't know if you find that in too many other places, other avenues in life." Alex B.

And of course, the jump to AAA, the final step before the Major Leagues, can be thrilling.

"It was pretty cool when I got promoted to AAA from High A. I was driving to the field like any other day and I got a call from my manager and he was like, 'Hey, what are you doing?' And I said I was driving to the field and he was like, 'Stop, you're going to AAA, your flight's leaving in a couple hours.' I was like, 'Whoa, how long am I going to be there?' and he said, 'I don't know, but bring your stuff.' So I pulled a U-ey, went back to my house and packed up what I thought I needed because I couldn't take everything. When I got to AAA it was amazing. The clubhouse was so much nicer, they packed up your bags for you, the food was way better, everything was better. And the game was a lot more polished. It was great. It turns out I was only there a couple of days. I went back down to High A and it gave me a unique perspective going back to a lower level. It was like child's play, the level of play and also the facilities. And then two weeks later I went up to AA." Kenny

"When I got called up to AAA, they flew us to Las Vegas and we stayed in the Golden Nugget in downtown Vegas. It was cool because we got to the baggage claim at the airport and we didn't get our luggage ourselves, they took it all for us so we didn't have to lift any of our luggage to the bus. The team members weren't even required to take the bus to the hotel. They got whatever other transportation they wanted. They rented their own cars, they Ubered, they taxied, it was pretty much a free for all unless you were taking the bus to the Golden Nugget. Definitely that was something I wasn't used to, coming from college. So I rode the bus and there were a couple of the higher level guys who rode the bus, and other than that it was just me and the two other guys who had come from Everett with me." Chris C.

But along certain dimensions, namely the travel and camaraderie, things actually get worse in AAA.

"In AAA you get to fly, but that's actually bad because you have to wake up and be at the airport at 4:00 AM. Especially because we were flying out of Omaha and you have to connect everywhere so the travel is longer. And the guys in AAA are older, they've been around the game a long time and in many cases they're bitter they haven't gotten a shot or they're upset they've been sent down from the big leagues." Kenny

"Nobody wants to be in AAA, nobody's happy to be in AAA, there are so many bitter guys. AAA is half made of people who are on their way up and half made of people who are on their way out. AAA is a different dynamic in the sense that it's a lot of older guys — the average age is now in the late 20's so you have people with families and wives. Grown men. These aren't kids anymore. They're still enjoying the game but once they've had a taste of the big leagues they know how much better it is. They're either working extra hard or they're extra bitter that they're not there at this point." Anonymous

****

"I felt like I was a special operations soldier and I just kinda got dropped into enemy territory trying to help out the AAA team."

Surprisingly, promotions aren't always good. While on the surface it may seem like a player is advancing up the system, in reality the organization may have no immediate plans for them to make the major league team. Some players are promoted to temporarily fill a roster spot or they're considered to be a positive influence on the culture of the locker room. These players will often move around the organization and play in higher levels than what their projected performance would suggest.

"I was in extended spring training before I got called up to AA Corpus Christi for an emergency outing. I think they had a 15-inning game the night before and they needed extra pitching so I and one other guy got called up. I got a phone call at probably 11:30 at night. In extended you wake up at six in the morning so I was going to bed pretty early, and I was not up for that phone call. But then my hotel phone rang and that woke me up and one of the coaches said, 'Hey Dave, pack your stuff, we need you to go to Corpus tomorrow.' When I got the phone call originally I thought oh cool I'm being called up to Quad Cities, which is A ball, but as soon as he said Corpus I was kinda like wait, what? It was cool, it was a really good experience. I pitched that night. The plan was originally for me to stay up for maybe a week or so, but I did pretty well in that first outing and did pretty well again in my second outing so I ended up staying for a month. I was on and off the roster getting to pitch whenever they needed a player. I completely skipped Low and High A. But I don't think that was the original plan. I kinda held my own there and it was big for my confidence and it helped me a lot going forward." David

"I was in extended spring training and my mom was in town and I was sitting by the pool at her hotel. We had dinner plans that night and we were going to hang out the next day after practice. And I'm not kidding I got a phone call by the poolside, and it's one of the coaches and he asked, 'What are you doing right now?' And I said, 'I'm hanging out with my mom at her hotel.' And he said, 'Can you make it down to the field soon because we're going to send you to help out the AAA team in Scranton, Pennsylvania.' I caught my breath a little bit and I answered, 'I can do that.' So I told my mom, 'I'm sorry but I'm

"It was at 3:30 PM when they called me and they got me on the next flight at 6:15 PM. I said, 'I love you, sorry about dinner.' "

going to have to cut our visit a little short, I'm going up to Pennsylvania.' So I went back and packed a quick bag. It was at 3:30 PM when they called me and they got me on the next flight at 6:15 PM. I said, 'I love you, sorry about dinner.' " Alex D.

"I was warming up in the bullpen one night in the Arizona Rookie League and our pitching coach got the call that apparently our AAA team in Tacoma had a late extra inning game and they were out of arms. He said to me, 'Hey, shut it off, you're not going to pitch tonight, there's a chance you're going up to AAA.' I didn't really know what to think. I had been doing pretty well and I was hoping to get sent up somewhere else. I was tired of playing against these man-children in the AZL, they were unbelievably talented but too easy to get out. Later that night they said go home, gather up your stuff, be back here in an hour and we'll have your itinerary. I had to get all my stuff together in a hurry, take the shuttle at 4:00 AM from the complex in Arizona to the airport and get on a 6:00 AM flight from Arizona to Tacoma. When I landed a few hours later I was picked up and taken to the field for the 10:30 AM game. I didn't have time to do anything, I don't even remember sleeping that night. I was thrown into the game in the 10th inning after our closer blew the save. Our bullpen was completely depleted and I was their only option left, they needed an arm. I got tagged for three runs on four hits or something like that. It was just a different level obviously. I had some adrenaline even though I was a little physically tired. It was definitely an experience. I guess looking back on that, getting an opportunity to play in AAA, that was something really special." Chris C.

Since everyone is basically competing for themselves, players can have mixed emotions when someone else gets called up.

"Anytime you're promoted it's exciting, everyone on your team is excited for you. Everyone obviously wants it, and when you see someone else get promoted you get motivated, you think, they're promoting people, that's good." Mark

"Other guys can be bitter even though players deserve to be promoted. It's a selfish game." Drew

Although there's a lot of excitement associated with a promotion, there are some team dynamics that have to be navigated.

"I would say the most stressful thing when you join a new team is finding a seat on the bus. There's definitely a pecking order and guys that have been there have their seats. Nobody really wants to double up despite what they say, you want to have your own seat for sure. Especially in the lower levels, there are a lot of guys and the team is trying to save money so they only have one bus. You have to kinda navigate where you can sit and who's going to be friendly and let you sit there, especially if you join the team on the road. I joined the team on the road and they had a long bus trip back and I had all my bags and stuff. The other part of it is you don't know anyone on the team that you're playing for, so you have to make new friends obviously and figure out team dynamics." Alex B.

"When I got to AAA it was a little intimidating walking in the locker room. I was just the little guy who just got off the flight an hour ago, coming in to cover an inning or two for the team. Everyone looked at me. These guys in AAA are grown men with families and kids and it's been their career for 10+ years and they're trying to make it back to the big leagues. They had incredible baseball experiences and here I am, my first year playing professional baseball, walking in trying to fit in with these guys. I was walking on eggshells a little bit and trying to mind my own business as best as I could, sitting in the back of the bullpen, making small, innocent talk." Chris C.

And there are some other lifestyle curveballs.

"I got promoted to Springfield (AA) while we were on the road in Tampa (High A). I had my baseball gear with me but all my other belongings were still at my apartment in Palm Beach. I didn't get that stuff for a long time." Danny

*"When I got called up to AAA we had just finished our last game in Tulsa (AA) and we were on the bus back home. My coach called me to the front of the bus and said, 'Hey,

you're not going home tomorrow, you need to go to Memphis for playoffs.' There had been September call-ups and they called an infielder up when the roster expanded, so I got to fill his spot. I had already bought a ticket to the Florida Georgia Line concert back home in San Diego for Friday because I was going to be home on a Wednesday. I had to figure out what to do with that. I don't remember if I was able to sell it or not. I might have sold it on StubHub." Tommy

In some cases, when you get called up the teams don't tell you how long you're going to be there. In fact, sometimes they don't even know themselves.

"You never really know, so you take it one day at a time. You know that you're probably not there to stay but at the same time there are guys who got sent up to AA and spent the last two months of the season there. You never know what the organization needs so you go and do your best at whichever level they send you to. For me it was take one day at a time. I tried not to think about it because in my situation anything was better than playing in the AZL." Chris C.

"I felt like I was a special operations soldier and I just kinda got dropped into enemy territory trying to help out the AAA team. I was told that I went to back up the catcher who was in AAA because the other guys who were there with him got bumped up because there were some injuries and older guys moving around at the major league level. So he was there by himself. I was only given an itinerary for one day and I didn't really know anything after that. I only packed for five or six days, and the rest of my stuff was still in Florida. I was living on the go and just trusting the process, the age old saying. It was just odd to me because I had been in extended. I expected one of the older, more experienced guys to get bumped up. I thought I was going to be in the bullpen for a few days and then I'd drop back down until they made other arrangements but they threw me out there for two games. I got two starts and I got my first RBI single the first night. I was a real boy! I was a little nervous, I was scared I was getting spoiled because we had that really nice complex in Florida and then they sent me straight to AAA. I was thinking to myself, 'Whenever the hard knocks start coming around I hope I'm ready for those too.' " Alex D.

"I had been playing for about a month in A ball in Midland, Michigan. After a game my manager told me they were sending me back down to Arizona the next day on a 5:00 AM flight. We live near there so my mom drove my car out and picked me up at the airport. It was Mother's Day and we were just hanging out at an outlet mall. I had been on the ground for two hours and I got a call from my coach saying, 'What I'm about to say is not a fucking joke. I don't know why, but you're going back to Midland.' The Midland team was still on the road, so I had left Cleveland and actually went back to the same place. On my way out I had told the manager I'd be back soon, and the next night I said, 'I told ya!' " Anonymous

"I remember when I got called up to AA, we were on a bus trip and every player got an envelope with meal money with their name on it. Mine said 'extra player.' That wasn't good." Danny

Just make sure to be prepared.

"There was another guy who got called up to AA with me, he was maybe 18 and from Panama and didn't really speak English. When he got the call he thought one of his buddies was messing with him, so he was like oh yeah, whatever, and hung up the phone. He didn't bring any stuff to the field the next day, he didn't pack. So we were both on this plane going to Corpus Christi and I had my suitcase and all my stuff and he had a backpack and that's it. He stayed for about a week. He borrowed some of my stuff and some of the coach's stuff." David

And whatever you do, make sure to get there.

"One guy who was in AA got the call — he'd been doing well, he was getting promoted to AAA. He was so excited he went out the night before with his friends and slept through his alarm and

"[He] slept through his alarm and missed his flight. And he missed getting promoted."

missed his flight. And he missed getting promoted. That really hurt him, because they brought up somebody else and that guy did well. The team was upset because they said, 'Look, this is part of being a professional. If we were going to call you up to the big leagues and you did that, that could cost the big league team a win, and this is serious stuff.' He never really recovered from that." Danny

Finally, there can be some hiccups in the call-up process, which exacerbates a process that's already nerve-wracking.

"We were in Colorado Springs (AAA), it was early July. I was having a decent year at the time, I was really starting to find my groove, starting to get hot. I guess it was just time for me to get called up. One day I got to the field and I saw I was in the lineup and started getting ready like a normal day. About an hour later they reposted the lineup and I wasn't in it. I was pretty much playing every day and it was rare for me to have an off day. The way things work, they don't really tell you exactly what's going on, they're pretty stingy with that information. But Mike Shildt, now head coach of the Cardinals, pulled me in the office and he said, 'You were in the lineup. Now you're out. You're a smart guy, you can probably figure it out.'[1] That was it. Everyone was congratulating me. I was in the locker room, just kinda hanging out, thinking I finally did it, take a deep breath, it was a great feeling. My parents were at the game and I texted my dad, 'Hey, I was in the lineup, I'm coming out, they haven't told me exactly why,' but he also could figure it out. The game started and all during the game guys were coming up to me, congratulating me, saying you'll do awesome. It was in Colorado so the ball was flying, the score was 13 to 11, the game was taking forever. I just wanted this game to be over so they could tell me officially and I could get on my way. But then in the 7th or 8th inning the trainer went up to the head coach and they made an in-game substitution. They pulled Dan Johnson who was playing first base out of the lineup for no apparent reason and they put someone else in. That was kind of weird. That doesn't really happen, he wasn't hurt,

---

[1] When a team makes the decision to call up a player to the big leagues, they will get taken out of the lineup for that night's game.

so clearly something had probably happened in the big league game, I think someone got hurt. And I figured OK, that's fine, he'll get called up too. When the game ended I was waiting around my locker for someone to grab me and tell me I'd been called up. I saw Dan Johnson go into the manager's office and come out and everyone was congratulating him. Then Mike called me into his office with a sad look on his face, just total disappointment. He just looked at me and said, 'I'll be completely honest with you, you were going up before the start of this game and something happened, they changed their mind.' Mike is one of my favorite coaches and I think he was just as pissed, maybe more, which was nice to know that he was feeling it for me too. He had my back. It's a pretty crummy thing to have happen. But there's nothing you can do, you just gotta keep going. I saw my parents outside the locker room, I was just kind of shaking my head, like, it didn't happen." Stephen

****

"I was not happy to be going down."

Demotions are generally not good. In the same way that promotions can create a chain of upward movement, demotions can create a chain of downward movement. If someone from a higher level team comes down, a spot has to be made for that player, sending someone else down to a lower level. Alternatively, a player being promoted might just be swapped with another player being demoted. The fact is, there aren't as many demotions because the team could just choose to release the player instead. Getting demoted is better than getting outright released, but nevertheless, it's not fun.

"I got demoted from High A to Low A, that sucked. I got called in after the game. They tried to frame it as a positive, that I was going to go down and get some more reps. And going down actually turned out to be a positive in my case because I was able to play more and find my groove. If I had stayed at the level I was at, I wouldn't have played as much." Kenny

"There was one time I was going down from Springfield (AA) to Palm Beach (High A) and it was an early morning flight. I had about 30 minutes before the flight and there were about 10 people in the terminal and only about four gates. I guess I had dozed off, because all of a sudden I heard someone calling 'Passenger Diekroeger, your flight is about to leave,' and I was like, what?? I looked at the time and I must have looked at the wrong board and I don't know what happened. I told them that was me and they were like, 'You've been sitting here the whole time? Seriously?' I told them I was so sorry. I was just out of it, I was not happy to be going down." Danny

Moving down is bad enough but sometimes there are logistical issues that make it even worse.

"I was being moved down from the New York-Penn League to the Gulf Coast League in Florida. They always pay for two bags but you have to keep the receipts and they reimburse you. So I kept the stubs but not the receipts and they wouldn't honor it. I had to eat the $60." Colton

"Two of my teammates got demoted when we were on the road. I lived with them so I had to get all their stuff gathered and give it to the clubbie who shipped it out to them." Colton

Some demotions are a function of the fact that a player has been assigned to a new organization. They aren't true demotions, they're more like "mental demotions." For instance, Marc had spent the previous season in High A with the Salem Red Sox before being released in Spring Training.

"I was picked up by the Angels during Spring Training and afterwards I was assigned to extended. I had probably four outings there, I was there maybe three weeks — that was brutal. It was a Saturday and my girlfriend was there visiting me. You get Sundays off, so we were making plans for the next day. At 9:00 PM the extended manager called and said, 'Hey congrats son you're going to Burlington.' I was like great, I'm going to Low A.

He said, 'Be at the locker room at 3:00 AM tomorrow because you've got a 5:00 AM flight.' That was something else. I got to Burlington, I had one outing and did fine. They were like, this is a waste of time having him here. I only pitched once because I was only there for five or six days, thank God. Now I'm back in High A." Marc

"I was with the Mariners and they already told me during Spring Training that I was going to AA in Little Rock, Arkansas. I was thinking, alright sweet I'm going to start this year in AA. Then I got traded to the Dodgers. I assumed I was going to their AA team in Tulsa but then I had a meeting with Andrew Friedman, the president of baseball ops and GM Gabe Kapler and they were like, 'We're going to send you to Rancho (High A) to start the year.' That's how they started the meeting, 'Drew, you're going to Rancho to start the year, how do you feel about that?' It was kinda weird, I mean, obviously they traded for me and they had a plan for me but I knew I was capable of playing at a higher level. They said, 'You're going to the California League to work on a new swing with the hitting coach who's there, we think it's better if we work on it at High A as opposed to AA.' I bought in but I was thinking, damn, I thought I was going to AA and now I'm going back to High A. That felt somewhat like a demotion but that was also a fresh start feeling so it was good. When I got promoted to Tulsa halfway through that year it was a big relief." Drew

****

"I feel like it's not allowed but everyone does it."

Because roster spots are limited, some players get put on the "phantom DL." The phantom DL (disabled list) is a tactic that teams use to put a perfectly healthy, non-injured player on the disabled list to clear a roster spot for someone else. The team is indicating that they still want the player around and don't want to release him yet.

"I'd say it's both a good thing and a bad thing. It's a bad thing because obviously if they liked you a lot you would not be on the phantom DL, they'd find somewhere for you to go.

But if they really didn't like you they'd just release you at that point. So if they put you on the phantom DL that means they don't like you enough for you to play, but they like your work ethic, they like you as a teammate, your mentality, your potential. So they put you on the phantom DL to keep you around in case somebody gets hurt." Anonymous

"It's different between the teams. With Boston, if you're on the phantom, that's a really bad sign for your career, it means they don't value you at all. But with the Angels, it's so different. I'd say half my team is just free agent signs like me. So they'll just kind of move guys around like crazy and load up a couple teams to where you have entirely too many players. There's one guy on the phantom right now, he's been doing well, they clearly care about him, but just because we have so many pitchers and he needs a little bit of rest, they put him on the phantom. With Boston it's a very bad sign to be there, but with the Angels you're getting rest. I feel like it's not allowed but everyone does it." Marc

"Once when I was in Bowling Green, the game was tied one to one and I was in the leadoff spot in the top of the 9th. I hit a long home run and then I was put on the phantom DL." Anonymous

After hitting a home run?

"That was definitely already planned. A couple days, maybe even a week prior they probably thought, hey, we're going to bring someone up or someone is coming off the real DL, so we're going to have to make room, someone else is going to have to move. I think if I had gone 4 for 4 with 4 home runs or had gone 0 for 4 with 4 strikeouts I still would have been on the phantom DL the next day. I was probably on the phantom DL for six of the total 20 months that I played. I'd say catchers are put on the phantom most often because you need a bullpen catcher and a lot of teams don't want their starting catcher and backup catcher both catching bullpens. So you keep an extra catcher around on the phantom DL to catch bullpens, that's usually pretty common. And pitchers are on there too because there are so many injuries. A lot of times they want a pitcher or two to stay with the team, keep throwing, stay healthy in case somebody gets hurt. Then they can just activate that *pitcher right away. He's on the team ready to go and teams don't skip a beat." Anonymous*

There's no designation for phantom DL so it can be confusing for the fans who see players being placed on what they think is the regular DL.

"I had fans asking me all the time, 'Hey, you just can't get off that DL, what do you keep injuring?' and I'd have to say, 'It's just a little ankle injury that I'm nursing.' And then these autograph hawks would see me at the next series and they'd say, 'You're back on the DL, you just can't stay healthy can you?' I couldn't say I was on the phantom DL." Anonymous

While it's not fun to not play and be put on the regular DL or the phantom DL, players continue to get paid and can still travel with the team.

"You're along for the ride but that's about it. When I was put on the phantom I'd just show up, never wear cleats out to the field. I'd pray the game would be as quick as possible or hope there would be a rainout. And pray that we didn't make the playoffs. I talked to a few people in the system and let them know I was pissed about the situation but I didn't really make a scene over it. I pretty much just hung in there." Marc

"We had picked up a guy, a former big leaguer, we owed him $6 million. He got put onto the phantom DL and he was getting $800,000 every two weeks. Rather than being a good teammate he would bring out a Gatorade bottle and get drunk every game. He'd say, 'Wanna know why I don't care that I'm on the phantom DL? This is why,' and he'd show us a picture of his paycheck." Anonymous

****

"It was really sad. It was the first time I actually cried when someone got moved or traded."

A player can be traded at any time but there are certain times of the year when that's more likely to happen.

"One of the really fun things about baseball more so than any other sport is the trade deadline, and mid-season trades happen all the time. You're not only playing to move up in your organization but you're playing to impress other teams that might have holes or might have guys to sell." Austin S.

Any player under contract can be traded between the end of the World Series and the July deadline. After the deadline, players must be put on waivers before they are able to be traded. (Placing a player on waivers means the team is willing to let the player be claimed by any team that wants him.) Because of this July deadline, there tends to be a lot of rumors and speculation leading up to it.

"We knew the Royals' big league team was doing well, but we knew they needed pitching if they wanted to make a World Series run. There were a lot of trade rumors on ESPN that the Royals were going to trade for a stud pitcher, and oftentimes when you trade for someone like that you need to give up minor league prospects. I was on the team that had a lot of Royals minor league prospects, so for a couple months we were always saying, 'Hey, Hunter you'd better enjoy your last day here, you're going to be traded to the whatever team.' He would be like, 'No, I don't want to get traded, it's going to be Mondesi.' So there was all this speculative banter over who was going to get traded. Like kids asking 'Are we there yet?' we'd keep asking the manager if he knew anything and he was like, 'I don't know.'" Kenny

> **"Like kids asking 'Are we there yet?' we'd keep asking the manager if he knew anything and he was like, 'I don't know.'"**

But trades can still happen at any time, including during Spring Training.

"I was two and a half weeks into Spring Training with the Mariners and I was the backup for every single big league game. It was really cool, but I was getting tired of sitting on

the bench just to be a defensive replacement. I wanted to play. So one day I was on the list but our farm director came in and said they didn't need me for the big league game anymore so I was thinking, nice, I get the afternoon off. I showered up and went back to my apartment. My roommate had to back up the big league game and he was super jealous I had the afternoon off. So I was playing video games and hours went by and around 5:00 I got a call from the farm director. He said, 'Hey Drew, this may come as a surprise but you've been traded to the Dodgers.' I was like what? Then it all made sense, no wonder they didn't want me backing up the big league game because I just got traded. He was like, 'Yeah, the Dodgers will call you and you're their property from now on. They'll tell you what to do and all I can say is thanks and come pack up your stuff and you'll head over there tomorrow.' So I turned my Xbox off and drove to the field and there were still a bunch of guys who were there and they were like, 'Dude, what?' It was wild. It wasn't that emotional, it was more emotional for some of my closer friends on the team. Everyone in the Mariners organization at the time kind of wanted to get traded, they were all super jealous. I was pretty stoked. I tried to call my family and nobody answered, literally no one was answering. Finally my brother Brett answered and was like, 'Dude that's awesome.' " Drew

"A trade is not necessarily awful, a trade can be very positive for some people but it can also be bad for other people. Sometimes you're traded to a team where there's less opportunity and in that sense it's bad. There are definitely pros and cons to each situation." Alex B.

One of the downsides of a trade is that it can be so quick that a player who is traded to another team may never see their teammates again.

"We had a Latin player traded in one of the big league deals between the Royals and Padres last year and they took him from our team. It is quick man, these things happen crazy fast. They might be at the field and then out of nowhere they get pulled into an office and told that they've been traded to someone else, and then that day their lockers are moved and they're off." Jack

"One of my super close buddies Luke got traded at the deadline, it was July 31st. It was really sad. It was the first time I actually cried when someone got moved or traded. We were in Springfield (AA) playing the Cardinals and you can walk from the hotel to the field there, so we were all in the clubhouse and he was still at the hotel. We were just hanging out, and someone was like, 'Luke just got traded' and I was like, 'Oh my gosh, no way.' We all checked Twitter and it was true. So I texted him, I said, 'bro' and he just said, 'I know man.' He came over 10 minutes later and walked into the clubhouse and started bawling because he loved everyone with the Dodgers. He made half our team cry. He was saying goodbye to everyone and he finally stopped crying when the trainer that we'd had for the last two years came out to say bye and he broke down again. I was like, oh my God, we had a game to play in 30 minutes and everyone was crying. He was the dude on our team, one of our best players, just jolly old guy to be around. We had been on the same team for the last two years, playing together every day. I was thinking, 'Damn, we just lost the best hitter on our team, the Dodgers just gave away a guy who always hit .300, he was a beast, he hit a bunch of home runs,' and boom, one day he's gone. I was just like, oh my gosh, I was not expecting that." Drew

So I guess he didn't stay around for the game.

"No, he just packed up his shit and left. He Ubered back home to Tulsa, a three-hour ride on the Twins' dime. Then he had to pack up all his stuff, put it in his car and drive 10 hours to Chattanooga. I remember him calling me saying, 'Dude, this place sucks, Tulsa is the best place ever compared to this.' But I think after it's all said and done he is really happy he's with the Twins because his opportunity to make it is so much better there. The Dodgers are so backed up with outfielders. The trade was really tough for him but I think afterwards he was pretty happy." Drew

Sometimes trades don't work out for anyone involved.

"One of my roommates – my fellow living room partner — was traded for a bucket of balls *to the Angels. He was in High A, doing OK, and he got phantomed. While he was on the phantom they sent him to Arizona to throw live batting practice to Kole Calhoun and it went fine. From there the manager called him in and said, 'Alright we got a flight for you, you're going to Short Season A now.' And this kid was 25 years old, already had time in High A, so he just said, 'I'm not getting on that flight.' And he just retired." Marc*

Another common time frame for trades to take place is during the winter meeting of general managers in December. Unlike the amateur draft that takes place in June, the Rule 5 December draft is for current professional players.[2]

In December of 2015, Mark Appel was part of a trade between the Philadelphia Phillies and the Houston Astros.[3]

"The Astros general manager gave me a call — this is a Saturday morning in the off-season — and he said, 'Hey Mark, I just want to let you know that we traded you to the Phillies. You know we're in need of a closer and Ken Giles was the guy that we identified and the guy we wanted to get, and the Phillies would not do the trade unless you were a part of it. We didn't want to give you up but we had to make a decision about that and we felt like it was best for our future as the Astros organization, so best of luck to you in Philly. You'll be receiving a phone call from Matt Klentak, the GM in Philadelphia.' That's basically how it happened, it was a less than a minute and a half phone call." Mark

---

[2] Minor league players who were signed when they were 19 or older and have played in professional baseball for four years are eligible, as are players who were signed at 18 and have played for five years. Teams that have vacancies on their 40-man roster draft in reverse order of the regular-season standings. A team that selects a player in the Rule 5 Draft pays $50,000 to the team from which he was selected. The receiving team must then keep the player on the Major League 25-man roster for the entirety of the next season, and the selected player must remain active (not on the disabled list) for a minimum of 90 days. If the player does not remain on the Major League roster, he is offered back to the team from which he was selected for $25,000. If his original team declines, the receiving team may waive the player. Once a player is selected, he is automatically assigned to his new organization's 40-man roster. mlb.mlb.com/mlb/minorleagues/rule_5.jsp?mc=faq

[3] December 12, 2015 the Philadelphia Phillies traded SS Jonathan Arauz and RHP Ken Giles to Houston Astros for LHP Brett Oberholtzer, RHP Harold Arauz, RHP Mark Appel, RHP Tom Eshelman and RHP Vince Velasquez.

Mark, who had been the #1 draft pick by the Astros in 2013, did not see it coming.

"I didn't really know. I kind of tuned out all of the off-season stuff and I didn't think too much about who was in the trade rumors and all that stuff. But the phone call from the Phillies felt good." Mark

****

"It's a business."

It's easy to see how the constant promotions, demotions, trades and uncertainty throughout the year begin to take a toll on the players.

"I've lost hope on the mound. I remember one time thinking, 'I'm in A Ball right now and I just gave up three home runs in an inning and what do I do from here? I guess I need to go back over my resume.'" Marc

"In pro ball they say you're one of three types of players. You're either a prospect, a suspect, or a no-spect." Kenny

One of the most frustrating aspects of baseball is not getting the opportunity to play every day.

"It all takes a toll mentally. It's like screw this, if I'm not going to play every day, there's no point in playing. Or trade me to another team, but you don't have the power to get traded to another team, other teams may not even want you. There are long bus rides, long nights, and you're thinking to yourself, what am I doing? In football you have the practice squad but you're not playing every day anyway. In basketball there's the G League, guys are playing every day down there because the teams aren't so big and there aren't as many of them. It's a little bit easier to have that visibility when you are playing every day." Lonnie

"When I got promoted from High A to AA, I felt the highest of highs. My wife and I were thinking I was on track to go to the big leagues the next year. Just keep playing, keep doing well, I was getting better, I was getting at bats. That's what I needed, live at bats. That's the only thing I was missing in my training because you can't simulate a live at bat. But then this is where everything falls off. The manager called me in the first day because he felt threatened by me, this is what I was told by the players. He said, 'I heard you came up to basically get our guys in line because they're out of line and I thought that was my job.' I was like, 'Dude, I don't know what the reason was that I was moved up, they just told me to come up here.' Furthermore, I was hitting like .400, .450 in my last 10 games before I got to AA, I was just crushing the ball. But my first day there with the hitting coach he tried changing my entire approach to the plate, giving me a big league kick, just changing everything. You just don't change or even talk about things like that to a guy who's doing well, especially in baseball. I'm already thinking, 'Whoa, this place sucks.' I was told a handful of times by my manager that I was going to play at some point, so I thought, OK, no problem, it's a long season, there are 300, 400 more at bats left in the season. All I need is 200+ consistent at bats, I'll get my experience. Throughout the season, he made me a couple promises, you're going to play every day from here on out, you're going to play every day for

"You just don't change or even talk about things like that to a guy who's doing well, especially in baseball."

the rest of this month. Those things never ever became true. I'd play two days and then they would bench me again. I would do well in those couple of days, I'd hit a home run, bat .400 for the four-ish days I'd play, and then I'd go back on the bench. I was basically a glorified pinch hitter for the rest of the season. I had 134 at bats in 38 games in High A Bradenton and then 124 at bats in 51 games in AA. Fewer at bats with 13 more games. I basically came in in the 9th inning, and the manager wouldn't give me any warning. He would tell me an at bat before. I found it was just not a place to succeed. You don't evaluate guys off one at bat, one pinch hit, and say how good they are. They need a consistent amount of at bats and especially someone like me who needed at bats. I was behind in at bats in my life and they weren't giving them to me." Tyler

The sad reality of professional baseball is there isn't equal opportunity. Guys who get more money have job security because the organization wants them to do well. Their odds of making it are higher. Others who sign for relatively small amounts have to compete harder to stay in the system. If a player isn't one of those high-round draft picks or one of those high international signs who got a big signing bonus, they really have to stand out and have to go above and beyond performance-wise to stand out and get call-up after call-up over some of the players with a lot of money invested in them.

"If there's one reason I would say the draft is really important it's that you're given more time to make errors. It's a business. If someone's invested $10 million in a company they're probably willing to let it ride, see if it's going to pay dividends, let it go a little longer than if they've invested $1,000 in a company. They're quicker to write off that $1,000 and say well, that money wasn't well spent." Cal

"I think the majority of your success depends on what round you're drafted in. I think the higher draft picks are definitely more inclined to go up a level as opposed to maintaining the level or even going a level down than the late draft picks. The biggest thing that you see is the amount of at bats that people get. You start to see oh, this person got paid x amount and it's interesting to see how much they play regardless of how good they are or how much they're struggling or how much they're striking out. When you start to see these guys who got paid a lot play on an everyday basis and after three to four months they're still struggling and there are people on the bench who are doing a lot better and still aren't playing every day, that's when the frustration starts to sink in. We had an ongoing joke, me and another infielder from the Dominican Republic who didn't get paid a lot, we'd say, 'Hey man, if you don't get two hits today you're not going to play tomorrow.' Two hits was the bare minimum in order to play the next day. There was one particular time — I remember this perfectly — when I had gotten two or three hits, three days in a row, it was epic. I was thinking, if I'm not playing tomorrow I'm going to lose it, I'm going to be so mad. And sure enough I didn't play the next day. And the guy who got paid more played the next day and I was like, you've got to be kidding me. There's really no way to find a groove if you're not even able to get in the lineup every day. I

think they just need to be more transparent with their players. They give everyone a false sense of hope that they're going to make it no matter how hard they try or how well they do." Lonnie

Frustration also stems from the fact that the system is so big.

"Honestly, I would argue to just drop the draft to 20 rounds and pay the guys you actually want. Don't be chasing these guys in the 30th round and giving them a false sense of hope and wasting their time playing for a couple years and getting a total of 100 at bats over the course of two to three years. You could easily cut out a league or two, you could easily just go A, AA, AAA and that's it. You don't need the Rookie ball, you don't need the Short Season, you don't need the Dominican Leagues and all this other stuff. There are just too many levels to get through in order to finally make it. You just don't need that many players in an organization." Lonnie

"I think the reason they have so many teams is there are towns that really like their minor league baseball and they're going to pay to watch these guys play. It's relatively inexpensive for the major league clubs to have these teams. They can pay us so little they might as well have the extra guys. Even if they get one star player out of those 30 guys it's probably worth it for them." Danny

Sometimes a player's prospects are a function of which organization they're a part of.

"A big margin team like the New York Yankees is financially willing and able to go trade and sign free agents and load from the top as opposed to smaller market teams like Milwaukee and Minnesota and Baltimore and teams like that. The New York Yankees' minor league system for me was kind of a double edged sword. On the one hand you had the best of the best, you had the best gear, you had great food, great service, they treated you fantastic, first class, A+ all the way. On the other hand their dependence on their minor league system isn't as high as a lower market team. They can go sign Jacoby

Ellsbury, they can go trade for Giancarlo Stanton. You're not competing with your fellow minor leaguers, you're competing with the best of the best across all of major league baseball when you're with the Yankees." Dom

"Coming up in the minors with the Giants they treat you better and have more resources than a small market team. But then again because they have more resources they are more likely to do what they did this off-season which is go get two outfielders and a third baseman and pitchers, whereas Cincinnati will promote guys from within. For us, it was easy to get promoted up to AAA but you really have to prove yourself and really have to make an impression to make the Major Leagues. They have $25 million to spend because money's not an issue. They can say is this guy worth it or should we go try to sign the best free agent available? It's a double edged sword for sure." Anonymous

And sometimes there's frustration with how the whole system operates.

"The minor league organizations have a hierarchy lifestyle as well. The staff in Low A is trying to make it to High A, and if they're in High A they're trying to make AA. That's how the entire job system works for the minor league staff. Everybody's trying to find a way to move up and they kind of get lost in what's the best for the team or what's the best for the players. Some guys are trying to hang out with the top draft prospects, stick onto them, get moved up with them, because they helped them with their swing, or they helped them with this, that goes a long way. It's a very weird dynamic." Tyler

****

Professional baseball is not always fair. Players are not always in control of their own destiny. For some players, the good outweighs the bad. The promotions keep coming and their performance continues to improve. For many others, the bad begins to outweigh the good, and there isn't a path to the top. What happens then?

Chapter II
Yer Outta Here!

Professional baseball is an up or out system. Not every player is going to make it to the top. Not every player is going to get the opportunities they want. Not every player performs they way they want. Frustration builds. It's a tough lifestyle and it wears them down. Despite the title of this book, however, most guys don't quit. Most get released. Some of them are surprised and some see it coming. Some are devastated and some are relieved. Other players will ask to be released and others just voluntarily retire. Many of their stories are shared below.

****

Releases can occur at any time. As noted earlier, a lot of players get released during Spring Training. That's when the organization has more players than they can assign to the minor league teams at the end of camp. There simply aren't enough spots in the organization to keep them all.

"I went to Spring Training in 2015 and was there for a couple weeks. It was just one of those days when I was excited for the day to be over. I ended up going in and they said they probably don't have a space for me. I was pretty relieved to be honest." Sam, released by the Seattle Mariners organization on March 23, 2015.

Sam continues:

"I had given a lot of my life to baseball but I knew I didn't love it to make it my career, I didn't love it enough to make it my life. I know guys who've made it their life. It was what should have happened and I'm at peace with it. If I could do it over I would do it again. I think baseball taught me a lot, it put me in a place where I got to meet my best friends, it put me in contact with a lot of people, it taught me a lot about failure. I wouldn't give it up." Sam

> **"Baseball taught me a lot, it put me in a place where I got to meet my best friends, it put me in contact with a lot of people, it taught me a lot about failure."**

Sam is now living in San Francisco and working for TPG, a global private investment firm.

****

The problem with getting released during Spring Training is the players have worked hard during the entire off-season to get themselves ready, and then three to six weeks in they get released. They've essentially invested the last six months on baseball rather than moving on in life.

"They definitely have to know after a season who they would prefer to get rid of, and they're better off just doing it then. It would be nice for them to let those people go, that

way they don't waste their time. For others, they do base some of this stuff on performance during Spring Training. Like if you did really well and then you came back to Spring Training 30 pounds overweight, and you can't do anything, they're going to be like, this guy is useless now. For me, I had done pretty well the season before so I didn't really expect it at all. My Spring Training was decent, and overall I think my performance the year before was good enough to at least make it through Spring Training regardless, but I got released the second to last day. I was in the locker room pretty early so no one was really there. There was a Post-It note on my locker so I went to the office and they were like, 'We have a lot of middle infielders, you should probably be getting more playing time, blah blah blah.' And I was like, 'Alright, sounds good man.' There's nothing you can really do about it, so you're just thinking, it looks like I'm going home." Lonnie, released by the Seattle Mariners organization on April 5, 2015.

Lonnie acknowledges:

"I don't know if there was that much I could have changed. If I had gotten drafted higher I would have been in a better boat. It took a while to realize that but then when I did I started to joke about it. A lot of people are really delusional and think they're going to make it. They play once every three days and they don't do well and they still think they're going to make it. At least for me I was more realistic, I was like, 'Alright I can continue to do this three, four, five more years and maybe have it pan out or I can use my Stanford degree,' which is something that a lot of people don't have in their back pocket. I was fortunate enough to have a Stanford degree." Lonnie

> "I was like, 'Alright I can continue to do this three, four, five more years and maybe have it pan out or I can use my Stanford degree.'"

Lonnie is now a Finance Manager at Western Digital in Southern California and is concurrently pursuing his MBA at USC.

************************████

Teams don't usually give the player any specific feedback on their performance and will articulate the player's release as a function of the size of the system.

"I was having a good Spring Training in 2016, I was hitting the ball well. I was with the AA Trenton squad and I showed up to the field just like any other day in March. Unfortunately Gary Denbo and Eric Schmitt, the farm director and assistant farm director, called me into the minor league office. They said, 'We're making decisions right now and we just have so many guys, there's not enough opportunities to go around and unfortunately we're going to have to give you your release. Thank you for your time and we wish you all the best.' In the moment I was upset, I just told them, 'Listen, I've outperformed other people, I feel like I'm getting better, I feel like I'm developing and progressing.' They said, 'We love having you here but it's a business. We're not always right 100% of the time but this is just the decision we're going to make.' Honestly it sucked, it was like 'ah Fuck.' But it happens, you know a lot of people say it happens to everyone eventually. So I went back and got my stuff." Dom, released by the Yankees organization on March 21, 2016.

Dom reflects back on his career:

"It was an awesome experience. I learned a lot of valuable lessons about discipline, teamwork, and accountability."

"It was an awesome experience. I'm grateful I had the opportunity to play baseball at the college and professional level. I learned a lot of valuable lessons about discipline, teamwork, and accountability. Celebrating with my teammates is what I miss the most." Dom

After working in the performance science department for the Dodgers for two years, Dom is now working for MVP Sports Agency in Los Angeles.

****

Many players just don't see it coming.

"I ended up getting released at the end of Spring Training which was a surprise because I thought the organization liked me. The back story is that during the off-season the GM of the Mariners got fired so they hired a new GM and he brought in his whole new staff, all new scouts, all new player development people. All the guys who had scouted me, drafted me and watched me play for the past couple years — they were all gone. The guys they brought in were more new age guys, they were real focused on stats and sabermetrics and all that, which was a departure from the old regime, which was more old school. So they invited me to this little camp before Spring Training started. It seemed like it was a good sign to be invited to that because it was a lot of the top players in the organization, and they told us we were going to be the leaders of the organization. So I was excited about that and it was good to be there. I actually had a really good Spring Training too, I hit really well, played good defense, I actually got to go play in the big league games three times. I caught really well, I got to catch a lot of the major league pitchers too, which was really fun. So everything was going really well. Then one day towards the end of Spring Training, just a few days before we were going to break camp, we had just gotten back from a scrimmage. I had a really good game, I hit a home run. We were eating and sure enough the grim reaper walked into the room — everybody gets nervous when he walks in — and I couldn't believe it, he walked right over to me and pulled me aside. He pulled me into a room with the head of player development and they told me they were going to release me. I put some pressure on them to give me an explanation for why they would invite me to that camp before Spring Training and tell everybody at this camp we were going to be the leaders of the organization, and then I have a great Spring Training and they release me. And they didn't really have an answer. I was surprised they couldn't give me reasons why." Wayne, released by the Seattle Mariners organization on March 28, 2016.

But after some follow-up, he was able get some specific feedback.

"They told me to go talk to my catcher coordinator, which I did. He told me some of the criteria they were looking at and it was really all stats based. There were a few stats from my previous season that didn't really conform to the new philosophy. So that's what it was about. They didn't really know me. I don't know how much they really watched me play during Spring Training but they could see the stats from the previous year. They were really big on walk-to-strikeout ratio, and I had a bad walk-to-strikeout ratio the year before. And that was something they talked about all the time during camp. And on-base percentage is a result of that. Theoretically if you have a good walk-to-strikeout ratio you're going to have a good on-base percentage. I think the previous regime had probably made the list for that pre-training camp before Spring Training. So I went back to the locker room and I packed up my stuff myself. A few guys were still hanging around the locker room and everybody was super sad for me. It's tough to tell everybody bye, especially guys I played two seasons in a row with and probably won't cross paths with frequently going forward. Not so much because I wouldn't be playing baseball anymore but you make a lot of good relationships, that part came to an end. That part was sadder than not having to take batting practice every day. I was alright at first but then when I got back to my hotel room, it all started to sink in. It was pretty sad." Wayne

> **"You make a lot of good relationships, that part came to an end. That part was sadder than not having to take batting practice every day."**

Wayne was offered an opportunity to stay with the Mariners.

"After they told me they were going to release me they presented another opportunity. They wanted me to be the bullpen catcher for the AAA team for the season and then after the season was over I would stay on board and move to the front office side of the club. I hated to be released but it was kind of flattering in the sense that they still wanted me to be a part of the organization. I was really disappointed to not be playing anymore but I was excited about the potential new opportunity. Bullpen catching was the first step to moving over to the front office. They also wanted me to be involved in coaches'

meetings, meet with the scouts that come in town and that sort of thing. I considered it, honestly it seemed like a lot of fun, getting to be around AAA guys, better cities, better stadiums, still getting to be around the game but not having to perform, not having to worry about my walk-to-strikeout ratio. And to me being a bullpen catcher is truly a role of servitude, a chance to be a servant and make a difference for other people and that was kind of attractive. I also spent a lot of time talking to the GM about what a career in the front office would look like, what the different career trajectories would be. I ended up discovering that pretty much every path to being a GM starts with being a scout. And that was not a life that I was desiring. So I ended up deciding not to do that, and ended up moving on, obviously, but it was definitely intriguing." Wayne

Wayne describes what he did next:

"After I got released, I realized that I had nothing to do for the next five months. I had my truck in Arizona, so I decided that before heading back home to Houston, I should drive up to Utah for some spring skiing. I spent three days in Brian Head, Utah, skiing by myself before starting the trek back to Texas. I had nothing better to do." Wayne

And some final reflections:

"Looking back, I feel tremendously blessed to have had the opportunities I did in baseball. My dream since I was a kid was to play professional ball, and I got a chance to fulfill my dream. I didn't make it to the big leagues, but I have a lot to be thankful for. I enjoyed the journey, both in the good times and challenging times, and I don't think I would have done anything differently." Wayne

Wayne works for a real estate private equity firm and lives in Redwood City, CA with his wife Kyle and their chocolate lab Gumbo. They try to get back to the Stanford campus as much as possible for football, volleyball, and baseball games.

****

There are some guys who aren't particularly surprised.

"I was in Spring Training in 2017 but unfortunately I saw the writing on the wall a little bit. I remember feeling like I did pretty well in Quad Cities (Low A) the year before but I saw other people getting moved up and obviously I didn't get the call. I was little older than a lot of the people at that level and it didn't seem like they had big plans for me and this could be it. It turns out it was. So I got in the car one morning with one of my best friends on the team. We had gotten drafted the same year, we came up together, we played together in the New York-Penn League and in Quad Cities. He gave me rides to the field every single day in Spring Training and one day I got in and he was like, 'Hey man, nice knowin ya.' I was like, 'What are you talking about?' and he said, 'I got a text from Eduardo the player development guy saying that I need to come see him in his office when I get to the field,' and I was like, 'Oh shoot, they're making the first round of cuts.' I hadn't gotten a text message but I wasn't convinced that I hadn't been cut because my phone wasn't really working that well at the time. I knew that my iPad got text messages so I texted my mom right away and I asked her, 'Do you mind checking the iPad at home really quick to see if I've gotten a text message?' and she was like, 'Yeah, you got a text from a guy named Eduardo.' I was thinking, shoot, I guess that means I'm done too. We got called in and it was pretty straightforward. The good thing about the Astros the entire way through was that they were really transparent about everything, they were always telling you where you stood, what you needed to work on, what you were doing well, how you stacked up against the other guys. I wasn't completely blindsided by it. They handled themselves pretty well. They basically said, 'Look, as you know we've got a lot of players here and we only have a certain amount of spots and unfortunately we had to make some tough decisions and we've gotta let you go.' And that was that, they kept it short, they kept it sweet. I don't think you really need to do anything more than that in that situation." David, released by the Astros organization in March, 2017.

David remembers this:

"Since I had kinda seen the writing on the wall the year before, I had spent a lot of time

in that off-season thinking about things and researching and trying to figure out what the next step might be for me when it was time. I felt prepared when it happened. It was really tough looking around at all my friends who had also gotten cut, because some of the guys were crying and some of the guys were all torn up. They were saying, 'I don't know what I'm going to do' and, 'I need to talk to my agent' and, 'Are you going to play Indie ball?' It was different for me coming from Stanford because I had graduated already. It was weird because at the time this was something I'd worked towards my entire life but I felt almost at peace with it. Besides obviously not playing in the big leagues I got everything that I ever wanted out of that experience. Working now, it's been an interesting transition to say the least. It's definitely two different worlds. When you're in the minors you wake up at probably noon every single day and you go to the field. After you get back from the field you either hang out with your friends, or you watch Netflix or read a book or something like that and go to sleep at three in the morning. It's definitely a lifestyle change but it's keeping me busy, that's for sure." David

> "It was weird because at the time this was something I'd worked towards my entire life but I felt almost at peace with it. Besides obviously not playing in the big leagues I got everything that I ever wanted out of that experience."

David now lives in New York City and works in credit risk management for an investment bank. He enjoys participating in the company's yearly softball game.

****

Marc was one of the players who got released during Spring Training but his career didn't end right away.

"I actually got released about two weeks before the end of my third Spring Training. I showed up at 7:00 AM and my pitching coach who I was pretty close with was waiting at the front door for me. He was like, 'Brake, come with me.' I was like, 'Ah, so this is it' *and he said, 'Yeah, dude.' So we went through the whole talk and then the farm director said he'd recommend me to every other team. Then I had the whole day to myself."* Marc, released by the Boston Red Sox organization on March 24, 2018.

Fortunately, that wasn't the end of his pitching career.

"I was ready to go tap into the real world, I had already written my resume before I had been released. I kinda saw it coming. The next day the Angels called, and a ton of independent ball teams called, but obviously if I was going to keep playing it was going to be with the Angels. After a lot of contemplation I decided to pursue the opportunity with the Angels. They flew me out three days after I agreed to sign with them." Marc, signed as a free agent with the Los Angeles Angels on March 29, 2018.

Marc went on to play the 2018 season with the Angels but it didn't go as well as he hoped.

"It was July and I was actually throwing really well and they put me on the phantom DL. They had guys who they wanted to give more chances to. There was a dude who threw high 90's so he had more upside than me, and there were guys who got more money so they were obligated to give them more chances. But seeing as I was pretty much back into my normal old form and they still put me on the phantom I was thinking, 'This is about as well as I can do and they still don't like me.' I came back and pitched pretty well again and then they put me back on the phantom with a couple weeks to go in the season. The second to last game of the year they brought me back to pitch in a meaningless game and I obviously wasn't great because I hadn't thrown off the mound for several weeks and I wasn't in exact pitching form. I had a little pop in my elbow — it was nothing serious but it scared the hell out of me. I came out in the middle of the inning and I called it a career. I knew that was it." Marc

But he didn't quit.

"What I was honestly expecting to happen was to go back to Spring Training again this year and get released during Spring Training. But when the farm director called me in November to tell me I was done, I actually thanked him. I told him, 'I appreciate you not wasting my time, having me train and get ready for the upcoming season and then release me during the spring.' It was a good move on their part to end things before I really had to worry about baseball again. It was funny, a week before the phone call I had literally started a job working for UPS for the five weeks or so in between Thanksgiving and Christmas. I was the guy who gets out of the car and runs the packages to the house. It's a pretty standard deal for minor league guys in the off-season." Marc, released by the Los Angeles Angels on November 13, 2018.

> "When the farm director called me in November to tell me I was done, I actually thanked him. I told him, 'I appreciate you not wasting my time.'"

Marc wraps it up:

"I'm done with baseball. After I was released it didn't seem appealing to try to play for yet another system. Now I'm applying for jobs and I'm pretty excited to get started in the real world. I miss it a lot less than I thought I would. I like playing catch every now and then but that's about it. The annual company softball game — that's something I'm looking forward to." Marc

Marc traveled around the Pacific Northwest, did some economic consulting work, and is now looking forward to the next chapter of his life.

****

Many guys make it through Spring Training but end up getting released during the season.

"My first year and a half I took it seriously and I did really well but I had had a couple shoulder surgeries and my arm was terrible and there were a lot of things that weren't going my way. In 2015 they sent me back down to Peoria (Low A) and I started off kind of slow. I wasn't very happy that I went back there and I was just kinda over it. I was sharing playing time and thought, 'Well this is stupid, I could be doing more with my life.' After one of the games one of the coaches told me, 'Hey, come into Coach so and so's office.' After games when guys get called into the office it's usually because you're getting promoted or you're getting released and I really didn't know what to think. I just walked in there and sat down and the manager said, 'I hate to tell you this, I've been debating on how I want to deliver this message because it's not easy to tell you this, but the Cardinals have decided to grant you your release.' And I literally said, 'Wow, isn't that a little premature?' But I completely understood. Then I just shook my hitting coach's hand and my manager's hand and went on my way. That was pretty much it. I was in Peoria so I was only a few hours from my parents' house, so my dad came down and got me." Justin, released by the St. Louis Cardinals organization on May 30, 2015.

Justin elaborates:

"Honestly when I got released I wasn't very upset. My initial reaction was like OK, I'm fine, I'm glad that they finally cut the cord because I wasn't really enjoying it very much. I did cry for a minute at some point when I was packing up my stuff because I realized I'm never going to do this again. I've moved on quite fast. I mean, if you're any good and you've played for a long time it's really hard to just quit, you kind of need someone to cut the cord, unfortunately. I'm happy I played in the minors for a couple years and I think that was long enough. Since I went through it I know I wasn't good enough to make it. I played for long enough in the minors to appreciate what it's all about and to see what it takes to make the big leagues and understand how hard it is to make it. I'm definitely glad I went through

> **"I played for long enough in the minors to appreciate what it's all about and to see what it takes to make the big leagues and understand how hard it is to make it."**

it and not long enough to where I feel like I wasted life. I don't feel like I wasted any part of my 20's." Justin

Justin moved back home to Chicago and works for Stryker, a medical technologies company.

****

"When I got released, we were in Tulsa (AA) on a road trip, it was the last day of the trip. Somehow we saw that a guy from AAA got added to our roster online so that meant somebody on our team was going to get moved down. I had a feeling it was going to be me because I wasn't playing that much, I knew I was the guy. I asked my manager what was going on and he said, 'I don't know anything but if I did I got your back.' So the game started, I was sitting on the bench. I got a chance to pinch hit and I actually got a hit. I got taken out and we ended up losing the game. And again after the game I asked him, 'What's going on? If I'm getting sent down I'd like to know,' and he wouldn't tell me anything. So we got on the bus to ride three hours back to Springfield and when we got home it was like 3:00 AM and I asked him again. He still said nothing, nothing. At the time I was staying at the hotel, so I went to bed in the hotel and then I got a text the next morning at 10:00 AM saying, 'Hey can you come by the field pretty soon.' I knew then that it was not a good sign because if you get called in at 10:00 AM it means you're getting released. If you are going to get moved down they tell you at night so you can take a flight the next morning and be with the team the next day. But this was in the morning. So I showed up to the locker room and I kinda knew what was going on. I sat down with the coach. He had gotten ejected the previous game and he started talking to me about how it was BS that he was ejected, and he didn't think it was right, and the umpire had no right to do that. And so I was sitting there knowing that my baseball career of 20 years is about to come to an end and he was there talking about how he was upset with the umpire for tossing him the night before. I asked him, 'Hey, look man, am I getting released?' and he said, 'Hold on,' and he kept talking and talking. Finally together we called the farm director who I had a pretty good relationship with and he told me I was getting released. So I got all my stuff packed up. They said I could fly out

whenever so I chose the next day. I had to call the guys in Florida to send my stuff home to me because I had gotten promoted while we were on the road and I didn't have any of my stuff." Danny, released by the St. Louis organization on August 3, 2017.

Danny has some further thoughts:

"Getting released was actually a freeing experience. Over the last few months of my career I was sitting on the bench a lot, so I had a feeling it was coming to an end. It was nice to be able to close the book on a great career and I immediately started getting excited about all the other things that were ahead in life. I had some great times in those few years with the Cardinals. There are so many memories and fun times with teammates I can look back on and laugh at. I'm glad I took the chance to pursue a childhood dream." Danny

> "I'm glad I took the chance to pursue a childhood dream."

In fact, his teammate and friend Justin remembers this exchange:

"It's funny, Danny texted me before his last season and asked me, 'So you've been out for a year now, what do you think, should I quit?' I knew exactly where he was at. He was in the same boat, not given too much money, kind of bouncing around. I told him, 'Honestly man, if you're still having fun and you still enjoy playing baseball whether you do well or do badly, then you should still play. If you're not enjoying it anymore, you're going to do just fine, you should just move on.' I was a year out and working and I said, 'Life is great post baseball. Baseball is fun but it's a lot more fun when you have money and you can do real things and you have weekends and a life.' " Justin

Danny now works as a software engineer for a cryptocurrency custody firm in Palo Alto, CA. He has weekends and a life.

****

Some players make it through the whole season but then get released sometime afterwards.

"That was really fun how that worked out. I was home at the end of September. I got a call from the farm director and he said, 'I'm sorry to tell you that we're releasing you.' It was extremely frustrating and extremely disappointing. You know, I want to take responsibility for whatever happens in my career but it was hard for me to convince myself that I could have done anything differently. They told me that I needed to pitch a different way. I couldn't help my arm from hurting, I had never felt pain like this before. I wasn't even halfway through the season but that's when I went back to Arizona and did the PRP treatment. I was like 'Yes sir,' and I did everything I needed to do. I worked my way back, I did rehab, I did my throwing program, I got back to throwing off the mound but apparently that wasn't enough. I think ultimately they wanted to minimize their liability and not be liable for any other treatments or follow up surgeries or anything having to do with my arm so they just decided to cut me loose and that was that. I would have respected them more if they told me as I was walking out the door rather than wait two weeks and call me. If you're going to release me at least say it to my face. I believe they knew they were going to release me two weeks before they did, when they let me go for the off-season. They can't release you as long as you're injured, they have to make sure you're completely healthy before they let you go. But they let me go home, they cleared me. I guess they did do me a nice courtesy by telling me then rather than waiting until the next year. He actually did mention that, he said, 'We want to let you get on and make plans if you want to go play for another team or if you just want to figure out where you're going to go from now.' So that was actually thoughtful of them but I don't know if I would quite give them enough credit to call them thoughtful." Chris C., released by the Seattle Mariners organization on October 12, 2018.

> "I would have respected them more if they told me as I was walking out the door rather than wait two weeks and call me. If you're going to release me at least say it to my face."

Chris is now living in Las Vegas where he works as a salesman for an aggregate parts company.

****

While the majority of minor league players' professional baseball careers end because they get released, some players choose to retire because they get injured.

"After my shoulder injury we were going to wait a couple months and rehab but at that point I didn't want to be sitting around in Arizona for the next one to two years. I still had some school to finish and I just said, 'It's time.' So I retired. I actually felt very comfortable with my choice. I felt like that was the right time in my life to make a change. I was still young, I still had school to finish, and I felt ready for that next step. I'm also so fortunate that I was able to attend a university like Stanford. Needless to say, it was comforting knowing that graduating from Stanford was my 'backup' plan." Eric, retired from the Los Angeles Dodgers organization on March 9, 2014.

Eric reflects back on that difficult decision:

"I look back on the last few years and I can't say I have any regrets. Baseball was a gigantic part of my life for so long. It was a little weird the following spring and summer when I wasn't playing. I don't miss the actual game that much. I mean, I DO NOT miss fouling a ball off my front ankle, never healing raspberries, or just the seemingly endless supply of bumps, bruises, and soreness. I do, however, miss the camaraderie that you develop with a close group of people and the competition. Nothing gets the adrenaline flowing like playing in a playoff baseball game (weeknight adult league basketball doesn't have the same effect). I've had so many amazing

> **"I DO NOT miss fouling a ball off my front ankle, never healing raspberries, or just the seemingly endless supply of bumps, bruises, and soreness. I do, however, miss the camaraderie that you develop with a close group of people and the competition."**

experiences, and have made so many friends and memories because of my involvement with baseball. My collegiate experience was shaped on the sport and it helped me achieve my childhood dream of becoming a professional baseball player. Looking back on everything, I'm incredibly fortunate for my support team. Being able to talk to my mom, dad, girlfriend (now wife), and so many others was a blessing. The time away from baseball has been some of the most memorable and rewarding time of my life. Instead of being away for 6-7 months, I was able to be at home and further develop my relationship with the person who would become my wife. I was able to graduate from a premier university and start my career in an industry that I absolutely love." Eric

Eric returned to Stanford as an undergraduate assistant coach for the 2014 season while he finished his degree. Upon completing his education, he transitioned into the non-profit sector.

****

In 2018, Andrew had been dealing with hip pain since before Spring Training.

"The pain became unmanageable and it started to limit my enjoyment and excitement about baseball. After a stretch of three months living in a hotel paired with two months of trying to get my hip healthy enough to pitch, I had surgery on July 5th. I flew back home to Seattle to begin the rehab, and in the process of rehabilitating my body I was rehabilitating my mind. I realized my future prospects in baseball were on a downward trend and I really felt like my ability to make baseball a career was pretty limited at that point. So I began to have conversations with my parents about wanting to make the transition out of baseball. I think it was both surprising and tough for them to hear because to their knowledge baseball was my dream and my passion, but I think the pain and the minor league lifestyle kind of eroded that dream and passion for me. There was no chance I was going back for the rest of that season, it's at least a six-month recovery. I knew I was done for the year." Andrew

And Andrew knew it might be over for good.

"It was kind of a weird feeling but I knew at that moment, walking off the mound after getting the last out, that it was over for me. It was more of a relief because it had been such a difficult five months, and I knew I was going to get the pain taken care of. I didn't really feel sad about it because I felt like I had given everything I could to the game and to my career. It just so happened that it didn't work out for me physically or in terms of my expectations of what it would be like to go through the process of playing professional baseball." Andrew

> **"It was more of a relief because it had been such a difficult five months, and I knew I was going to get the pain taken care of."**

Andrew made the phone call a few months later.

"In September I started working full time for a company in California but the Cardinals were still thinking that I was going to come back the next season and play. I was giving myself an opportunity to see if I got the baseball bug back. If I felt like I really wanted to get back out there and throw or get on the mound then it would be an indication that my gut reaction after surgery was wrong and I really did want to be back on the field. But September and October rolled through and I really had no desire to go back out and play. So in early November I decided, alright, I gotta call the Minor League Coordinator. He was the guy you didn't really want to talk to because he held the fate of minor leaguers in his hands with all the promotions and demotions. We called him Scary Gary because more often than not he had bad news. I had maybe said Hi to this guy in the hallway one time during Spring Training, I doubted he even knew who I was. I was at work that day, just sitting there thinking eventually I've got to make this call and pull the plug. I called him and I was incredibly nervous but I got his voicemail, which made me more nervous because he had to call me back. About an hour later he returned my call and I had to explain, 'Hey this is Andrew Summerville, one of the players in the Cardinals organization.' I went on to explain very candidly that after getting my hip operated on, it gave me some time to reflect and allowed me to recognize that there were promising opportunities for me with

this business, it was something I really wanted to take advantage of. To his credit he was really really thoughtful and considerate when I told him that. There wasn't an ounce of anger or malice towards me for having decided to move on. He was really respectful of my decision. He said that it was more common than he would like, to have Stanford guys say they want to move on to other things. He said, 'It's one of the reasons why you guys go to the school you do, to get the education so you have the ability to do other things.' And he appreciated my desire to take advantage of the opportunity at hand and wished me all the best. He said if there's any way he could help out, please let him know. So I was scared all for naught. It was still a frightening conversation to have to have, but he wasn't scary after all. He was awesome, a really considerate guy. Just that 15-minute interaction with him would eliminate the title of Scary Gary." Andrew Summerville, retired from the St. Louis Cardinals organization on November 6, 2018.

Andrew is now living in Palo Alto, CA and working for a Stanford-born company called Pando, which helps athletes and individuals hedge away career risk by helping them pool income with their peers.

****

Some players choose to retire but not necessarily because of an injury. The problem with retiring too soon is that most minor league contracts are set up so players have to play at least three years in order to keep the full amount of their signing bonus. (That's to prevent a player from turning around and signing a contract with another team.) Thus, if a player wants to retire before the three year mark of his career, then he would be better off getting released. But in some cases, knowing a player truly wants to retire, a team will go ahead and grant the player a release. That's how this player's career came to an end.

"By my second Spring Training, I had lost the passion for it, I had lost the fun aspect of it. It became more of a job and an obligation than it was a fun game for me. The season before we were playing 140 games, taking those 10-hour bus rides, making barely enough money to do anything with and not really seeing too many rewards from it. That

last season I think the month of June I hit .120. And I'm such a homebody, I wanted to be closer to home. It wasn't really a single thing, it was just kinda the lifestyle and everything put together, it wasn't for me anymore. I knew that the day when that came around was the day I was going to stop playing. And I was having some issues with my shoulder from throwing. I was just not really excited to go about it, I kinda wanted to finish up my degree and move back home and move on to the next chapter. It was built into the contract that you had to play three years to get the whole signing bonus but I had only played two. If you quit, you didn't get your signing bonus but if you got released you would get your signing bonus. That was one of the things I'd talked to the team briefly about in January. And when I got to Spring Training they had brought in some outfielders, and there was some outfield position battles. There were a lot of young guys and they had brought in two or three other young really talented outfielders throughout the lower levels of A, High A, and AA. It was just young up above me and they had just brought in more. So I had an honest conversation with the minor league player development guy about that and then he released me, so it was kind of nice. I'd like to think it made their decisions just a little easier to get one outfielder out of the mix. I just facilitated the process." Anonymous

> "It wasn't really a single thing, it was just kinda the lifestyle and everything put together, it wasn't for me anymore. I knew that the day when that came around was the day I was going to stop playing."

After his release, he felt this:

"It was a great relief, getting away from it all and seeing Snapchats from my friends at 3:00 AM on a bus in the middle of nowhere. I liked seeing some of that stuff and thinking, 'ha ha ha.' And one thing that really helped me was after I was released I started coaching with my high school in June right away, for their summer season, so I was still involved with baseball. That was the thing I was going to miss the most, being around baseball and messing around and having fun with the team. Coaching really *made the transition super smooth. I work with the same coaches at my high school that I played for. It's nice being back around, telling the kids, 'I was in your shoes, I did a bunch of the things that you guys are trying to do.' It was an easy transition for me to get involved in that, it was a huge help. That's why I'm still doing it."* Anonymous

****

Brant spent three years moving around the Dodgers organization but didn't see a path to the major league level.

"For me it was a mutual thing. I called the team in early December to see where I was going to land in Spring Training, what their initial thoughts were. They told me that I was going to be in the same position as last year, meaning AAA and being on the phantom DL, not having a spot. I kinda said, 'Well that's a waste of my time,' and the guy said, 'Yeah, it is a waste of your time, I'll go ahead and grant your release if you want so other teams can pick you up.' I agreed that was the best course. So it was a mutual release. They would have liked to have me back but they granted my release." Brant, released by the Los Angeles Dodgers organization on December 19, 2017.

Brant went on to play Independent ball for the Lincoln Saltdogs and Evansville Otters. He is now with the San Francisco Giants in a major league support staff role, which includes bullpen catching, advanced scouting, and working as an assistant catching coach.

****

In 2015, Kenny was playing with the Northwest Arkansas Naturals, an affiliate of the Kansas City Royals.

"I was in AA and I was playing well at the time. One day I walked into the clubhouse and I looked at the roster and thought I'd see my name, but I didn't see my name, I saw the name of a guy from a level below on the roster. I thought, 'Oh shoot, they must have

called Torres up.' He was in the lineup and obviously I was on the bench. It was at that moment that I realized that the success that I had had in AA was really for naught, and they valued Torres more than me. I didn't ask the manager yet, but in the next day or two I asked him what was going on and the good news is, he was really frank with me. He said, 'Look, you're not one of their guys anymore, but the organization really does value having you around and the only thing you can do now is play your best for the rest of the season and be a team player.' So I thought about that for the next month, and I had another conversation with him about what that meant for my future. I was trying to figure out whether I should stay or not. Over the course of that time I wasn't playing much and basically I transitioned my mindset from being intently focused on being a major leaguer to realizing that this was the end of the road. I decided with at least a month left in the season that I was done." Kenny

But he didn't walk away mid-season.

"I was lucky that I knew I would have the last month to make the most of it and I did. It was a great time, I was a team player, I enjoyed it. We had a great playoff run, it was a lot of fun, we popped champagne and all that. On the last game of the season, my coach did a very kind thing. We were getting smoked like 10 to nothing in the last game of the championship series, the season was about to be over and we were about to lose. I wasn't playing but in the 6th or 7th inning the manager called me over and said, 'Hey, do you want another at bat?' And I said no, because I felt like I had ended on a good note, my last game I hit pretty well and I went 2 for 4. I thought that was a really kind gesture that he thought of me and gave me that chance, but I said, 'Nope, I'm good.' I remember everything about that last game, the last time I put my uniform on, the last time I walked out of the tunnel, the last time we were walking back. But it was fine. I wasn't that emotional, maybe I was just happy to go out on a positive note. I

> "I remember everything about that last game, the last time I put my uniform on, the last time I walked out of the tunnel, the last time we were walking back."

didn't tell my teammates because I didn't want it to be like, 'Hey, this is the last time I'll ever see you.' I just said, 'I'll see you next year.'" Kenny

Kenny called the team and made it official four months later.

"I remember calling the assistant GM from the boardroom of the investment firm where I was interning. It was an odd mix of emotions being in the next chapter of my life and putting a close to the previous one. It was hard to hold back tears. It was one thing to say to myself I'd never return to competitive baseball, but it was another to say it out loud to the organization. And it was even harder to share the news with the folks at the training facility where I had trained for over eight years. I had a long conversation with the lead trainer as we looked out over the facility where I battled to the absolute core for years of my life. And as I remembered the heavy squats, the explosive jumps, the great times and the bad, I couldn't keep it together anymore. I just started bawling." Kenny, retired from the Kansas City Royals organization on January 12, 2016.

Kenny now lives in San Francisco and works for Makena Capital Management in Menlo Park, CA.

****

Tyler resumed his professional baseball career in 2018 with the Pirates organization after spending four years in the NFL. After being promoted to AA Altoona, things started to go downhill.

"The entire vibe I was getting was it was a place to fail. I got extremely frustrated with what was going on based on how well I'd been doing. I started questioning my own talents and skills. Maybe this was too much for me? I found myself getting worse as a person, physically and mentally. I wasn't able to work out because I never knew when I was going to play, there was no communication. I went to a little bit of a dark place because even on the home games I was saying goodnight to my kids at 11:00 AM because I wasn't going to see them until 11:00 PM and they'd be sleeping. And then I was on the road and I wasn't

seeing them and I was leaving my wife and two kids who were both under two years old in a dorm room with no TV and no internet. It was just a tough position for my entire family. There was no amount of money that was paying for this lifestyle. I don't care if they gave me $500,000, a million dollars to do this lifestyle, I wasn't happy at all. I was missing things, missing my kids, missing all my friends and family because there was no easy way to get to Altoona. It gave me a lot of perspective and I realized what quality of life meant and it was the opposite of what I was going through." Tyler

But Tyler didn't quit.

"I'll never quit, I'll never end my sports career on quitting. I was going to finish out my obligation, that's how I was raised, you start something you finish it. About a month before the season ended, I sent my family home early so they could get a breath of fresh air, be back in California near family and friends." Tyler

In February of 2019, Tyler called the Pirates to tell them he was retiring.

"They tried to explain to me that they were changing some things — new coaching, new philosophies. But I told them that wasn't the issue, I'm just at a different place in life. I'm looking forward to a better quality of life, there's no changing that aspect of it. So they tried for a second to convince me to stay and then they accepted it. If I had any doubts I would not have retired but I'm looking forward to being around my family and seeing my kids grow up, that's what's important to me at this point in my life. It was different when I was 21, obviously. Even as I'm looking at what industries to work in, I'm getting a lot of good job offers that require a lot of travel, they're good money, but that's not what I want to do. Sometimes you have to go through some trials and tribulations to truly appreciate what's going on. I'm glad to be where I'm at." Tyler, retired from the Pittsburgh Pirates organization in February, 2019.

> **"I'm looking forward to being around my family and seeing my kids grow up, that's what's important to me at this point in my life."**

Tyler is now living in San Diego, CA with his wife Kristen and their two children Jaxon Jet and Conway Bo.

****

And finally, this narrative began with Mark being drafted as the number one overall selection in the 2013 draft. After five seasons in the minor leagues, Mark made the decision in February of 2018 to take a break from baseball.

"I was hurt, that was a huge factor, because when you're on the DL you're just sitting there and you aren't playing the game that you thought you would be playing. You just feel really removed from competition and it wasn't what I expected pro ball to be. I don't think anybody ever expects to be hurt. And I realized that because I was hurt, I was going to be spending most of the next year on the DL again and the DL is pretty isolating. You're living in a hotel room, there aren't too many people around, you have to work every day, even on Sundays. It can become very repetitive and you're far away from the people you love. I'm a relational person so I love being around the people that I love, my family and friends, and I was really starved of those relationships. I just made the decision that I may not go back and play baseball. I don't know if I would call it retirement but I knew that I needed to at least take a break and step away and reevaluate and spend time in Houston with my family. That was really weighing on my heart for a while. It seemed like every time I gathered momentum playing pro ball, something would happen. I would get hurt, I would have an appendectomy, I would blow my shoulder out, I would have elbow surgery, something like that, and it really wore me down. So I realized that — and again, this goes back to my value system — I would be much better served getting to focus an entire year on physical, emotional, mental and spiritual health as opposed to trying to rehab a hurt shoulder that ultimately may need surgery. I felt like I was beating my head against the wall just putting in all this work, all this effort and not seeing any results from that. That's what it came down to. The times that I enjoyed myself the most were the times when my family was visiting me or my girlfriend was visiting me. There are people in my life from college and pro ball that will be lifelong friends and when you miss out on their engagements and their weddings and things like that, you do it joyfully because you're chasing this dream, and everybody understands. But you want to be in two places at once. I realize that being hurt

was not what I ultimately signed up for and if I'm going to be hurt, then I'd rather be hurt in Houston around relationships that I know are lifelong and life giving. Getting to be a part of my church at home and getting to have really good community around me was a huge driving factor of why I decided to take a break." Mark, voluntarily took a break from baseball in February, 2018.

> "Getting to be a part of my church at home and getting to have really good community around me was a huge driving factor of why I decided to take a break."

Mark still isn't sure if he's going back or not.

"I don't know if I'll go back. It might be retirement, but for the time being it's great to be able to focus on those relationships. It's great to be able to focus on figuring out what things I like and don't like outside of baseball. It's great to be working a new job for the first time, and thinking about the future and thinking about going to business school. And I'll see where my shoulder is as well. There's still a lot that is so unknown with the future but I have a lot of peace and I have a lot of confidence in the situation I'm in right now and that really goes a long way. I know that I'll only try to go back when I'm in a place that I can and I want to fully invest in it and in a place where I believe I'm going to be a contributor to whatever team I'm playing for. Being able to be mentally and emotionally and physically and spiritually prepared to do that again would be great. The game is not going to get easier just because you take time off." Mark

Mark now lives in Houston, TX and is spending time with family, serving in his local church, and pursuing business opportunities as an entrepreneur.

Chapter 12
Grand Slam!

Of all the calls in baseball, undoubtedly the most exciting is the call-up to the Major Leagues. About 14% of minor league players get to experience the thrill of being told that they're going to the big leagues. Here are three instances where that happened.

****

In early July of 2015, Stephen Piscotty thought he was being called up during a game with the AAA Memphis Redbirds, but it didn't happen that day. Two weeks later, it did.

"We were in Iowa. As opposed to two weeks earlier when I was hitting really well, this time I was not. I don't know if I was rattled from the previous situation, but I wasn't really expecting it because I was struggling. We had an off day, and I was with a couple of

guys having pizza. We just got to the restaurant and the manager Mike Shildt called me and said, 'Hey, can you meet me in the hotel lobby?' and I was like, 'Yeah sure I'll be right over.' So I went over and met up with Mike and the hitting coach Mark Budaska. He said something along the lines of, 'Alright, it's your time, you've been called up.' He congratulated me and said I was going to do great, I was ready. Then they got me all dialed in with the travel plans and whatnot. And I was on my way." Stephen

> "He congratulated me and said I was going to do great, I was ready."

Who did he call first??

"I called my mom. She knew something was up because even though we texted back and forth all the time, something's gotta be going on for me to give her a call. As soon as she picked up she was like, 'Hey, what's going on? What's up?' I asked if she could get dad on the phone too. They were in South Dakota for a family wedding. I could just hear the excitement in her voice trying to find my dad. 'Where's Mike?? Go find him!!' That was pretty funny. I remember being in the hotel hallway, just kind of sitting there on the floor. You've got roommates on the road so I was outside just trying to get a little privacy. They both got on the phone and I gave them the good news. They were screaming and hollering, all excited. There was a lot of family around them, everyone was cheering and celebrating. It was really cool, I couldn't have asked for it to go much better than that." Stephen

When a player is called up, he has to meet up with the major league team immediately, and it's not always at their home city.

"I had to get to Chicago where the Cardinals were going to be playing. One of the fortunate things for me was the big league team had an off day so it gave me and my family time to get to Chicago. I flew out really early in the morning and had the day there. I remember not having the right clothing because we were on the road. I went to

Banana Republic to get a bunch of shirts, I had to get some shoes, I had to look good. In the meantime my family was flying in, the game was the next night. My agent Brodie flew out, he got the tickets and the BP passes and made sure everything was taken care of so they could just enjoy it. So many people were able to come out, it was really cool." Stephen

And just because a player has made it to the big leagues, it doesn't mean there aren't still some logistics to work out.

"I was called up because Matt Holliday got hurt, and basically I was pretty certain I'd be there for the rest of the year but you just never know. It happens all the time, a guy gets called up for a week and then gets sent down. You try not to move out everything. I think it was a good month before everything in my apartment in Memphis was shipped out. When you get called up they put you in a hotel at your home city — it's called '7 and 7.' You get 7 days in a hotel and 7 days of meal money. It gives you time to figure out what you're going to do. Then Pete Kozma, who I was pretty close with throughout the minor leagues, offered to let me stay in his apartment, he had an extra room. I ended up doing that and didn't have to worry about signing a lease and all that stuff." Stephen

Stephen Piscotty made his major league debut with the St. Louis Cardinals on July 21, 2015.

****

On April 9, 2018, Alex Blandino was playing for the Louisville Bats, the AAA affiliate of the Cincinnati Reds.

"It was our second game of the season, it was in the fifth inning and I was 0 for 2 with a strikeout in that game. My manager came up to me and said, 'Hey, I'm going to take you out and put this other guy in because we need a little better production out of the leadoff spot.' And I was like, uh OK. I was kinda surprised and a little upset because

that shouldn't really happen, especially so early in the year. Then a couple of minutes later I went into the clubhouse and the guys were like, 'Did you hear?' And I was like, 'Did I hear what?' And they were like, 'Suarez broke his thumb.' Suarez was the third baseman for the Reds. I didn't know but I kind of had an idea that's why I got pulled from the game. My skipper sat me down an inning later in the dugout and said, 'Hey, you know why we pulled you out?' and I was like, 'Because my at bats were so bad?' I kinda knew he was joking with me. I hadn't even gotten a hit yet during the season, it was our second game and I was 0 for 4 so far. Then he said, 'You don't have any hits yet so we're just hoping you can save that first one of the year for the big leagues. Congrats.' Then everyone congratulated me. It was still during the game and everyone was like, 'Dude, go call your parents or something, go make some phone calls.' " Alex

> "You don't have any hits yet so we're just hoping you can save that first one of the year for the big leagues."

Like Stephen, Alex had to meet his team on the road.

"I had to meet the team in Philadelphia so the next morning I drove an hour and a half from Louisville to Cincinnati so I'd have my car there. Then I took a flight from Cincinnati to Philly to meet the team. I was in Philly for the road trip and then I flew back to Cincinnati with the team." Alex

Alex Blandino made his major league debut with the Cincinnati Reds on April 10, 2018.

Because of the constant movement of players between AAA and the major leagues, it would be convenient if the AAA teams were located within a short distance of the major league's home city. Unfortunately, that's not always the case. The distances range from about 36 miles between the AAA Tacoma Rainiers and the Seattle Mariners to 2,800 miles between the AAA Fresno Grizzlies and the Washington Nationals. Of the 30 AAA teams, half of them are under 300 miles from their major league city (about a five-hour drive). For the rest of the teams, the players being called up have to get on a plane.

****

In June of 2017 Austin Slater was boarding a bus with the Sacramento River Cats, the AAA affiliate for the San Francisco Giants.

"We were boarding a bus at 5:00 in the morning going to the airport. Before we got on the bus my manager was following me around for five minutes asking me all these questions about if I'd paid my rent in Sacramento and how much rent was in San Francisco and all this stuff. I was like, 'I don't know, it's 5:00 in the morning and I'm just trying to get on the bus.' As I was walking up the steps he said, 'No, you need to get off the bus, you're going to San Francisco.' That was pretty cool. I called my parents and gave them the good news and then got in the car and met the team in San Francisco. That day they had an off day so they were flying to Philadelphia. It worked out nice for my family because it was on the East Coast and they could all get there from Jacksonville, Florida. That was a pretty special moment. I started the next day, which was really nice." Austin S.

"He said, 'No, you need to get off the bus, you're going to San Francisco.'"

Austin Slater made his major league debut with the San Francisco Giants on June 2, 2017.

Back in Chapter One, we learned that Austin was disappointed with where he had been drafted because he was in the middle of a college playoff game and wasn't able to answer his phone.

"It's funny, I probably got drafted in the best situation I possibly could have as far as the

organization goes. The Giants do a great job supporting their players, not being cheap or cutting corners. They were also kind of thin in position players so it was a perfect storm and it worked out perfectly." Austin S.

As opposed to the starting AAA salary of $2,250 per month, the minimum salary for major league players in 2018 was $545,000. When a player is called up, he immediately begins earning money at that rate.

"You go from making three grand a month to three grand a day. The discrepancy is ridiculous." Alex

"It's nice to check your bank account for the first time after the first two weeks, that's for sure." Austin S.

So maybe it IS all worth it in the end.

Roster of Players

The following bios describe what the players did after playing baseball at Stanford University.
*Photos courtesy of MiLB

Mark Appel

Mark Appel was drafted as the #1 overall pick of the 2013 MLB Amateur Draft by the Houston Astros. As a pitcher, he spent three years in the minor leagues with the Astros, playing for the Tri-City ValleyCats (Short Season A), Quad Cities River Bandits (Low A), Lancaster JetHawks (High A), Corpus Christi Hooks (AA), and the Fresno Grizzlies (AAA). In December of 2015, Mark was traded to the Philadelphia Phillies. He then played for the GCL Phillies (Rookie) and the Lehigh Valley IronPigs (AAA) before taking an indefinite leave from baseball after the 2017 season. He now lives in Houston, TX and is spending time with family, serving in his local church, and pursuing business opportunities as an entrepreneur.

Alex Blandino

Alex Blandino was drafted in the first round of the 2014 MLB Amateur Draft by the Cincinnati Reds. In his four years as an infielder in the minor leagues he played for the Billings Mustangs (Rookie), Dayton Dragons (Low A), Daytona Tortugas (High A), Pensacola Blue Wahoos (AA) and the Louisville Bats (AAA). Alex made his major league debut with the Reds on April 10, 2018. He is currently a second baseman for the Cincinnati Reds and spends his off-seasons with his family in San Francisco, CA.

Sahil Bloom

Sahil Bloom graduated from Stanford in 2014 with an M.A. in Public Policy and a B.A. in Economics and Sociology. He was a pitcher on the Stanford Baseball Team from 2009-2013, twice earning the Bruce R. Cameron Award for Excellence in Academics, Athletics, and Leadership, before finishing his career as a graduate assistant coach in 2014. Sahil joined Altamont Capital Partners, a Palo Alto-based private equity fund in 2014, and currently serves as a Vice President of the firm. Sahil lives with his wife Elizabeth in the Bay Area.

Marc Brakeman

Marc Brakeman was drafted in the 16th round of the 2015 MLB Amateur Draft by the Boston Red Sox. He pitched for the GCL Red Sox (Rookie), the Greenville Drive (Low A) and the Salem Red Sox (High A). He then signed as a free agent with the Los Angeles Angels in March of 2018. As an Angel, he played for the Burlington Bees (Low A) and the Inland Empire 66ers (High A). Since his release in November of 2018, Marc has traveled around the Pacific Northwest, done economic consulting work, and is now looking forward to the next chapter of his life.

Chris Castellanos

Chris Castellanos was drafted in the 33rd round of the 2017 MLB Amateur Draft by the Seattle Mariners. He pitched for the AZL Mariners (Rookie), Everett AquaSox (Short Season A), Clinton LumberKings (Low A) and the Tacoma Rainiers (AAA). After being released in October of 2018, Chris moved to Las Vegas where he works as a salesman for an aggregate parts company.

Danny & Kenny Diekroeger

Danny Diekroeger was drafted in the 10th round of the 2014 MLB Amateur Draft by the St. Louis Cardinals. He spent four years as an infielder in the minor leagues and played for the State College Spikes (Short Season A), Peoria Chiefs (Low A), Palm Beach Cardinals (High A) and the Springfield Cardinals (AA). After being released in August of 2017, Danny went to Burning Man, adopted a rescue pit bull named Sky, and completed his Master's degree in Computer Science at Stanford. He now works as a software engineer for a cryptocurrency custody firm in Palo Alto, CA.

Kenny Diekroeger was drafted in 4th round of the 2012 MLB Amateur Draft by the Kansas City Royals. He spent four years as an infielder in the minor leagues and played for the Burlington Royals (Rookie), Lexington Legends (Low A), Wilmington Blue Rocks (High A), Northwest Arkansas Naturals (AA) and the Omaha Storm Chasers (AAA). After retiring in 2016, Kenny attended the Stanford Graduate School of Business and graduated in June of 2018. He now lives in San Francisco and works for Makena Capital Management in Menlo Park, CA.

Alex Dunlap

Alex Dunlap was drafted in the 29th round of the 2017 MLB Amateur Draft by the Washington Nationals. As a catcher, he played for the GCL Nationals (Rookie), Hagerstown Suns (Low A) and the Syracuse Chiefs (AAA). He is still playing with the Nationals organization and spends his off-seasons with his family in Houston, TX.

Tommy Edman

Tommy Edman was drafted in the 6th round of the 2016 MLB Amateur Draft by the St. Louis Cardinals. As an infielder in the minor leagues he has played for the State College Spikes (Short Season A), Peoria Chiefs (Low A), Palm Beach Cardinals (High A), Springfield Cardinals (AA) and the Memphis Redbirds (AAA). Tommy is still playing with the Cardinals organization and lives in San Diego with his family during his off-seasons.

Tyler Gaffney

Tyler Gaffney was drafted in the 24th round of the 2012 MLB Amateur Draft by the Pittsburgh Pirates. After spending his first summer with the State College Spikes (Short Season A), Tyler took a break from baseball to play his senior season as a running back for the Stanford football team. He was drafted by the Carolina Panthers in the 6th round of the 2014 NFL draft. In July of 2014, Tyler was claimed off waivers by the New England Patriots where he was a part of two Super Bowl championships. In August of 2017, he was signed by the Jacksonville Jaguars. After suffering a third knee injury he retired from football and resumed his professional baseball career in March of 2018. He then played for the Bradenton Marauders (High A) and the Altoona Curve (AA) before announcing his retirement. Tyler is now living in San Diego, CA with his wife Kristen and their two children Jaxon Jet and Conway Bo.

Colton Hock

Colton Hock was drafted in the 4th round of the 2017 MLB Amateur Draft by the Miami Marlins. Colton has pitched for the GCL Marlins (Rookie), Batavia Muckdogs (Short Season A), and the Greensboro Grasshoppers (Low A). Colton currently plays with the Marlins organization and trains in the off-season in Nashville, TN.

Drew Jackson

Drew Jackson was drafted in the 5th round of the 2015 MLB Amateur Draft by the Seattle Mariners. As an infielder, he played for the Everett AquaSox (Short Season A) and the Bakersfield Blaze (High A). In March of 2017, Drew was traded to the Los Angeles Dodgers. As a Dodger he played for the AZL Dodgers (Rookie), Rancho Cucamonga Quakes (High A) and the Tulsa Drillers (AA). In December of 2018, Drew was claimed off waivers by the Philadelphia Phillies and traded to the Baltimore Orioles. He spends his off-seasons with his family in the San Francisco Bay Area.

Dom Jose

Dom Jose was drafted in the 24th round of the 2014 MLB Amateur Draft by the New York Yankees. He was an outfielder for the GCL Yankees (Rookie) and the Charleston RiverDogs (Low A). After being released in March of 2016, Dominic worked for the Los Angeles Dodgers as a Research & Development Liaison. He now lives in Los Angeles and works for MVP Sports Group in Beverly Hills, CA.

Lonnie Kauppila

Lonnie Kauppila was drafted in the 16th round of the 2013 MLB Amateur Draft by the Seattle Mariners. As an infielder, he played for the AZL Mariners (Rookie), Everett AquaSox (Short Season A), Clinton LumberKings (Low A) and the High Desert Mavericks (High A). Following his release in April of 2015, Lonnie took a role as a financial analyst at Western Digital. He is currently working for the same company as a Finance Manager and is concurrently pursuing his MBA at USC.

Jack Klein

Jack Klein was drafted in the 34th round of the 2017 MLB Amateur Draft by the Kansas City Royals. An outfielder in college, Jack converted to being a pitcher for the AZL Royals (Rookie) and the Idaho Falls Chukars (Rookie). He was released in November of 2018 and now lives in his hometown of San Francisco, CA.

Sam Lindquist

Sam Lindquist was drafted in the 37th round of the 2014 MLB Amateur Draft by the Seattle Mariners. He pitched for the Everett AquaSox (Short Season A) near his hometown of Seattle and was released in March of 2015. He went on to finish his degrees in Human Biology and Psychology. He now works for TPG, a global private investment firm in San Francisco, CA.

Stephen Piscotty

Stephen Piscotty was drafted in the supplemental first round of the 2012 MLB Amateur Draft by the St. Louis Cardinals. He was an outfielder for the Quad Cities River Bandits (Low A), Palm Beach Cardinals (High A), Springfield Cardinals (AA) and the Memphis Redbirds (AAA). He made his major league debut with the St. Louis Cardinals on July 21, 2015. Stephen was traded to the Oakland Athletics in December of 2017. He is currently an outfielder with the A's and lives with his wife Carrie in the Bay Area.

Cal Quantrill

Cal Quantrill was drafted in the 1st round of the 2016 MLB Amateur Draft by the San Diego Padres. He has pitched for the AZL Padres (Rookie), Tri-City Dust Devils (Short Season A), Fort Wayne TinCaps (Low A), Lake Elsinore Storm (High A), San Antonio Missions (AA) and the El Paso Chihuahuas (AAA). He is still affiliated with the Padres and spends his off-seasons with his family in Port Hope, Ontario, Canada.

Justin Ringo

Justin Ringo was drafted in the 28th round of the 2013 MLB Amateur Draft by the St. Louis Cardinals. He was a first baseman for the Johnson City Cardinals (Rookie) and the Peoria Chiefs (Low A). After being released in May of 2015, Justin moved back home to Chicago and began working for Stryker, a medical technologies company. He lives with his wife Dani and their two dogs, Winston and Olive, in Chicago, IL.

David Schmidt

David Schmidt signed as a free agent with the Houston Astros in June of 2015. He pitched for the Tri-City ValleyCats (Short Season A), Quad Cities River Bandits (Low A) and the Corpus Christi Hooks (AA). He was released in March of 2017. He now lives in New York City and works in credit risk management for an investment bank. He enjoys participating in the company's yearly softball game.

Austin Slater

Austin Slater was drafted in the 8th round of the 2014 MLB Amateur Draft by the San Francisco Giants. He was an outfielder for the AZL Giants (Rookie), Salem-Keizer Volcanoes (Short Season A), San Jose Giants (High A), Richmond Flying Squirrels (AA) and the Sacramento River Cats (AAA). He made his major league debut on June 2, 2017 with the San Francisco Giants. He is still an outfielder for the Giants and spends his off-seasons training in San Francisco, CA.

Eric Smith

Eric Smith was drafted in the 18th round of the 2012 MLB Amateur Draft by the Los Angeles Dodgers. As a catcher, he played for the Ogden Raptors (Rookie) and the Great Lakes Loons (Low A). He retired after a shoulder injury in March of 2014. He returned to Stanford as an undergraduate assistant coach for the 2014 season while he finished his degree. Upon completing his education, he transitioned into the non-profit sector.

Jake Stewart

Jake Stewart was drafted in the 9th round of the 2012 MLB Amateur Draft by the Detroit Tigers. He was an outfielder for the Connecticut Tigers (Short Season A) and the West Michigan Whitecaps (Low A). After his release in March of 2014, he returned to his hometown of Fort Collins, CO to coach his high school team. He now works at Gray Creek Development and lives with his wife Kayla in Fort Collins.

Andrew Summerville

Andrew Summerville was drafted in the 12th round of the 2017 MLB Amateur Draft by the St. Louis Cardinals. He pitched for the State College Spikes (Short Season A) and the Peoria Chiefs (Low A). He retired in November of 2018 and is now living in Palo Alto and working for a Stanford-born company called Pando. Pando helps athletes and individuals hedge away career risk by helping them pool income with their peers.

Wayne Taylor

Wayne Taylor was drafted in the 16th round of the 2014 MLB Amateur Draft by the Seattle Mariners. He caught for the Pulaski Mariners (Rookie), the Clinton LumberKings (Low A) and the Tacoma Rainiers (AAA). He was released in March of 2016. Wayne got married in July of 2017 and is now living in Redwood City, CA with his wife Kyle and their chocolate lab Gumbo. He works for ASB Real Estate Investments, a real estate private equity firm. He and Kyle try to get back to the Stanford campus as much as possible for football, volleyball and baseball games.

Chris Viall

Chris Viall was drafted in the 6th round of the 2016 MLB Amateur Draft by the New York Mets. He pitched for the Kingsport Mets (Rookie), the Brooklyn Cyclones (Short Season A) and the Columbia Fireflies (Low A). He is still affiliated with the Mets and spends his off-seasons with his family in Santa Cruz, CA.

Brant Whiting

Brant Whiting was drafted in the 30th round of the 2014 MLB Amateur Draft by the Los Angeles Dodgers. He was a catcher on the AZL Dodgers (Rookie), Great Lakes Loons (Low A), Rancho Cucamonga Quakes (High A), Tulsa Drillers (AA) and Oklahoma City Dodgers (AAA). Following his release in 2017, Brant went on to play Independent ball for the Lincoln Saltdogs and Evansville Otters. He is now with the San Francisco Giants in a major league support staff role, which includes bullpen catching, advanced scouting, and working as an assistant catching coach.

Austin Wilson

Austin Wilson was drafted in the 2nd round of the 2013 MLB Amateur Draft by the Seattle Mariners. He was an outfielder for AZL Mariners (Rookie), Everett AquaSox (Short Season A), Clinton LumberKings (Low A) and the Bakersfield Blaze (High A). In December of 2016, Austin was selected by the St. Louis Cardinals in the Triple A phase of the Rule 5 draft. He played for the Palm Beach Cardinals (High A) before being released in July of 2017. He is now working for a startup in Venice Beach, California and lives in Los Angeles.

Acknowledgments

First and foremost, I want to thank the 28 young men who agreed to share their experiences with me. Our conversations became the heart and soul of this book. They were all so fun and engaging to speak with and I am forever grateful for their time and willingness to speak with me. My sons Kenny and Danny both deserve shout-outs for providing not just the initial stories that started this whole idea but for their ongoing help throughout the process.

I want to thank Adam Kluger for his professional wisdom and experience which helped me get this from a rough draft into a published work, Bernadette Marciniak for her countless hours of design and editing, and Sean Buttimer for his editing as well. It was a pleasure to work with all of them.

I was also fortunate to be able to work with the talented Anthony Lanza, who provided me with the cover design and the illustrations.

Without Kenny's and Sarah's enthusiasm and feedback on the earliest draft (which they read while driving across the country), this would never have made it beyond a first draft. I also couldn't have done this without Kenny's ongoing willingness to provide data on demand.

I owe a big thanks to my sister Susan, who slogged through this as my first editor and was always available to provide feedback, to Lisa and Laura for their editing contributions, and to Kate, who listened intently and asked me so many thoughtful questions while we drove home from Kirkwood.

Thank you to Maura Sincoff, who met with me very early on and gave me some great ideas and feedback.

I very much appreciate Bob's willingness to read an early draft and give me the thumbs up, which meant a lot, given that he's read pretty much every sports book ever published.

Many many thanks to the Hens, for listening to my readings and encouraging me to keep this project going. (Or was that just the wine talking??)

I also want to thank my friend Mikey for taking an interest in this and for introducing me to Sue, who eagerly put me in touch with Andy, who generously gave me his time and perspective as a minor league baseball team president.

Most importantly, I want thank my husband Ken for providing constant support and for forcing me to take breaks every time he walked into my office "just to see how I was doing."

And finally, to our extended family of baseball parents, coaches and friends with whom we shared this baseball journey, thank you for enriching our lives with your friendship and providing us with a lifetime of memories that we'll never forget.

Made in the USA
Coppell, TX
27 March 2021